Frederick Hayes
Halloween 1974.

Gokhale, Gandhi and the Nehrus
Studies in Indian Nationalism

by B. R. Nanda

Mahatma Gandhi
The Nehrus
Socialism in India (*ed.*)
Nehru and the Modern World (*ed.*)

Gokhale, Gandhi and the Nehrus

Studies in Indian Nationalism

B. R. NANDA

London · George Allen & Unwin Ltd
Ruskin House   Museum Street

ISBN 0 04 954018 1

Printed in Great Britain
in 10 point Times Roman type
by Unwin Brothers Limited
The Gresham Press
Old Woking   Surrey

To
S.M.P.

Preface

The essays brought together in this volume touch upon certain important figures and aspects of the nationalist movement in India in the closing years of the nineteenth and first half of the twentieth century. Some of them were contributed to seminars: on the partition of India convened by the London School of Oriental and African Studies; on Gandhi, by the American Association of Asian Studies; and on 'Socialism in India' by the Nehru Memorial Museum and Library, New Delhi. Friends, whose opinions I value, feel that these papers, though originally written for fellow historians, would be of interest to a wider audience. 'Gokhale's Year of Decision' appeared in the *Journal of Indian History* in 1965. The 'Social Thought of Gokhale' was the text of a lecture delivered during the following year. The biographical sketches of Gokhale and Motilal Nehru were occasioned by their centenaries. 'Jawaharlal Nehru as a Writer' is an amplified version of an article contributed to the *Hindustan Times* in 1966.

Though these essays vary in their origins, they pertain to a period in which I have had a long-standing interest; indeed, they are by-products of larger projects. They will, I hope, be of interest not only to students of Indian nationalism, but also to the general reader. The men and events discussed in this book are not really so remote from our times, nor are they so unconnected with each other as they may appear to be at first sight. The Gandhi-Nehru partnership exercised a momentous influence on the course of Indian history. The partition of India was a traumatic experience for the people of the Indian sub-continent, the understanding of which should have a liberating effect on the minds of men. Gandhi, Gokhale and the Nehrus were contemporaries, who had not a little to do with each other. The two Nehrus and Gokhale, with their rational and secular outlook, should be of special interest to a generation still struggling to shake off the burden of the past.

I must acknowledge my debt of gratitude to the India Office Library for use of the papers of Lords Hamilton, Elgin, Curzon, Lansdowne and Morley; to the National Archives of India for the

Gokhale Papers; to the Nehru Memorial Museum and Library for the Nehru Papers; and to the Gandhi Memorial Museum for the Gandhi Papers.

Grateful acknowledgment is made to the following for permission to reprint material used previously:

The University Press of Hawaii. (An abridged version of 'Gandhi and Nehru' appeared in the *Meanings of Gandhi* edited by Paul F. Power).

The Director, Indian Institute of Advanced Study, Simla. ('Relevance of Gandhi' appeared in *Gandhi: Theory and Practice, Social Impact and Contemporary Relevance* edited by S. C. Biswas.)

Allen & Unwin ('Nehru and Partition of India' appeared in *Partition of India* edited by C. H. Philips and M. D. Wainwright.)

The Statesman Ltd, Calcutta. (The biographical sketch of Gopal Krishna Gokhale appeared in the *Statesman* in May 1966.)

The Hindustan Times Ltd, New Delhi. (An abridged version of 'Jawaharlal Nehru as a Writer' appeared in the *Hindustan Times* in 1966.)

B. R. NANDA

Contents

Chapter 1

Gopal Krishna Gokhale (1966)

I

When Gokhale died in February 1915, at the age of forty-eight, the Calcutta *Statesman* wrote that 'Mr Gokhale was the greatest leader that India has ever produced – perhaps her greatest man'. The young poetess Sarojini Naidu, who had been to Gokhale what she was to be to Gandhi, a daughter, a disciple and a friend, wrote:[1]

> Heroic heart! lost hope of all our days!
> Need'st thou the homage of our love or praise?
> Lo! Let the mournful millions round thy pyre
> Kindle their souls with consecrated fire,
> Caught from the brave torch fallen from thy hand,
> To succour and serve our stricken land,
> And in a daily worship taught by thee,
> Upbuild the Temple of her Unity,

Sarojini Naidu echoed the feelings of 'educated India', of Congress veterans such as Dadabhai Naoroji, William Wedderburn and Pherozeshah Mehta; of young politicians such as Tej Bahadur Sapru, C. Y. Chintamani and M. A. Jinnah; and above all, of M. K. Gandhi of South African fame, who had recently returned to India and was to mourn the death of his 'master' Gokhale by going bare-foot for a year.

Today, Gokhale hardly figures in popular imagination except vaguely as a member of that 'gullible' group of politicians, the Moderates, whose compromising politics are supposed to have been first eroded by the Extremist tide and finally washed away by the Gandhian deluge. This is of course a very inadequate view of what actually happened; it was pardonable at a time, when in the intensified phase of the nationalist movement in the 1920s, political alignments had to be sharply redrawn. In the case of Gokhale, apart from the eclipse which overtook the whole Moderate tribe, some of the heat and dust of Maharashtrian politics at the turn of the century have lingered and added to the difficulties of an objective assessment. Nearly two decades after the transfer of power, as men and events fall into historical focus, it should be possible to see his life and times in clearer perspective.

Gopal Krishna Gokhale was born on 9 May 1866, at Kotluk a small village in Ratnagiri District, the home of Chitpavan Brahmans and the traditional nursery of Maharashtra's patriots. His early years were shadowed by tragedy and poverty. He lost his father when he was thirteen. But for the extraordinary generosity of his elder brother, he would have had to give up his studies. As a student, he led a hard and frugal existence, sometimes cooking his own meals and saving kerosene by reading under the street lamp. He was a quiet, industrious and ambitious boy, but his scholastic record was not particularly distinguished. Though he gave evidence of a prodigious memory in his college days, his intellectual powers were to unfold themselves a little later. He toyed with the idea of taking the ICS examination. He joined the Engineering College in Bombay, but left it after a few weeks. For a year he attended the law classes in Bombay and may have ended up as a lawyer or a judge, if in January 1885, he had not taken a step which seemed almost insane to his family: he became a teacher at the paltry salary of Rs 35 a month in Poona's New English School, run by a band of young patriots who were called 'Indian Jesuits'. It was the example of Bal Gangadhar Tilak and Gopal Ganesh Agarkar, which had attracted Gokhale to the New English School. When the Deccan Education Society was formed soon afterwards, Gokhale became its life member. At the age of twenty he began to teach in Fergusson College, Poona. He was the 'professor to order', and could switch from mathematics to English literature, from history to political economy. He was a painstaking and popular teacher, but his talents and ambitions could not be contained within the classroom. Luckily for him, he caught the eye of Ranade, and in 1890, when he was barely twenty-four, became the secretary of the Sarvajanik Sabha, the premier political association of western India and the editor of its quarterly journal. Thirteen years' apprenticeship, which terminated only with Ranade's death, gave Gokhale a good grounding in Indian politics and economics. It also gave him an excellent start in his political career. Ranade enjoyed the confidence and respect of the top Congress leadership; to be known as his protégé was a decided asset to a young politician. Close association with Ranade also drew Gokhale into the bitter controversies over issues of social reform, which rent the public life of Poona in the 1890s and generated a poison which was to spill into provincial and national politics for two decades. There were confrontations between the two parties over the Age of Consent Bill in 1891 and the Poona Congress Session in 1895. Ranade's party suffered a serious set-back in 1896 when the Sarvajanik Sabha was captured by Tilak and his adherents.

Early in 1897, Ranade sent Gokhale to London to appear before the Welby Commission. His written evidence was an excellent exposition of the Indian case. However, it was in his oral evidence, under the searching examination of British experts that he came off best. His grasp of fundamentals as well as details, quick wit and courage impressed the Commission. Gokhale's political stock rose sky-high, but soon afterwards it crashed over what came to be known as the 'apology incident'. While in England he had, on the basis of letters from some friends in Poona, made allegations against British soldiers engaged in plague operations; and when he was unable to substantiate these allegations, he expressed unqualified regret for his mistake. He was denounced by British critics as a 'seditionist', and by his political rivals as a weakling. For a time, he became a back-bencher in the Indian National Congress, and it almost seemed that his political career was over.

Gokhale staged a spectacular come-back by entering the Bombay Council in 1899 and the Imperial Council in 1901. The Council chamber was the forum where he could show his talents to the best advantage. His first speech on the Government of India's budget in March 1902 marked him out as the most outstanding non-official member of the Imperial Council. He came to be known as the 'Leader of the Opposition'. The Imperial Council had a permanent majority of British officials or their nominees, and the Viceroy – the supreme head of the executive – presided over its deliberations. The half-dozen Indian gentlemen, most of them titled and dependent upon the favours of the Government, were hardly the stuff of which an 'opposition party' is made. It is a tribute to Gokhale's charm and persuasive eloquence that in several critical divisions in the last lap of Curzon's viceroyalty, he was able to carry most of his Indian colleagues with him against the Government. Curzon whose policies Gokhale had strongly assailed, paid the highest tribute to him on 16 March 1915, when he told the House of Lords, that he had 'never met a man of any nationality more gifted with parliamentary capacities. Mr Gokhale would have obtained a position of distinction in any parliament in the world.'

Gokhale's rise to political eminence was henceforth meteoric. In December 1903, he was elected Joint General Secretary of the Indian National Congress at the Madras session. Two years later, when he was only thirty-nine years old, he had the distinction of being the youngest President of the Indian Congress at its Benaras session.

These were the years of a new political ferment. Thanks to a series of unpopular measures in the closing period of Curzon's regime, particularly the partition of Bengal, the political temperature in India had risen. The premises and policies of the Congress leadership were being questioned by the younger generation. At the Benaras Congress in 1905, a head-on clash was almost miraculously avoided. A crisis was averted in December 1906 by the desperate expedient of inviting the eighty-year-old Dadabhai Naoroji to come from England to preside over the Calcutta Congress. In the events which led a year later to the split between the two wings of the Congress, Gokhale played an important, though not a dominant role. The tragedy at Surat was the outcome of a clash of principles as well as of personalities, of mistrust as well as miscalculation. It was Pherozeshah Mehta who had the decisive voice in the counsels of the Moderates at Surat, but it was Gokhale who had to bear the brunt of the schism in the Congress which followed.

Gokhale's emergence as a national leader in 1905 coincided with a crisis in the Indian National Congress. It also coincided with the return to power of the Liberal Party in Britain and the appointment of John Morley as Secretary of State for India. Gokhale had first met Morley in London in May 1897. During the next three years, while the proposals for constitutional reforms were being forged, Gokhale visited England several times and explained the Indian point of view to the Secretary of State. Gokhale's influence on the final shape of the Minto-Morley reforms was less than was assumed at the time: it was exaggerated by Tory and Anglo-Indian critics eager to embarrass Morley, and by Indian Moderates anxious to clutch at every straw in the wind. It is, however, arguable that, but for Gokhale's passionate advocacy in and outside the Imperial Council, the constitutional caravan might have been brought to a standstill by the conflicting pressures on Morley: his own liberal instincts, the resistance of.India Office, the doubts and fears of a conservative Viceroy and the dilatory tactics of the civil service in India. From 1910 onwards Gokhale did his best to make the Minto-Morley reforms a success. The 'Surat Split' in the Congress, the elimination of the Extremist wing and the growth of terrorism and official counter-terrorism, brought political life to a low ebb. There was, however, no rest for Gokhale. He laboured for the abolition of the indenture system in Natal, for moral and financial support to Gandhi in his struggle on behalf of the Indian community in South Africa, and for the extension of elementary education. In 1912, he was appointed a member of the Islington Commission on Public Services. The same year he visited South Africa. In the final phase of the Indian struggle in South Africa in 1913–14, which culminated in the Gandhi-Smuts Pact, Gokhale played a crucial role behind the scenes as the adviser of Gandhi, as well as of the Viceroy, Lord Hardinge. The strain of those anxious months combined with his labours on the Royal Commission to finally break a constitution already undermined by chronic diabetes and long years of incessant toil. On 19 February 1915, at the age of forty-eight, Gokhale died.

The attitude of British statesmen towards Gokhale had a peculiar ambivalence. They admired his encyclopaedic mind; they respected him for his courage and incorruptibility; they appreciated his professions of loyalty to the Empire, but they were baffled and exasperated by his insistence on Indian claims to self-government. In March 1903 Lord Curzon – who usually found it difficult to admire anyone except himself – described Gokhale in a private letter to the Secretary of State 'as a very able and courageous person, a Mahratta Brahmin, a Congressman . . . highly cultivated and not unreasonable'.[2] A few months later, while communicating to Gokhale the bestowal of the CIE, in the New Year Honours list for 1904, Curzon wrote: 'I only wish that India produced more such public men'.[3] Curzon's admiration was to be soon tempered by indignation when Gokhale offered the stoutest resistance in the Imperial Legislative Council to the Universities and Official Secrets Bills.

Curzon's successor, Minto wrote to Morley: 'He [Gokhale] is all you say about ability, but whether he is a genuine article, I can't tell'.[4] It is a strange paradox that during the years when Gokhale was under heavy fire in the Extremist press in India as a British lackey, his movements were being watched and letters opened by the CID. It may seem incredible, but it is true that even in

London it was not unusual for Gokhale, after having been closeted for several hours with the Secretary of State in the India Office, to be shadowed back to his hotel by a detective.

II

Gokhale's politics were the politics of Dadabhai Naoroji and Womesh Chandra Bonnerjee, of Allan Hume and William Wedderburn, of D. E. Wacha and Surendranath Banerjea. These 'Founding Fathers' of the Indian National Congress had greater vision, courage, and political acumen than later generations have tended to allow. In the years before the First World War, when the prestige of the British Empire was at its height, and the bureaucratic monopoly of power seemed almost absolute, when the politically conscious class in India numbered less than a million, and the number of full-time workers was not large enough to be counted on the fingers of one hand, the strategy followed by the Congress leadership was not merely sensible, but the only practical one. In the conflict between two generations of Congress politicians Gokhale did not join the rebel band of angry young men; instead he became the ablest spokesman of the Old Guard.

It is not possible here to recapitulate the controversies of those days, but it is necessary to remind ourselves that the terms 'Moderates' and 'Extremists' were party labels, and did not necessarily represent degrees of patriotic fervour. Gandhi, who spent a month early in 1902 in Calcutta during the session of the Imperial Council, has left a pen-picture of Gokhale at work: 'He never wasted a minute. His private relations and friends were all for the public good. All his talks had reference only to the good of the country and were absolutely free from any trace of untruth or insincerity. India's poverty and subjection were matters of constant and instant concern to him.'[5] 'I recognise no limits', Gokhale declared, 'to my aspirations for our motherland. I want our people to be in their own country what other people are in theirs.'[6] He visualised an India 'of expanding industry, of awakened faculties, of increasing prosperity and of more widely distributed comfort and wealth'. He believed, he said, in the almost 'illimitable capacities' of his countrymen. But he did not oversimplify the task of political or economic reconstruction: he was not a simplifier. He wrote to a friend in September 1909:

'Our problem is indeed an enormously difficult one. I sometimes think that no country in the world has ever been called upon to face such a problem as ours. Endless divisions and sub-divisions in the country, the bulk of population ignorant, and clinging with a tenacity of which only those who are of them can have an adequate conception, to old modes of thought and sentiment, which are averse to all change and do not understand change; seventy millions of Mohammedans more or less hostile to national aspirations, and all power lodged in the hands of a fleeting body of foreign officials, most of whom generally represent Tory principles at their worst – this is the situation today. Out of this mass, an India has to be evolved, strong, free, united, democratic, and qualified generally to take her proper place among the nations of the world.'[7]

The fact that violence lay so near the ostensibly tranquil surface of Indian life deeply disturbed him and strengthened his faith in political evolution through constitutional processes. The divisive tendencies of Indian politics weighed heavily upon his mind. He himself was remarkably free from sectarian and religious pre-judices and usually succeeded in enlisting the support of his Muslim colleagues in the Imperial Council. However, he had seen at first hand the mixture of blandishment, intrigue and propaganda on the part of Messrs Ameer Ali and Aga Khan, and their British friends, which preceded the incorporation of separate electorates in the Minto-Morley Reforms. When Sarojini Naidu told Gokhale in 1912 that Hindu-Muslim unity would be achieved in five years, Gokhale replied: 'Child, you are a poet, but you hope too much. It will not come in your life-time or mine. But keep your faith and work [for it] if you can.'[8]

Gokhale was proud of the ancient culture of his country, but he shared the faith of his mentor Ranade, and indeed of the first generation of Congress leaders, that India could take her place in the comity of nations only by imbibing the political thought of the West and adopting its representative institutions and methods of economic development. He pinned his hopes on education for the masses, and was one of the few nationalist leaders who tried to master financial and economic problems. He was an excellent speaker, but he knew that there were limits to what speeches and slogans could achieve, that politics to be effective have to be something more than a diversion for the leisure hours or the week-end. During the first twenty years of its existence, the Congress had been able to get few full-time workers. But where were these workers to come from? It occurred to

B

Gokhale that in a country, where thousands turned their backs upon personal ambitions and material comfort for the salvation of their souls, it should not be difficult to recruit a few political *sanyasins* (monks). When he wrote in the preamble of the Servants of India Society that 'politics should be spiritualised', Gokhale (who in his early years had been an agnostic and whose attitude to religion resembled that of Jawaharlal Nehru) was not laying down a metaphysical proposition, but seeking to apply the spirit of religion – its utter devotion and renunciation – to a secular purpose. His own example was the best advertisement for the society he founded. In 1904, he had fulfilled the twenty years' vow of voluntary poverty as a life-member of the Deccan Education Society; in 1905, he took the vows of a Servant of India, and undertook to train young men as 'national missionaries'. Among those who became his disciples were V. S. Srinivasa Sastri, G. K. Deodhar, Thakkar Bapa, N. M. Joshi and H. N. Kunzru. And among those who were attracted to the Society, but could not join it were C. Y. Chintamani, M. R. Jayakar, Rajendra Prasÿad, and Gandhi. Like Gandhi but long before him, Gokhale had shed those ties of family and property which make cowards of most men. When Gokhale spoke of his 'home', he meant the headquarters of the Servants of India Society, where he lived with his disciples, and not the little house down the street where his two motherless daughters were being brought up by his widowed sister.

No dish is colder or less appetising than that of dead controversies. For us, who are preoccupied with the menace of a nuclear disaster, the Indo-Pakistan conflict and the population explosion, it is not easy to interest ourselves in the pros and cons of the Age of Consent Bill, the Minto-Morley Reforms and the Surat Split, which obsessed a bygone generation. The problems with which Gokhale grappled, and the controversies in which he wore himself out, have only an academic interest today. But his rational, secular and almost scientific approach to Indian politics and economics, his complete freedom from social obscurantism, his belief in the disinterested pursuit of politics and in constitutional democracy, have acquired a new relevance in the post-independence era. And across half a century, we can still feel the magnetism of the man who was the disciple of Ranade, the colleague and rival of Tilak, the mentor of Gandhi and the hero of Motilal Nehru, Sapru and Jinnah; always reasoning and reasonable, knowledgeable and modest, gentle and generous, often racked by illness and anxiety, pacing up and down the room to think of the precise word to express a thought, waking through the night to prepare a speech he was to deliver next morning, and till the last day of his life squeezing the last ounce of his energy in the service of his country.

Chapter 2

Gokhale's
Year of Decision (1965)

I

1897 was an eventful year for Gokhale. It suddenly lifted him
into the limelight, revealed him as one of the most promising
young politicians, and then almost as suddenly seemed to consign
him to oblivion. A review of the sequence of events which made
such an impact on him is rewarding for the light it throws not
only on Gokhale's character and career, but also on the tangled
politics of Maharashtra and Indo-British relations in that critical
year.

Gokhale was one of the four Indians selected to appear before
the Royal Commission on Indian Expenditure in the spring of
1897. Among the members of this Commission, which was
presided over by Lord Welby, were three ardent advocates of
Indian aspirations in England: Wedderburn, Dadabhai Naoroji,
and W. S. Caine.[1] They had laboured for years to secure an
inquiry into Indian affairs, and specially into the inequitable
distribution of financial burdens between India and Britain. They
were keen to ensure that the Indian case before the Commission
was presented in the best possible manner by the ablest men
available. They would have liked Justice M. G. Ranade to come
to England.[2] The proposal was acceptable to the Commission
as a whole, but it did not find favour with the Government of
India[3] and eventually D. E. Wacha from Bombay, Surendranath
Banerjea from Calcutta and G. Subramania Iyer from Madras
were deputed to London. Ranade himself was unable to go, but
decided to send Gokhale as a representative of the Deccan Sabha
of Poona.

Gokhale left India in the first week of March 1897. He was
well equipped for his mission. Not only did he carry voluminous
notes compiled by that painstaking headmaster-economist, G. V.

Joshi, but he had behind him nearly a decade of apprenticeship to Ranade, and valuable experience acquired during seven years as Secretary of the Poona Sarvajanik Sabha, and as editor of its quarterly journal. His written evidence before the Welby Commission, with its solid, statistical core (derived mostly from blue-books and official sources) was a masterly exposition of the Indian case; he dwelt on the economic exploitation of India which was the recurrent theme of Naoroji and R. C. Dutt, but his assault was on a broad front, taking in its sweep the economic, financial and political policies of the Government of India. However, it was in his oral evidence, under the searching examination of old India hands like Sir James Peile, that he came off best. His extraordinary grasp of fundamentals as well as details, sense of proportion, quick wit, and courage made an excellent impression on the Commission. 'Permit me to say', wrote Caine to Gokhale, 'that I have never seen a cleverer or more masterly exposition of the views of an educated Indian reformer on all the subjects dealt with.' It was (Caine added), 'a splendid and unique service to your country for which your countrymen ought to be grateful'. Ranade was glad to get good reports of the performance of his disciple. 'Professor Gokhale is our rising man', he wrote to a friend on 21 May 1897.[4] Wedderburn, to whose care Ranade had commended Gokhale, was simply delighted with the young professor from Poona, who was to become his confidant and lifelong friend. Wedderburn did his best in the next two months to initiate Gokhale into the political world of London, by arranging interviews with people who mattered in Indian affairs in and outside the Parliament, and by giving him an opportunity to address public meetings. Gokhale met, among others, T. P. O'Connor, Sir W. W. Hunter, Sir George Birdwood, and John Morley. He visited educational institutions, spoke on social subjects, met politicians holding different political views, rubbed shoulders with celebrities in the National Liberal Club, and paced the corridors of the House of Commons and saw it at work. He sensed the favourable impression he had made on the great veterans of the Indian national movement in England, on Wedderburn, Hume, Naoroji and Caine. Was it too much to hope that he might before long be in the House of Commons like good old Naoroji, who was now over seventy and well past his prime? The words 'G. K. Gokhale MP', had a pleasant ring. Gokhale was young, and optimistic and the future looked bright, but just then six thousand miles away, back in his hometown, there were rumblings of a storm which was to wreck all these fancies.

II

In his evidence Gokhale had referred to the terrible famine of 1896–7, which was officially described at the time as the most disastrous in a century.[5] More than half a million square miles of the country inhabited by nearly ninety-seven million people were affected, and some of the worst hit districts were in the Deccan. Wedderburn, Naoroji and their friends on the British Committee of the Congress, who kept a watching brief for India in England, were naturally anxious about conditions in India; it was their pressure which led to the foundation of the Lord Mayor's Fund for famine relief. Not less important than immediate relief was the problem of focusing attention on the basic economic issues of India, of breaking through the spell of official optimism, and of underlining the terrible poverty which made it impossible for the hard-pressed peasantry to withstand failure of a single harvest.

In western India, to the rigours of famine were added the terrors of bubonic plague. Its first assault on India, like the one on Hong Kong two years earlier, was particularly fierce. When Gokhale left for England early in March, several towns in western India including Karachi, Bombay, Surat and Poona were in the grip of the epidemic. Mortality was heavy; medical science had yet much to learn about the prevention and treatment of this scourge. Those were the days when, in the words of the poet Gadkari,[6] one had to be more afraid of a dead rat than of lions and tigers.

With the spread of plague in India, European ports threatened to shut out British ships bearing produce from India. Claims of commerce no less than those of humanity dictated urgent measures for the suppression of the epidemic.[7] Lord George Hamilton, Secretary of State for India, pleaded with Lord Elgin, the Viceroy, to stamp out the dreadful disease, and not to allow the sanitary considerations to be subordinated to the political. This was no time to be squeamish about caste and social prejudices.[8] After some initial misgivings, the Government decided on a drastic campaign against plague.

In the second week of March 1897, the Bombay Government decided to form a Plague Committee, with Mr W. C. Rand, ICS, as Chairman, and Lt-Colonel C. R. Phillipps and Surgeon-

Captain W. W. O. Beveridge as members. Consisting of a senior civilian, a military officer and a doctor, the Committee was well equipped to combat the epidemic in Poona.

The Plague Committee was authorised to supervise, and in some respects almost to supersede the local bodies exercising jurisdiction over the city, cantonment and suburban areas, to amend municipal bye-laws, to incur expenditure, to search and fumigate buildings, to segregate persons suspected of the disease, and even to demolish or burn infected huts or temporary structures. It was made obligatory to register every death; in case of default, any member of the funeral party could be detained by the police!

Lord Sandhurst, Governor of Bombay, who had taken much of the initiative in this campaign, called a meeting of leaders of various communities and parties in Poona, informed them that stringent measures were proposed, including the house-to-house search for patients with a view to their isolation and treatment in hospitals. There was an air of expectancy and even apprehension in Poona, but there was at first little disposition to criticise the Government for measures which obviously were in the interest of the town. Even Tilak's papers pointed out the cruel necessity of the proposed operations, if the town was to be purged of the epidemic.[9]

The Operation Plague started in Poona rather dramatically. In the early hours of a March morning, the Budhwar Peth and part of Shukrawar were taken up by the military – about 200 cavalry and 100 infantrymen – for inspection. The streets were blockaded. At that early hour, some of the shop-keepers, who lived in outlying parts of the town, had not arrived. Their shops were forced open, disinfected, and left unattended. Between the British and Indian soldiers there was a division of labour; the former confined themselves to 'inspection' and the latter to disinfection of buildings. The medical member of the Plague Committee, Dr Beveridge, who had been well acquainted with the course of plague operations in Hong Kong, felt that a native agency for inspection was as likely to fail in Poona as it had done in Hong Kong, that only the British soldiers were capable of strict impartiality in segregating the sick. Whatever the reason for employing British soldiers for house-to-house searches, it was a tactical blunder of the first magnitude. The soldiers could hardly realise that if an Englishman's house is his castle, the Brahman's house is his temple. The young Tommy, who stepped with his shoes into rooms reserved for offering worship or taking food, did not even know that he had committed a sacrilege. Nor could he see any harm in a mild pleasantry – such as when he lifted a flower from an idol to throw it on a trembling young Brahman maiden.[10] Nevertheless, these were heinous offences in the eyes of the Brahmans of Poona, even if they occurred occasionally. The Poona press at once became critical of the Plague Committee; there were numerous allegations: soldiers were alleged to have opened metal safes and cash boxes in search of patients, and to have burnt not only the personal belongings and beddings of diseased persons, but even their account books and sewing machines.

Complaints were carried to Rand but without much effect. 'If anyone takes a complaint to Mr Rand orally', wrote a local paper, 'he simply laughs and sends the complainant away. If anyone sends a written petition, he gets a stereotyped reply that his allegations are false.'[11] The same paper accused Rand of behaving 'like the Sultan of Turkey'. Tilak, who had been present in a deputation, which had waited on Rand, castigated him in the *Kesari* and asked indignantly, 'What people on earth, however docile, will continue to submit to this sort of mad terror?' Though Rand may not have been 'one of the most courteous and kindly men', it is not necessary to assume that he was trying deliberately to oppress the people. He knew he had a disagreeable and thankless job and he was determined to do it quickly. His reputation with the people of Poona was not high; their experience had shown that he was no friend of the Brahmans or of the educated community. Indeed, in common with most of his British colleagues in the civil service, he entertained a lively distrust of Poona Brahmans; so far as Rand was concerned, the germs of sedition seemed to have infected them long before the plague came to Poona. Inspection and segregation, if they were to be effective, were processes which could hardly be popular; it was not easy to distinguish between a really aggrieved person and one who was out to sabotage the operations, and Rand had no intention to get involved in a long argument.

Failing to secure redress through representations, deputations and complaints in the press, the people of Poona sent up a memorial to the Governor of Bombay. The initiative was taken by the Deccan Sabha, which had been founded only recently in November 1896 under the inspiration of Ranade to serve as the mouthpiece of the moderate politicians of Poona, who were wedded to loyal and constitutional methods. The memorial

which also bore the signatures of some leading members of the
Anjuman Association, the premier organisation of local Muslims,
referred to the 'irregular and oppressive high-handedness of the
special agency employed by the Plague Committee', which had
resulted 'in a reign of terror' in Poona. Among the grievances
were the rough and ready methods used by the soldiers, who
carried off to hospitals not only patients, but even their relatives
and passers-by; the indignity of public stripping of men and
women for 'inspection'; disregard of social and religious susceptibilities; the forcible opening of houses and business premises,
and the wanton destruction of property. The enclosures to the
memorial contained some specific cases in support of the allegations. Finally, there was a demand for the redress of grievances,
and the substitution of the Plague Committee by 'such other
agency as will be more amenable to control, on the plan followed
in Bombay with such success'.

The memorial was dated 10 May 1897; the next ten days were
spent in collecting signatures, and the memorial was submitted
to Lord Sandhurst on 21 May. Gokhale read it in London, when
he was engaged in a lecture tour organised by the British Committee. He could recognise the signatures of the more important
men who had signed. There was V. M. Bhide, President of the
Deccan Sabha (of which Gokhale himself was one of the secretaries), a retired judge, a former head of the Poona Sarvajanik
Sabha, and a highly respected spokesman of the moderate and
reforming party in the town. There was Koopooswamy Mudaliar,
elevated by the Government to the rank of a First Class Sirdar
of the Deccan, a popular figure among the local Europeans, and
one of the richest men in Poona, who as a rule took little interest
in politics. Then there was Nawab Abdul Ferojkhan, President of
the (Muslim) Anjuman Association. That Hindus and Muslims,
despite recent communal tension in the town, should have agreed
on a joint representation was a measure of the resentment roused
by the operations of the Plague Committee.

The memorial was mailed to Gokhale by his friend H. N. Apte,
a famous Marathi novelist, and at that time one of the secretaries of the Deccan Sabha. When Gokhale left Poona early in
March, Apte had promised to keep him posted about developments at home, but he left the town just before the Rand Committee went into action. He wrote to Gokhale:

'I was compelled to leave the place bag and baggage. A rumour was afloat that military search parties were to make house-to-house visitation in the city, and this terrified me as I had at that time in my house my sister suffering from fever for several months. It was no doubt an act of cowardice thus to take to one's heels at that time, but I preferred to discharge the duty of looking after those in my charge, to remain[ing] wilfully indifferent to their interests.'[12]

Apte's letter made ominous reading, but the Deccan Sabha in its memorial to Lord Sandhurst had also mentioned that in 'a few cases the modesty of Native Ladies has not been respected'. There were other complaints of alleged misconduct by soldiers. Pandita Ramabai, a prominent Christian social worker in Poona and Bombay complained in the *Bombay Guardian* that one of her girls had been taken to the Plague Hospital, and had not been heard of again. 'God knows', she wrote, 'how many young girls of good character have been . . . obliged to go to the Plague Hospital and Segregation Camp and be ruined and lost for ever.'[13]

The contents of the Deccan Sabha memorial were disquieting, but by the time Gokhale read them in England, Operation Plague in Poona was over; the house-to-house inspection for isolation of the sick had been completed; the soldiers had been withdrawn; the mortality had perceptibly declined; the epidemic – deceptively as it turned out – seemed to have been suppressed; the people of Poona could breathe again. But just as the end of this unhappy chapter was in sight, a tragedy occurred, which brought fresh trials not only for the town, but also for its leaders, including Gokhale.

III

The tragedy occurred soon after midnight on 22 June 1897. It had been a crowded and memorable day, marking as it did the sixtieth anniversary of Queen Victoria's reign. There could be little real rejoicing for a people afflicted by famine and plague, but there was a reservoir of a real reverence and affection for the Great White Queen. Colour and pageantry were much in evidence in the European quarter of the town. In the afternoon Governor Sandhurst held a levee, which was attended by high European officials, the principal chiefs of the Deccan and 'some Native Gentlemen', including the 'Hon'ble B. G. Tilak, Member of the Governor's Legislative Council'. Ganesh Khind, the

Poona residence of the Governor, which had been brilliantly illuminated, was the scene of a state banquet followed by a reception. Huge fires on the hills beyond blazed merrily, lighting up the countryside for many miles. Finally, as a fitting close to a day of joyous celebration, came a spectacular display of fireworks.

Soon after midnight a string of carriages began to file out of the gates of Ganesh Khind. Among these was one carrying Mr W. C. Rand to his rooms in the Western India Club; it had gone only a few hundred yards when, at a spot lined by an avenue of trees, somebody climbed on to the back of his carriage and shot him with a pistol. Lt Ayerst, whose carriage was immediately behind Rand's was shot almost simultaneously. Ayerst died at once, but Rand lingered on for a few days.

It is not easy today to realise the impact this outrage made on European opinion in India and Britain. The attack on the 27-year-old Lt Ayerst, a junior officer in the Commissariat Department, seemed to be a case of mistaken identity, but in the case of Rand, there was an immediate suspicion of a political motive. The European community was deeply stirred; sympathy for the victims of the tragedy mingled with indignation against native, particularly Brahman wickedness. Memories of 1857 flooded back. In European clubs and offices and homes there were whispers on the gravity of the crisis; everyone seemed to agree that this was no time for weakness or misplaced kindness. The Bishop of Bombay, preaching in St Paul's Church, Poona, on the Sunday following the tragedy, sensed the feeling of his audience and tried to assuage it: 'It was unjust to lump all Natives together in our loathing of those who are guilty. . . . After all these years . . . do they [the natives] suppose us capable today of letting loose a military vengeance, indiscriminately for the shedding of Christian blood?'[14]

The news of the Poona murders was bad enough to earn banner headlines and editorial comment in the British press. 'Poona', wrote the *Daily Mail* (1 July) 'of course has long been notorious as the hotbed of southern India fanaticism; a town and district where the crafty, mutinous, semi-educated Brahman walked at large, and freely propagated in newspaper and bazaar his faith in the liberation and regeneration of India on high caste lines.' Two days later, the *Morning Post* (3 July), after darkly hinting at the possibility of a 'Second Mutiny', ascribed the 'disturbances' in India to the fact, 'that for twelve years all sorts of *Babus* have been allowed by the special permission of Lord Ripon to scatter broadcast, whatever venomous lies it occurred to them to utter'. The *Daily Mail* (1 July) held the 'Brahman editor' responsible for the Poona outrages, and observed that 'assassination by the pen may in the long run, prove a deal more formidable to British rule in India than assassination by the sword'.

'Assassination by the pen' was no journalistic hyperbole. Within a few hours of the Rand-Ayerst murders, Lord George Hamilton, Secretary of State for India, had inquired telegraphically from Lord Sandhurst, the Governor of Bombay: 'Do you connect these outrages with the incendiary tone of the press?'[15] Ten days later, Hamilton urged Viceroy Elgin to take strong measures as 'public opinion in the Parliament and press and elsewhere was uneasy'.[16] Hamilton had good reasons for anxiety. The year 1897 was 'full of the tricks of malevolent fortune'.[17] Famine and plague had ravaged large parts of India, and strained local administrations to the limit. A surprise raid on an armed escort accompanying a political officer on 10 June had not only resulted in the loss of British lives,[18] but had the ominous sign of a tribal rising on the north-west frontier. On 16 June Assam and Bengal were rocked by a terrible earthquake. In Shillong, the capital of Assam, most of the public buildings and private houses were razed to the ground; in Cooch Behar only one house was left standing, and in Calcutta, the damage to buildings was considered so serious, that it was considered unsafe to fire a sixty-gun ceremonial salute on the Queen's Jubilee.[19] It was on the very night of the Jubilee that Rand and Ayerst had been shot down at Poona. A week later there was a riot at Calcutta in which local Muslims, outraged by nothing more than the execution of a legal process (which put a Hindu landlord in possession of property on which a mosque had been constructed), vented their fury on European inhabitants in Calcutta.

It is not surprising that, overwhelmed by bad news in such quick succession, Hamilton should have hastened to inquire from the Viceroy about 'disposition of native troops' and whether there was any connection between the tribal trouble in the north-west and the riot in Calcutta and the assassinations in Poona. The Viceroy consulted his Council and sounded the Governors, but discounted dangers of a mutiny. Nor did he favour hasty legislation against the Indian press or grant of more executive powers to the Bombay Government to deal with the emergency. 'Sandhurst', wrote the Viceroy about the Bombay Governor, 'has such ample military and police resources at his command that he can enforce anything which he thinks necessary, while in the Regulation of 1827 he has summary powers of arrest and imprisonment which . . . probably exceed those of the Czar of Russia.'[20]

As the police were unable to lay their hands on the assassins of Rand and Ayerst immediately, the Bombay Government announced a reward of Rs 10,000 for clues leading to their discovery. The Bombay Governor wrote to the Viceroy:

'Investigations are proceeding and, so far as we have got indications, point to Brahmanism as being at the bottom of the plot. . . . My colleagues and I are unanimous in thinking strong action most necessary. We have resolved as a beginning to put into Poona, a punitive police force of 50 Europeans and 150 Natives. We are further considering the desirability of disarming Poona City . . . while it might be necessary to put into force the power to arrest and detain persons as state prisoners. . . .'[21]

IV

The imposition of the punitive police on Poona, the smear campaign against educated Indians as a class, the outcry in the Anglo-Indian and Tory press for repressive measures, and hints from the Secretary of State for India in the Parliament that legislation to curb the 'native' press was being contemplated, were developments which caused Wedderburn much concern. The question was not only of affording some relief to the unfortunate people of Poona who had been harassed by famine, plague, house-searches – and now by punitive police. An effort was clearly necessary to prevent new chains being forged for the Indian press: if the Poona assassinations could be put in the local context of plague operations, and the bubbles of a widespread conspiracy and an imminent mutiny pricked, the threatened legislation against the Indian press might perhaps be staved off. Wedderburn decided to press for a public and impartial inquiry into Poona affairs. He convened a meeting of the Indian Parliamentary Committee in the Conference Room of the House of Commons on 1 July, and invited to it the four Indian delegates who had appeared before the Welby Commission. It fell to Gokhale, as the representative of the Deccan, to do most of the briefing to the

MPs on the background of events in his home-town, and on the reasons which made a public inquiry essential. After the meeting Gokhale gave an interview to a representative of the *Manchester Guardian*. The report of this interview, which appeared on the following day (2 July), constituted a sharp and unequivocal indictment of the entire Plague Administration: it had the same air of certainty and fighting spirit which had marked his cross-examination by the Welby Commission a few weeks earlier. 'British soldiers', the *Manchester Guardian* quoted Gokhale as saying, 'ignorant of the language and contemptuous of the customs, the sentiments and the religious susceptibilities of the people', had been 'let loose' upon the town; 'they had wantonly destroyed property, appropriated jewellery, burnt furniture, entered kitchens and places of worship, contaminated food, spat upon idols or broke them by throwing them on the ground, and dragged women into streets for inspection before removal to hospitals'. 'My correspondents', added Gokhale, 'whose word I can trust absolutely, report the violation of two women, one of whom is said afterwards to have committed suicide rather than survive her shame.'

The Wedderburn-Gokhale strategy in highlighting the local significance of the Poona murders by seeking a public inquiry was a rational one, but in the irrational, almost hysterical atmosphere created by the murders themselves it had no chance of success. A public inquiry into Poona affairs at any time would have been difficult to secure; but after 23 June it was ruled out. For the Government to concede such an inquiry in July 1897 would have been to cast a slur on the record of Rand (who was lying in hospital in a grave condition when Gokhale gave his press interview), to question the honour of the British soldiers, and even to impugn the administration of Lord Sandhurst who was closely associated with the direction of plague operations.

Hostile critics at once seized upon that part of the indictment of plague operations, which was the most difficult to prove: the alleged violation of women by the British soldiers. The major issue of the conduct of plague operations in Poona and the justification for a public inquiry were relegated to the background, and Wedderburn and Gokhale found themselves the chief targets of a scathing press campaign. Meanwhile, on the very day Gokhale addressed the Indian Parliamentary Committee, the Secretary of State had telegraphed to the Governor of Bombay for information. Lord Sandhurst's reply of 4 July was emphatic:

'Gokhale is Poona Brahman, his associates are known to be disaffected and to have done much to obstruct and defame plague operations. Probably question in Parliament is prompted by desire to gain some sympathy with Poona Brahmans, a section of whom are suspected to be promoters of Poona assassinations.'[22]

On 13 July, in reply to a question by Sir James Fergusson, the Secretary of State read from a telegram sent by Lord Sandhurst: 'Regarding Gokhale's letter alleging violation of women, from all inquiries I have made, I am convinced this is still more gross and malevolent invention than that about stripping of women'. Wedderburn, who was not present in the House of Commons when this question was answered, at once wrote a letter to *The Times*[23] bearing personal testimony to Prof. Gokhale's 'highest character for integrity and his public spirit', and justifying a public inquiry into Poona affairs. Gokhale himself wrote to the *Manchester Guardian* on 14 July, explaining the context of the allegation about the misconduct of the soldiers and the ground on which he had based it.

Gokhale's letter to the *Manchester Guardian* was published on 15 July. The following day he left for India. However, he already had some idea of the severity of the storm which had broken over his head. Not only was he being branded as an arch-liar and a slanderer, but a campaign of vilification had opened against Poona Brahmans, indeed against educated Indians as a class whose claims for greater association with the administration of the country he had so ably advocated before the Welby Commission. If (as seemed likely) the allegation about the violation of the two women by the soldiers could not be proved, would it not give a handle to Anglo-Indian opponents of Indian reform, who never lost an opportunity of denouncing Indian politicians as untrustworthy and irresponsible? Would it not make the task of good old Hume, Wedderburn, and Naoroji in putting across the Indian case to the British people even more difficult?[24]

When Wacha joined Gokhale aboard the *Caledonia* on 18 July, at Brindisi he found him in a deep depression.[25] With his head stooped low, the young professor paced the deck, brooding on the cruel turn of events which had brought his triumphant trip to England to a disastrous conclusion. A group of Europeans from Aden recognised Gokhale and went out of their way to insult him. Wacha and Lawrence (a British civilian who was on his way to India) did their best to comfort Gokhale. Before landing in

Bombay, Gokhale had an unexpected visitor: Vincent, the Commissioner of Police who came aboard to probe Gokhale for fuller details of the allegations and, if possible, for the names of his correspondents in Poona. Gokhale was polite but firm; he would not oblige the Commissioner of Police, though he assured him that he proposed to act in a straightforward manner.

After meeting Ranade and other friends in Bombay and Poona Gokhale realised at once that there was no chance of his being able to substantiate the allegations. In the peculiar conditions of Indian social life, two months after the completion of the plague operations, production of evidence would have been difficult under the best of circumstances. But after the imposition of punitive police on Poona, the arrest of Tilak, and the deportation of the Natu brothers,[26] few people would have dared to defy the authorities. Though it was impossible to be sure, the chances of Gokhale being prosecuted were remote; his allegations had been made in England in good faith in general terms and avowedly on the basis of reports received from correspondents in India; moreover, he could not be charged with defaming a particular individual. If his case was legally tenable, did he not have a moral duty? 'The very fact' he recorded later, 'that the injured parties had no legal redress against me made my responsibilities as a gentleman all the greater.'[27] The moral argument was reinforced by a political one: if the controversy on Rand and the soldiers continued, it could only further stoke up the fires of racial antagonism in Poona. If by a frank withdrawal of the charges Gokhale could close the controversy would it not lower the political temperature and afford a sorely needed respite to that hapless town?

Within five days of landing in Bombay, Gokhale had mailed to Lord Sandhurst 'a full statement containing explanation, full retraction' and 'an unqualified apology' which was directed to all, 'to H.E., the Governor, to the members of the Plague Committee, and to soldiers engaged in plague operations'.

For Gokhale, the 'Apology' was a bitter cup of humiliation. He drained it to the dregs, but it seemed to do him little good. The wrath of the Government was not visibly abated. On 4 August Lord Sandhurst spoke in the Bombay Legislative Council in terms of irony and scorn about the 'apology and withdrawal made by a gentleman, whose name was prominently for a few days before the public'. On 5 August Sir M. Bhownaggree made a stinging attack on Gokhale in the House of Commons: 'There had appeared before them the precious Mr Gokhale, who under the guidance of the Hon. Member for Banff [Wedderburn] defiled the threshold of this building.'[28] Nor did the apology go down well with the Indian press. A few papers such as the friendly *Dnyan Prakash* (9 August) or the *Indian Spectator* (8 August) praised Gokhale for acting like a gentleman, but many papers were frankly critical. 'Whatever may be said in favour of the rising publicist', wrote the *Kaiser-i-Hind* (8 August) 'this much is certain that he has much compromised his reputation.' The *Gujarati* (8 August) referred to Gokhale's 'absolute, frank, and helpless self-condemnation'. Tilak's papers were far from sympathetic. The *Mahratta* (8 August) could not appreciate why 'the humiliated professor', had withdrawn all the charges, when he was unable to substantiate one of them. The *Kesari* (10 August) expressed the fear that Gokhale's 'overwhelming apology', and the repudiation of the joint memorial by the Muslims of Poona, had lent support to Governor Sandhurst's charges against the people of Poona. In a private letter to a friend, Tilak, who had meanwhile been arrested and placed on trial for seditious writings, made a disparaging reference to Gokhale: 'I think in me they [Government] will not find a *Kutcha* [raw] reed as they did in Professor Gokhale.'[29]

With political factionalism developed to a high degree in Poona, there was no dearth of men willing to embroider on the story of the apology. It was suggested that Gokhale had agreed to apologise under a threat from the Commissioner of Police who had met him on arrival at Bombay, that the draft of the apology had been made out by Bennett, the editor of *The Times of India*. It was argued that Gokhale had lowered the prestige of his country, that he had shown want of courage, that he had irretrievably damaged the Indian cause in England.

Gokhale was very lonely and unhappy, talked of giving up public life, and wrote long letters to Hume, Wedderburn, Naoroji, and Caine to whom he opened out the anguish of his heart. They were all sympathetic and realised his predicament. Caine,[30] Naoroji[31] and even Hume[32] pointed out that the apology was much too long and much too humble, but they admired his public spirit and did not see why he should talk of retiring from politics. 'We look upon you', wrote Hume to Gokhale, 'as a martyr to the cause', and advised him to 'disregard the ravings alike of the Anglo-Indians and Indian lick-spittles'.[33] Naoroji urged him to remain 'cool and calm'. Wedderburn acknowledged his own part

C

in the affair: he had failed to foresee the risks of mentioning anything that was not capable of legal proof. 'Among us', he told Gokhale, 'we made the mistake – it was a venial one – we were trying to protect the weak against the strong, and in such work we must expect sometimes to get hard knocks . . . the very ferocity of the attack upon you testifies to the importance and value of the work you did in England on behalf of your countrymen.'[34]

These were comforting words, but they could not solve Gokhale's immediate difficulties. On return from England he was excommunicated from the Chitpavan Brahman community for breaking the taboo on foreign travel. Thus he became a social outcaste just at the time when he was being reduced to a political outcaste. He feared his opponents would go to any length to discredit him; he was haunted by the fear of a public affront which would only rub salt into his wounds. In the last week of August, the Bombay Presidency Association[35] called a special public meeting to honour him and Wacha for their work in connection with the Welby Commission. Gokhale was proud of his work in England and would have loved to be present at the meeting, but thought it prudent to stay away.

As the Amraoti session of the Indian National Congress in December 1897 approached, friends urged Gokhale to attend it: to deliberately avoid it would be an act of cowardice, perhaps of political suicide. Gokhale was not well; the pain in his heart, caused by an accident at Calais in March, had revived and the week's quarantine for plague before entering Amraoti was a great trial.[36] Nevertheless he persevered in his resolve to attend the Congress. Unfortunately for him his worst fears were confirmed. The hostile demonstration, which he had dreaded all along, came when his name was proposed to be included in the list of speakers. He was denounced as a traitor by some delegates from Bengal, who were supported by their friends from the Deccan.

Gokhale's cup of humiliation and sorrow brimmed over; once again he reviewed the whole course of events which had led to the fatal interview and the apology in a letter to the press. It was a long, eloquent and even moving document; its concluding paragraph affirmed:

'Public duties, undertaken at the bidding of no man cannot be laid down at the desire of any one. . . . One is always glad of the approbation of the public of what one has done. . . . But it is not the highest purpose of existence, nor nearly the highest. If it comes – to use the words of Herbert Spencer – well, if not, well also, though not so well.'[37]

He was indeed hungering for public understanding, if not public appreciation. It might seem at first that he was wallowing in self-pity. Those who told him to lie low and let the incident be forgotten did not know Poona;[38] he knew his hometown too well to cherish any such illusion. The apology was going to be a very handy stick to beat him with. It is true that in his statements, and letters to friends he preferred to put the matter on a public plane, but he would have been more than human if he had not been conscious of the personal aspect of the crisis. Only two years before, in the winter of 1895–6, he and his friends had been squeezed out of the Poona Sarvajanik Sabha. In February 1896 he had confided to a friend: 'I have grown absolutely sick of public life in Poona . . . personally I wish now to wash my hands of all political work in Poona. There is so much selfish and ignoble here, that I would fly from it to the furthest extremities of the world if I could.'[39] With the foundation of the Deccan Sabha in November 1896 his party had made a fresh start. It was however, the visit to England in 1897 which had really put fresh heart into Gokhale, and opened new political vistas to him; he had even seen visions of fighting for his country from a seat in the House of Commons. But suddenly, after that fatal meeting of the Indian Parliamentary Committee and the press interview in London, his fortunes had suffered a drastic reversal. The high praise he had earned for his evidence before the Welby Commission was forgotten; in the eyes of the Europeans he was a slanderer; in those of his own countrymen he was a coward. 'You must be prepared', W. S. Caine wrote to Gokhale on 29 October 1897, 'if you came to settle in this country [England], to be constantly spoken of as the fellow who slandered the British soldiers.'[40]

It was at the Amraoti session of the Congress that Gokhale's fortunes touched their nadir. He saw the virulence of his opponents and the heavy odds against which he would have to recover the ground he had lost. Was history going to repeat itself? Would he be edged out of the Indian National Congress, just as he had been edged out of the Poona Sarvajanik two years earlier?

This was Gokhale's moment of truth. His extreme sensitiveness, and disdain for the rough and tumble of politics wrestled with his sense of self-preservation. 'The best part of our nature', he wrote to a correspondent in January 1898, 'is manifested not in what we enjoy but what we endure. There is a sublimity and moral elevation in undeserved suffering, which nothing can equal, and which is almost its own reward.'[41] This was almost a Gandhian approach, but high idealism alone was not enough to sustain him against the vicissitudes of politics. The flame of ambition had to be rekindled. During these weeks Gokhale went through much searching of heart, but emerged a stronger, if a sadder man. On 5 February 1898, he committed to his diary a remarkably ambitious programme. 'By the grace of Sree Guru Dattatreya', he solemnly recorded, he 'would endeavour humbly but firmly' to acquire 'yoga, knowledge of History, Philosophy, Astronomy, Geology, Physiology and French', and would 'try to become a member of Bombay, the Supreme Legislative Council and the British Parliament. In all these assemblies I will try to do good to my country by all means in my power.'[42]

Though the diary entry goes on to include even the preaching of a new religion, what is really important is the reassertion of Gokhale's intellectual and political ambitions. He was no longer thinking of retiring from the field of battle; he was bracing himself to face the obduracy and malice of his opponents and the fickleness of public opinion. Though he never acquired the cool reassurance of political gladiators who emerge completely unruffled from the heat and dust of political controversy, he was able to shed some of his ultra-sensitivity. He also realised that knowledge and courage were not enough; they needed to be tinged with caution, if the political struggle for Indian reform was to be waged on a long-term basis.

Henceforth Gokhale's speeches and writings though solidly based on facts and figures acquired a marked tendency to understatement; this was a great asset to one whose best political work was to be done in legislative chambers or in private negotiations with British statesmen.

V

In 1899, Gokhale was elected to the Bombay Legislative Council. In 1901, he sought the assistance of Sir Pherozeshah Mehta in securing the Bombay seat in the Imperial Legislative Council, which he had thought of as a prelude to a parliamentary career in England. Nothing had wounded him more, he confided to Mehta, 'than Bhownaggree's denunciation of me in the House of

Commons as a despicable perjurer.[43] The words burnt into my heart and the night I read them, I made up my mind, as soon as I was free from my pledge,[44] to devote myself to the furtherance of our political cause in England, to which I had, without meaning it, done much serious injury.'

Gokhale's election to the Imperial Legislative Council did not prove, as he had expected, a stepping-stone to the House of Commons. Nevertheless, it was a turning point in his career; it provided him with a forum where he could show his talents to the best advantage, and quickly win recognition as a statesman. The crisis in 1897, which had threatened to sweep him off the political stage also provided the dynamic for his spectacular comeback and for the important role he was to play in the political evolution of India for more than a decade.

Chapter 3

Social Thought of Gokhale (1966)

I

In the published speeches and writings of Gokhale social problems do not figure much. Nor have biographers and historians considered the subject important enough to discuss it in any detail. It would, however, be rash to infer from this that Gokhale was indifferent to social problems. He held clear and strong views on the issues of social reform that confronted the Hindu society in his time; his approach to these issues was influenced by the men and institutions with whom he came into contact during his impressionable years, and by the priorities he set himself in the course of a comparatively short but intensely crowded public life.

Gokhale was born in 1866 and grew into manhood in the 1880s, an important decade in Indian social and political evolution, when the country was stirring into a new life. The awakening was not a painless process. In the social sphere the spirit of inquiry and scepticism had begun to foster doubts about institutions, conventions and taboos which had been hallowed by long tradition and a powerful priestly class. To picture the hidebound condition of the Hindu society in the latter half of the nineteenth century requires an effort of imagination. The strait-jacket of custom and superstition was firmly wrapped round the community and strangled initiative and freedom. An elaborate ritual prescribed behaviour not only in public but in private.

The historian, G. S. Sardesai, a contemporary of Gokhale, has recorded[1] how as a child he was stopped from entering his house and forced to bathe if he had happened to touch a person of a low caste; how at meal-times he had to wear clothes made of 'pure textiles', i.e. silk or wool; and how he could not have a hair-cut except on auspicious days. Little boys in Maharashtra had their ear-lobes pierced; such was the importance attached to this custom that in Marathi the word for non-Hindus was, *Avindha* (those whose ear-lobes had not been pierced). There was a strong taboo against foreign travel. Instructions on what, when and where to eat, were taken to ridiculous lengths. At the annual sessions of the Indian National Congress, the more orthodox delegates carried or cooked their own food, and ate behind closed doors, away from the unholy gaze of their colleagues. The more affluent of the Congress delegates took care to provide themselves not only with Brahman cooks, but Brahman cooks of particular sub-castes. All this may appear amusing to us, but it was not a laughing matter for those over whom hung the Damocles' Sword of excommunication from the caste. That was a dreadful weapon mercilessly wielded against those who dared to defy the ortho-doxies of the day. What it meant in terms of physical and mental suffering to its victims may be gleaned from the pages of Bipin Chandra Pal's autobiography. When under the influence of Bramho Samaj, Bipin Chandra began to champion widow re-marriage and other social reforms, his father, who had married a second time in old age, was furious. He wrote to his son:

'My first mistake was to send you to an English school. My second mistake was to resign from judicial service . . . to find facilities for your English education. . . . My third mistake was to send you to Calcutta after you passed the Entrance Examination, and I have committed a fourth blunder by marrying at this age. But I hope that by this marriage I have created unrivalled opportunities for the pursuit of your religion, so that you may . . . have the satisfaction of giving away your own widowed stepmother in marriage.'[2]

How strong the grip of religion was on that generation is shown by an entry in the diary of a British officer of the Indian Civil Service, H. M. Kisch. On 29 November 1876, he witnessed a strange scene on the Grand Trunk Road in Dubra, Govindpur Sub-division in Bengal:

'A very large number of pilgrims are to be seen passing down the Grand Trunk Road from northern and western India to the Shrine of Juggernaut in Orissa. The mode in which the pilgrimage is performed is strange. The pilgrims measure their bodies along the whole length of the road. They begin their journey in a standing posture, then fall on their faces, stretch out their arms and make a line in the dust on the road. They then get up, walk as far as the line they have just made, then fall down again on their faces and make another line, and carry on the same mode of progress for the whole journey, say from Lucknow to Juggernaut. Supposing a man to be able to cover 8 feet from his feet to the extremities of his hands when stretched out, he must in order to travel one mile fall down 660 times. At this rate it is found that a pilgrim can travel about 4 miles a day, and many men have to spend a year or two on the pilgrimage before they can reach the sacred shrine.'[3]

It was not only on their personal lives that the beliefs of the people made an impact. The story of Sham Charan Pal, published by the *Indian Social Reformer*,[4] was a remarkable instance of the passions aroused by a fanatical insistence on the superiority of the Brahmans in the social scale. Sham Charan Pal was arrested on the charge of murdering a Brahman and committed to the 'sessions'. He was too poor to engage a counsel, but his wife begged a famous barrister, Ghose, to defend him. The acquittal by the Court notwithstanding, the man was nearly lynched. In the words of Ghose:

'On the termination of the trial, the Judge declaring that, in his opinion, the man was innocent, the prisoner had the greatest difficulty in getting out of the court house; he would probably have been mobbed, if I had not myself spoken to the crowd and escorted him, protecting him all the time with the walking stick I had in my hand. I brought him from the Howrah Court-House to my own house in Calcutta where his young wife was anxiously waiting to hear the result of the case.'

Of the evils which corroded Indian society, the worst were probably those which stunted its womanhood. Singing and playing were unthinkable for most girls, and so were reading and writing. It was not uncommon for them to be married off at the age of five or six; ancient Sanskrit texts had been twisted to mean that parents, who did not marry off their daughters before they attained puberty, were . . . doomed to eternal perdition. Early marriage was practically universal; it was the root cause of illiteracy, but its most serious consequence was the terrible institution of the child widow. Little girls, who hardly knew the meaning of marriage, were condemned to life-long mourning for boy-husbands on whom they had probably never set their eyes. The problem of child widows was not an academic one. In 1895 a writer in the *Quarterly Journal of the Poona Sarvajanik Sabha* estimated that among the Deccan and Konkani Brahmans one out of five women was a widow, and one out of thirty widows was under nine years of age.[5]

II

It was in this society that Gokhale was born and brought up. It is possible that, like most of his contemporaries, he would have acquiesced in its taboos and accepted its injunctions. Tolstoy once remarked before his 'conversion' that his philosophy of life was that 'one should live so as to have the best for oneself and one's family and not to try to be wiser than life and nature'. That indeed is the philosophy of most people in all countries and at all times; if it was not adopted by Gokhale it was due to an exceptional circumstance, which took him off the beaten path. It was a happy accident that the Rajaram College at Kolhapur did not provide for the full BA course, and Gokhale had to spend a few months in the Deccan College at Poona, and later in the Elphinstone College, Bombay. The stay at Elphinstone College left a deep impression upon Gokhale. Contact with English professors broadened his outlook; new vistas unfolded before him; he was fired with a spirit of inquiry which not only whetted his intellectual appetite but enabled him to take a fresh look at things around him. He decided not to use his degree as a passport to a coveted post under the Government or to a lucrative career at the bar, but pledged himself to serve on a subsistence wage as a teacher, first in the New English School and then in the Fergusson College, run by the Deccan Education Society of Poona.

Another important formative influence on Gokhale was his close contact with two of the most forward-looking minds in Maharashtra in the closing years of the nineteenth century. One of them was Gopal Ganesh Agarkar and the other was Mahadev Govind Ranade. Both of them made a deep impression on Gokhale when he was serving his apprenticeship in public life.

Agarkar was a free-thinker and a rationalist, who had nourished himself on the philosophy of Mill and Spencer; a logician, who had the courage of his convictions and made no secret of his agnosticism, and even atheism. He made a frontal assault on Hindu orthodoxy, challenged its cherished beliefs and questioned its time-honoured rituals. He had no use for the caste system, and

unequivocally denounced untouchability and infant marriage. As
we read Agarkar today, we feel he was fifty years ahead of his
time. He did not see why a Hindu widow should be denied the
privilege of a *kumkum* mark on her forehead. He did not see
why girls could not have the same facilities for education as
boys. He failed to see why women could not be employed on the
same terms as men. There was nothing apologetic or half-hearted
about his pleas for social reform. The long and bitter quarrel
between him and his one-time friend B. G. Tilak may have owed
something to differences of temperament, but Agarkar's views
on social reform went far beyond anything that Tilak could
accept. Their conflicting opinions were at first reflected in the
columns of the *Kesari*, until Agarkar broke away from it, and
founded *Sudharak*, a bi-lingual weekly, the Marathi section of
which was edited by Agarkar and the English section by Gokhale.
In the *Sudharak*, as in the crusade for reform, Gokhale was
Agarkar's partner.

Agarkar spearheaded the assaults on the orthodox party; he
was also the chief victim when the counter-attack came. The
tension between the advocates and opponents of reform reached
its height in the early months of 1891 over the Age of Consent
Bill. Maharashtra and Bengal were convulsed with a mass hysteria
over what seems today a modest, almost innocuous bill in the
Imperial Council raising the legal age of consent (not marriage)
for girls from ten to twelve years. It was insinuated by the opponents of reform that the British Government, with the connivance,
if not the incitement of the reformers, had laid a diabolical plan
to undermine Hindu religion and society. The fact was that Lord
Lansdowne and the Government of India had been most reluctant
to trespass on the delicate area of religious belief and social usage,
and were willy-nilly pushed into it by the pressure of public
opinion in England which had been roused by Malabari's
tenacious propaganda in that country, on behalf of the hapless
Hindu widows.[6]

The Age of Consent Bill passed through the Imperial Legislative Council, thanks to its standing official majority, but the
sequel surprised the government as well as the reformers. The
reformers were described as renegades, denounced in the press
and on the platform and ostracised by their neighbours. In Poona,
Agarkar was the target of a smear campaign, the highlight of
which was the burning of his effigy with an egg in one hand and
a bottle of brandy in the other; the effigy was taken out in a pro-

cession and burnt on the outskirts of the town. Agarkar's ordeal as a social reformer left a deep impression on Gokhale. It gave him a glimpse of the volcanic properties of Hindu orthodoxy in matters of social reform and of the exceptional virulence and ruthlessness of the opponents of social reform in Poona.

A deeper and a more pervasive influence than that of Agarkar was that of Mahadev Govind Ranade whom Gokhale recognised as his *guru*; 'at whose feet' – the words are Gokhale's – he sat for fourteen years. One of the first and the finest products of university education in nineteenth-century India, Ranade attempted a living synthesis of the best that the cultures of India and the West had to offer. Like Ram Mohun Roy before him, and Gandhi after him, Ranade had the genius to see the Indian predicament as a whole. There was hardly an aspect of India's past, present or future on which Ranade did not exercise his mind. He argued:

'You cannot have a good social system while you find yourself low in the scale of political rights, nor can you be fit to receive the political rights and privileges unless your social system is based on reason and justice. You cannot have a good economical system when your social arrangements are imperfect. If your religious ideas are low and grovelling you cannot succeed in economical, political and social spheres. This interdependence is not an accident but the law of nature.'[7]

Ranade's versatility was extraordinary. Besides being a distinguished judge, who could hold his own with his European colleagues on the bench of the Bombay High Court, he was well versed in Hindu philosophy and European literature; he was a historian of the Maratha revival and a perceptive commentator on economic and financial developments in India and abroad; he was one of the founding fathers of the Indian National Congress. He was also a deeply religious man, whose sermons at the 'Prarthana Samaj' meetings brought tears to the eyes of his audience.

Almost the first cause which Ranade had espoused at the age of twenty was social reform; it was also the cause which obsessed him on his death-bed forty years later. He had recognised the strength of religious superstition and priestly vested interest behind social evils. He tried to reason his generation out of this bondage. He refuted the argument that a practice was right simply because it was longstanding. 'Above all mere ordinances and institutes [of religion]', he wrote, 'stands the law eternal, of

justice and equality, of pity and compassion, the suggestion of
the conscience within and of nature without us.'[8] 'We can never
forego', he affirmed, 'the right of every human being to act in
concert with others of his own way of thinking and make the
effort to better our condition with the light that is given to us,
and with the help that religion and history afford us.'[9]

Ranade's devotion to social reform equalled that of Agarkar,
but he did not have Agarkar's militancy. Agarkar was a born
rebel, a combative journalist who delighted in polemics, and
neither expected nor received any quarter. Ranade's scholarly
and judicial mind, instinctively shrank from public controversy,
preferring the hope of a slow conversion to the risks of a head-on
confrontation. He had a sense of history and could take long-
term views; he had been influenced by Darwin's theory of evolution which in his youth had changed the intellectual climate of
the western world. He learnt to view society as an organism which
was susceptible to the laws of growth and decay. The reforms
in Hindu society which he advocated were intended to lop off
the diseased overgrowth and excrescences and to restore vitality
and energy to the social organism. Ranade paved the way for
these reforms by writing articles, delivering lectures, reinterpreting
ancient texts, enrolling field workers. In 1887, he founded the
National Social Conference, which met every year at the same
place, as the Indian National Congress, and provided a national
forum for social reformers.

III

Having had a glimpse of the society into which Gokhale was
born, of his formative influences, and of the two men who were
the mentors of his youth, it is easier to explain Gokhale's own
attitude to the burning social problems of his day. One of the
earliest and the clearest expositions of his views came in a paper
he read at an Educational Congress in the women's section of
the Victorian Era Exhibition in 1897 when he was in London to
appear before the Welby Commission. He began by posing (as
Ranade was wont to do) the problem of transition from the old
to the new, which faced India at the close of the nineteenth
century:

'A great Eastern civilisation, stationary for many centuries, is
being once again galvanised into life by reason of its coming into

contact with a younger and much more vigorous civilisation of the West. The retention of all that is great and noble in our national life, as it has come down to us from the past, and the fullest absorption of what is great and noble in the life of the West . . . this is now the work which has to be accomplished before we can once more hold our head high as a nation.'[10]

Gokhale's main theme in this lecture was female education in India. He put the problem in perspective by pointing out that the bondage of caste and custom tried

'to keep us tied down to certain fixed ways of life and fixed modes of thought, and which so often cripples all efforts at the most elementary reforms. . . . One peculiarity of the Indian life of the present day is the manner in which almost every single act of our daily life is regarded as regulated by some religious notion or another. We must eat, and sleep, and even stand and sit, and walk only in accordance with certain religious beliefs; and the slightest departure from the accepted ideas in these matters is understood to increase the difficulties in the path of our salvation.'[11]

He acknowledged that these ideas had a firmer hold on the minds of women, and 'the combination of enforced ignorance and overdone religion made them willing victims of unjust customs and even opponents of reform'. 'It is obvious', Gokhale concluded, 'that . . . a wide diffusion of education, with all its solvent influences among the women of India is the only means of emancipating their minds from this degrading thraldom to ideas inherited through a long past.'[12]

Gokhale made no secret of his views on the social problems facing the Hindu society in his day. Indeed he was not prepared to make any concession to entrenched priesthood; he claimed an equal position for women. He supported the introduction of co-education in Fergusson College; he educated his daughters and defied the convention of the time by not marrying them at an early age. On marriage which, being tied up with religious beliefs and injunctions, was one of the most explosive subjects, Gokhale spoke in accents which even today sound modern. In January 1912, while speaking in the Imperial Legislative Council on Bhupendra Nath Basu's Civil Marriage Bill, he looked forward to the day when grown-up boys and girls would choose for themselves, and care neither for caste nor creed:

'It is quite true that the Bill represents ideas which are in advance of the views of the bulk of the Hindu and Muhammaden communities today; but I am quite sure that with the spread of higher education among Indian women, with late marriages coming more and more into vogue – and late marriages mostly lead to choice marriages, i.e., to free choice by the marrying parties – with these things coming, with the dignity of individual freedom realised better and better, and last but not least, in the steady fusion of different creeds and different races, which is bound to take place under the stress of our growing nationality . . . the day cannot be far distant when a measure like the one before us will find its way to the Statute Book.'[13]

Gokhale was thus looking forward to not only 'choice marriages', but to inter-caste, inter-communal and inter-regional marriages as well.

IV

The emancipation of women through the abolition of infant brides and child widows, provision for girls' education, and raising the age of marriage and permitting widow remarriage was a major plank in the social reform movement. The improvement in the condition of the 'untouchables' was another. The disabilities of the untouchables, like those of women, had become intertwined with religious sentiment. Gokhale spoke on this subject with great feeling and great courage on 27 April 1903, when he moved a resolution on the uplift of the depressed classes at the Dharwar Social Conference. It was, he said 'absolutely monstrous that a class of human beings with bodies similar to our own, with brains that can think and with hearts that can feel',[14] should be perpetually condemned to servitude and mental and moral degradation. He quoted from one of Ranade's speeches, in which, while speaking on the grievances of Indians in South Africa, he had asked whether the sympathy with oppressed and down-trodden Indians was to be confined only to those countrymen of theirs who had left India. Was this sympathy not to be extended to 'our own people of low castes who suffered oppression'? Gokhale ridiculed the specious argument brought forward by some people that the caste system in Indian society was in any way comparable to the class structure in Western society, and ended with the stern warning: 'If you were to stand where you were a thousand years ago, the system of castes need not be modified in any material degree. . . .'

Five and a half years later, in December 1908, in one of his rare interventions in the proceedings of the National Social Conference at Madras, Gokhale deplored the fact that fifty years after the introduction of Western ideas and university education, the condition of the depressed classes had not improved. He recalled how in Japan where Western influence came later than in India, the Order of Jeeta, which corresponded in some ways to the depressed classes in India, had been abolished by a proclamation of the Mikado: within forty years the people belonging to the Jeeta class had been completely assimilated within the Japanese society.

V

Whenever Gokhale commented on social problems of his time, he did so unambiguously. These problems did not seem so simple to him and his contemporaries as they may seem to us today. Nevertheless, Gokhale himself seems to have had little difficulty in making the transition from the old to the new, from the traditional to the modern. In the clarity and radicalism of his social thought he was an apt pupil of Agarkar, but in propagating them, he did not show Agarkar's persistence and pugnacity. Gokhale's interest in the movement for social reform of his day was in fact spasmodic. Even when he was the joint editor of the *Sudharak*, and the battle of words between the orthodox and reform parties in Poona raged fiercely, Gokhale preferred to write on political subjects, leaving social issues to the caustic pen of Agarkar. Gokhale did not attend the annual meetings of the National Social Conference regularly even though it was run by his master, Ranade. He was not present at the session held at Bombay in December 1889. In 1890 at the Calcutta session he was seen on the dais with the prominent leaders of social reform, but his name does not figure in the records of the Conference proceedings for 1894, 1895 or 1899. In December 1900 he deputised for Ranade by reading his inaugural address at the Lahore session. Ranade died a few days later, and Gokhale in the next fourteen years attended only three meetings of the National Social Conference: in 1901, 1902 and 1908.

Gokhale's lukewarm interest in the social reform movement calls for an explanation. Fortunately we have the evidence of

R. P. Paranjpye, a young colleague and friend who had questioned Gokhale on this subject.[15] It transpired that Gokhale had been married at an early age, but the girl, whom an elder relative had selected for him, was found to be suffering from leprosy. Gokhale provided for her maintenance, but never lived with her, and a few years later on the insistence of an uncle married again. Though his first wife died soon afterwards, the fact that he had married a second time in the life-time of his first wife was considered a great blot upon him. This incident made him an easy target, and Gokhale to avoid embarrassment to his friends in the social reform movement, preferred to keep himself in the background.

Paranjpye's explanation offers an important clue to the working of Gokhale's mind. But besides this skeleton in his domestic cupboard, there were good reasons why Gokhale should have hesitated to jump into the arena of social reform. Despite his admiration for Agarkar and devotion to Ranade, Gokhale's real interest had always been in politics, not in social reform. The call of politics came to him very early with the persistence and urgency with which it was to come to young Jawaharlal Nehru. Like Nehru, Gokhale had fine sensibilities; he loved poetry and knew the pleasures of reading and writing, but these pleasures had to take second place when the cause of Indian nationalism beckoned. Dinshaw Wacha has left a vivid pen-portrait of the 26-year-old Gokhale waving to the crowds from the coach carrying Dadabhai Naoroji through the streets of Poona in 1893.[16] It was obvious even in those early years that Gokhale's whole being vibrated to the excitement of politics. Like Nehru, Gokhale needed a mighty purpose to hold him. Social reform could hardly satisfy his patriotic fervour. It is as difficult to imagine Gokhale arranging widow remarriages as to imagine Jawaharlal Nehru running the Harijan Sevak Sangh.

To a man who had set his political sights high, another consideration could not have been absent. During the 'apology incident' in 1897, Gokhale had discovered that a warm heart was not enough for politics, and that a cool head was equally important. He had also seen how tricky the ground was in social reform, especially in Poona: a careless step and one could go under. In 1897 Gokhale had learnt to his cost how easy it was to commit political *hara-kiri* in the fickle climate of Poona's factious politics. It took him some years to restore his political fortunes, and it is not surprising that in 1901, he should have declined to accept the reins of the social reform movement which Ranade pressed upon him from his death bed. Ranade wrote from Lonavla on 3 January 1901, just a fortnight before his death:

'My dear Gopalrao, our great want is that young men with great promise of usefulness do not step in the place of the older men who are disabled for active duties. In the political as also in the social sphere, this want is much felt and in my moments of self-communion, I feel that you have it in your power to console any passing despondency one might feel on this account.'[17]

Even this last desperate appeal from the Master failed to move Gokhale. The mantle of social reform fell not on Gokhale but on Chandavarkar. In 1901 Gokhale had recovered from the shadow of the apology incident, but not until 1905 did he attain a position in the counsels of the Indian National Congress, and Imperial Legislative Council and the British Committee of the Congress in London, which made him politically invulnerable. But this pre-eminence brought its own burden of responsibilities which completely absorbed, and indeed exhausted him, leaving scarcely any time for social reform.

Paradoxically, even though Gokhale did not figure among the prominent social reformers of his time, his contribution to the cause of social reform was significant. The National Social Conference, which had been run by Ranade heroically almost single-handed, had by 1905 become an anaemic organisation, with a narrow social base and little activity in the field. Gokhale saw with an unerring instinct that further progress, whether in the political or in the social sphere, depended upon educating the mass of the Indian population through a band of dedicated workers – political *sanyasins*. By spelling out his non-sectarian, rational and secular politics, by campaigning for universal elementary education, and by spotting and training 'his Servants of India' for full-time work in the field Gokhale paved the way for a new phase of the social reform movement. It was left to his disciples Thakkar Bapa and N. M. Joshi – and above all to Gandhi – to give a broader base and a new orientation to social reform in the post-Gokhale era.

D

Chapter 4

Motilal Nehru

I

The Nehrus came from Kashmir, but had settled in Delhi at the beginning of the eighteenth century. Motilal's grandfather Lakshmi Narayan became the first vakil of the East India Company at the Mughal Court of Delhi. Motilal's father Ganga Dhar was a police officer in Delhi in 1857 when the Mutiny took place. In September 1857, as the victorious British troops shelled their way into the town, the Indian population streamed out in panic. Some encamped in the suburbs of Delhi, others bade goodbye to it for ever. Among the fugitives who took the road to Agra were Ganga Dhar, his wife Jeorani, their two daughters Patrani and Maharani, and their sons Bansi Dhar and Nand Lal. Having lost everything in the upheaval of 1857, Ganga Dhar had to start life afresh, but he did not live long. Early in 1861 he died at the age of thirty-four. Three months after his death, his wife gave birth to a son. He was named Motilal.

The death of her husband was a terrible blow to Jeorani. It was one of those catastrophes under the weight of which many an Indian family of ancient lineage has been known to sink into permanent oblivion. Luckily Bansi Dhar and Nand Lal were plucky boys, and though still in their teens, were able to stand on their own feet. Bansi Dhar secured a job as a judgement-writer in the *Sadar Diwani Adalat* at Agra and rose to the position of a subordinate judge. Nand Lal became a teacher, and later the *Diwan* (chief minister) in the small feudatory state of Khetri in Rajasthan. Since the eldest brother was in government service and liable to frequent transfers, Motilal was brought up by Nand Lal. Between these two grew up a strong bond of affection, a happy blend of the filial and the fraternal, of which the Hindu joint family, with all its faults, furnishes perhaps the finest example.

In 1870 Nand Lal quitted Khetri, qualified as a lawyer and began to practise law at Agra. When the High Court was transferred to Allahabad, he moved with it.

Meanwhile Motilal was growing up into a vivacious lad. From Kazi Sadruddin, the tutor of the Raja of Khetri, he learnt Arabic and Persian; in the latter his proficiency at the age of twelve was striking enough to command the respect of men much older than himself. He passed the matriculation examination from Kanpur and joined the Muir Central College at Allahabad. Athletic, fond of outdoor sports, especially wrestling, brimming over with an insatiable curiosity and zest for life, he took to the playground and the places of amusement, and between whiles attended his classes. His career in school and college was not notable for scholastic attainments. On the contrary, his quick wits and high spirits landed him in many an escapade from which he was extricated by Principal Harrison and his British colleagues in the Muir Central College, who had taken a strong liking to this intelligent, lively and restless Kashmiri youth. The contact with his British professors turned out to be a strong formative influence in Motilal's life. It implanted in him an intelligent, rational, sceptical attitude to life, and also a strong admiration for English culture and English institutions. Thus equipped, Motilal found no difficulty in challenging the conservative, caste-ridden and hidebound society into which he had been born.

Motilal sat for his degree examination, thought – wrongly as it turned out – that he had done his first paper badly, and decided to stay away from the rest of the examination. His college career thus ended ingloriously. If this casual, carefree and irresponsible mood of adolescence had been prolonged it might have been Motilal's undoing. Fortunately, he pulled himself together, decided to become a lawyer, worked hard at his legal studies and topped the list of successful candidates in the vakils' examination in 1883. He set up as a lawyer at Kanpur and made a good start, but the district courts of Kanpur did not offer sufficient scope to his talents and ambition. Three years later he moved to Allahabad where he could have a wider field for practice at the High Court, and also be near his brother Nand Lal, who had built up a lucrative practice.

Once again fate dealt a cruel blow to Motilal. In April 1887 Nand Lal died at the age of forty-two, leaving behind him five sons and two daughters. At the age of twenty-five Motilal found himself at the head of a large family, its sole breadwinner.

II

A star-crossed destiny seemed to haunt Motilal's early years; it had robbed him of his father before he was born, and then taken away his beloved brother in the prime of his life. But Motilal was not the man to be overwhelmed by adversity. The death of his brother had increased his burdens, but it also gave a keener edge to his ambition. He rapidly climbed the ladder of success. He was scarcely forty when his income reached five figures. He was one of the four brilliant *vakils* – the others being Pandit (later Sir) Sunderlal, Munshi Ram Prasad, Jogendranath Chaudhuri – who were admitted to the roll of advocates of the Allahabad High Court in 1896. Henceforth Motilal's position as one of the foremost lawyers in northern India was assured. A chief judge of the Allahabad High Court, Sir Grimwood Mears attributed Motilal's pre-eminence in his profession to

'a profusion of gifts; knowledge came easily to him, and as an advocate he had the art of presenting his case in its most attractive form. Every fact fell into its proper place in the narration of the story and was emphasised in just the right degree. He had an exquisite public speaking voice and a charm of manner which made it a pleasure to listen to him.'

Sir Grimwood did not mention, and perhaps did not know the infinite pains which Motilal took over the preparation of his briefs.

Motilal's optimism and self-confidence hastened his success at the Bar; his success further enhanced his self-confidence. Looking back, he could not help feeling that he had triumphed against heavy odds. He did not suffer from false humility; he enjoyed his success enormously and visibly, and took full credit for it. He valued money, prestige and the good things of life, and was glad to be able to command them.

Indeed, there was nothing he seemed to lack. His wife Swarup Rani was a flower of Kashmiri womanhood. The birth of a son – Jawaharlal – in 1889 was an occasion for great rejoicing; two daughters Sarup and Krishna born in 1900 and 1907 completed the family. In 1900 Motilal purchased a house, 1 Church Road, rebuilt it, and named it *Anand Bhawan* (the abode of happiness). A rise in the standard of living was paralleled by a progressive westernisation, a process which was accelerated by visits to Europe in 1899 and 1900. Thoroughgoing changes, from knives and forks at the dining-table to European governesses and tutors for the children, ensued. Of the taboos prevalent among Kashmiri Brahmans none was perhaps stronger than that relating to overseas travel. On his return to India, Motilal refused to perform what was called the ceremony of 'repentance and purification'. He treated his outraged opponents with open contempt. 'I know what your *biradri* [caste] is', he wrote to one of the prominent leaders of the community, on 22 December 1899, 'and if necessary I will ruthlessly and mercilessly lay bare the tattered fabric of its existence.'[1] He was excommunicated, but took no notice of the fiat of the leaders of the community. His defiance helped to put out the dying embers of orthodoxy.

In May 1905 Motilal again sailed for Europe, this time with his whole family. He returned in November of the same year after sending Jawaharlal to Harrow School. From Harrow Jawaharlal went on to Cambridge where he took a tripos in Natural Sciences before being called to the bar. In June 1912, two months before the return of his son to India, Motilal confided to his brother that he was looking forward to an early retirement 'in peace and comfort after a most strenuous life of active work extending over thirty-five years'.[2] Little did he know that the last years of his life were to be the most crowded, the most strenuous, the stormiest and the most memorable of his life. If he had indeed been able to enjoy his well-earned retirement, he might have lived to a ripe old age, holding his court in *Anand Bhawan*, entertaining his friends, holidaying in Kashmir or the south of France. His children and grandchildren would then have cherished his memory as that of a fascinating, if somewhat formidable and mercurial patriarch. And in the bar libraries of his province, and more particularly of Allahabad, he would have been remembered as a brilliant lawyer, who had lived well and laughed well – one of those fortunate few who had made and spent a fortune at the bar. Motilal was destined for a larger role than that of a genial patriarch or a local celebrity. He was to become one of the heroes of India's struggle for freedom.

III

Strangely enough, Motilal's early incursions into politics were reluctant, brief and sporadic. The list of 1,400 delegates of the Allahabad Congress (1888) includes: 'Pandit Motilal, Hindu, Brahman, Vakil High Court, NWP [North-Western Provinces]'.

He attended some of the subsequent sessions of the Congress, but unlike his Allahabad contemporary Madan Mohan Malaviya, he was no more than a passive spectator. He was so absorbed in his profession that he had neither the time nor the inclination to participate in active politics. It was the tug of war between Moderates and Extremists in the aftermath of the partition of Bengal which drew Motilal into the arena and, strangely enough, on the side of the Moderates. In 1907 he presided over a provincial conference at Allahabad. His presidential speech was a vigorous onslaught on the Extremist ideology. 'We are constitutional agitators', he said, 'and the reforms we wish to bring about must come through the medium of constituted authority'. He avowed his faith in the *bona fides* of the British:

'John Bull means well – it is not in his nature to mean ill. . . . It takes him rather long to comprehend the situation, but when he does see things plainly, he does his plain duty, and there is no power on earth – no, not even his kith and kin in this country or elsewhere – that can successfully resist his mighty will.'[3]

In 1909 Motilal was elected a member of the UP Council. He attended the Delhi Durbar in 1911 in honour of the visit of King George V and Queen Mary. He became a member of the Allahabad Municipal Board, and the Vice-President of the Seva Samiti. He served as a member of the All India Congress Committee, and as the President of the UP Congress. Nevertheless, it was not politics but domestic and professional preoccupations which were the dominant interest of his life. From 1912, when Jawaharlal returned from England, there were forces at work – both at home and in the country – which were to lead Motilal into the maelstrom of national politics.

The First World War generated deep discontent in several sectors of Indian society which found a focus in the Home Rule Movement. Motilal had been reluctant to join the Home Rule League, but the internment of Mrs Besant in June 1917 by the Madras Government brought him into the fray. He became the President of the Allahabad branch of the Home Rule League and presided over a provincial conference convened to protest against the internment. Now began a gradual but perceptible leftward shift in Motilal's politics. In August 1918 he parted company with his Moderate friends on the constitutional issue, and at the end of the year took an active part in the proceedings of the Bombay Congress which demanded radical changes in the

Montagu-Chelmsford Reforms. On 5 February 1919 he launched a new daily paper, the *Independent*, as a counter-blast to the well-established but moderately-edited *Leader*.

The emergence of Gandhi on the Indian political stage changed the course of Indian history; it also profoundly influenced the fortunes of the Nehru family. The Rowlatt Bills and the publication of the Satyagraha pledge in February 1919 deeply stirred Jawaharlal; he felt an irresistible call to follow the Mahatma. Motilal was not the man to be easily swept off his feet: his legal background predisposed him against an extra-constitutional agitation. Deliberate disobedience of laws seemed to him preposterous and the idea of his only son courting imprisonment was simply unthinkable. It was clear to both father and son that they were at the crossroads. Neither was prepared to give in, but at Motilal's instance Gandhi intervened and counselled patience on young Nehru.

Shortly afterwards events marched to a tragic climax in the Punjab: the holocaust of Jallianwala Bagh was followed by martial law. Motilal did what he could be bring succour and solace to that unhappy province. He gave his time freely, at the cost of his own legal practice, to the defence of scores of hapless victims of the martial law, who had been condemned to the gallows or sentenced to long terms of imprisonment. He also served with Gandhi on the unofficial committee set up by the Indian National Congress to inquire into the Punjab disturbances. C. F. Andrews who saw the committee at work noted: 'It was painful to see how shock after shock went home, when they [Gandhi and Motilal] both examined, as trained lawyers, the evidence put before them.' 'Amritsar', wrote Andrews, 'shook the very foundations of the faith on which Motilal had built up his life.'

Elected to preside over the Amritsar Congress (December 1919) Motilal was in the centre of the gathering storm which pulled down many familiar landmarks during the following year. He was the only front-rank leader to lend his support to non-co-operation at the Special Congress at Calcutta. Motilal's fateful decision to cast in his lot with Gandhi was no doubt influenced by the tragic chain of events in 1919. But even in the heyday of his Anglicism he had a strong vein of pride. As the President of the Moderates' Conference at Allahabad in 1907 he had deprecated 'mean cringing, fawning flattery of those in power'. 'You have grievances', he told the delegates, 'and you must like men demand redress. Be brave, unbending, persistent.'[4] Apart from his pride, and the force of events, there was another vital factor without which he may not have made, in his sixtieth year, a clean break with his past and plunged into the unknown. This was the unshakeable resolve of his son to go the way of Satyagraha. Motilal loved the good things of life, but he loved his son even more.

Immediately after the Calcutta Congress Motilal resigned from the UP Council, abandoned his practice at the bar, curtailed the retinue of servants in *Anand Bhawan*, changed his style of living, consigned cartloads of foreign finery to public bonfires and put on home-spun *khadi*. All this he did without any air of martyrdom. Indeed he was soon savouring the new simplicity with the same gusto with which he had relished the luxuries he had voluntarily renounced.

In December 1921 both father and son were arrested and sentenced to six months' imprisonment. In February 1922 came the anti-climax, when Gandhi first announced and then suddenly cancelled mass civil disobedience. In March the Mahatma himself was arrested, tried for sedition and sentenced to six years' imprisonment.

When Motilal came out of gaol in the summer of 1922, he found that the movement had declined, the Congress organisation was distracted by internal squabbles and the constructive programme could not evoke the enthusiasm of the intelligentsia. Motilal felt that the time had come to revise the programme of non-co-operation so as to permit entry into legislative councils. This revision was resisted by those who regarded themselves as the faithful followers of the Mahatma. A long and bitter controversy, which nearly split the Congress, ensued. However, Motilal and C. R. Das, who had founded the Swaraj Party in January 1923, had their way, and contested the elections at the end of that year. The Swaraj Party emerged as the largest party in the Central Legislative Assembly as well as in some of the provincial legislatures and from 1925 onwards became the political wing of the Congress.

IV

The spotlight shifts for the next six years to the Legislative Assembly where Motilal was the Leader of the Opposition. With his commanding personality, incisive intellect, great knowledge of law, brilliant advocacy, ready wit and combative spirit, he seemed to be cut out for a parliamentary role. The Legislative Assembly, however, was no parliament. It was a hybrid legislature elected on a narrow and communal franchise; it had a solid bloc of official, nominated, European and Indian members who took their cue from the irremovable executive. At first Motilal was able to secure sufficient support from the Moderate and Muslim legislators to outvote the Government. He ruled his own party with an iron hand, but found his task increasingly difficult from 1926 onwards when communal and personal squabbles made politics sink to the lowest ebb.

Towards the end of 1927, with the appointment of the Simon Commission, came a political revival. The exclusion of Indians from the Commission united Indian parties in opposition to the Government. An All-Parties Conference was convened by Dr Ansari the Congress President, and a committee, including Tej Bahadur Sapru and headed by Motilal, was appointed to determine the principles of a constitution for free India. The report of the committee – the Nehru Report as it came to be called – attempted a solution of the communal problem which promised to command general assent, but eventually was repudiated by a vocal section of Muslim opinion led by the Aga Khan and Jinnah.

Motilal, who was happily free from the sectarian passions of many of his contemporaries, held strong views on the place of religion in politics, and expressed them in December 1928 with his characteristic bluntness:

'Whatever the higher conception of religion may be, it has in our life come to signify bigotry and fanaticism, intolerance and narrow-mindedness. . . . Its chief inspiration is hatred of him who does not profess it. . . . Can any sane person consider the trivial and ridiculous causes of conflict between Hindu and Muslim, or between sect and sect, and not wonder how anyone with a grain of sense should be affected by them? . . . Religion as practised today is . . . the greatest separatist force. It puts artificial barriers between man and man and presents the development of healthy and co-operative national life. . . . Its association with politics has been to the good of neither. Religion has been degraded and politics has sunk in the mire; complete divorce of the one from the other is the only remedy.'[5]

The Nehru Report, representing as it did the highest common

denominator among a number of heterogeneous parties, was based on 'Dominion Status'. This was regarded as a climb-down by a radical wing in the Congress led by Jawaharlal and Subhas Bose who founded the 'Independence for India League'. The Calcutta Congress (December 1928) over which Motilal presided was the scene of a head-on clash between those who were prepared to accept Dominion Status and those who would have nothing short of complete independence. A split was averted by a *via media* proposed by Gandhi, according to which if Britain did not concede Dominion Status within a year, the Congress was to demand complete independence, and to fight for it, if necessary, by launching civil disobedience.

The way was thus opened for Gandhi's return to active politics and for the revival of *Satyagraha*. While unfurling the Congress flag at Calcutta in December 1928, Motilal told a group of young volunteers: 'Soldiers of Liberty, old as I am, let me assure you that you will always find me at the post of duty. I will be there always in the thick of it.'[6] He was at first more amused than impressed by Gandhi's plans for the breach of the Salt Laws, but as the movement caught on, it found him – against the advice of his doctors – in the centre of the storm. He was arrested and imprisoned; but his health gave way and he was released. But there could be no peace for him when most of his family was in gaol and the whole of India was passing through a baptism of fire. In the last week of January 1931 Gandhi and the Congress Working Committee were released by the Government as a gesture in that chain of events which was to lead to the Gandhi-Irwin Pact. Motilal had the satisfaction of having his son and Gandhi beside him in his last days. On 6 February 1931 he died.

V

Motilal did not live to see the end of the struggle into which he had thrown his all. During the twenties when the national movement reached its lowest ebb, and the Mahatma took to the spinning-wheel and his *ashram*, the Swaraj Party kept up the spirit of resistance to foreign rule. In the face of the contrary winds which were blowing over the land, Motilal helped to keep the torch of freedom burning and to pass it on to others – to Gandhi, and to his own son. He played his part in the national struggle, bore great burdens and suffered many scars. But he was a born fighter who battled against the superstitions, the sectarianism and frailties of his own countrymen with the same tenacity with which he challenged a mighty Empire.

Embattled nationalism, like war, inevitably narrows the energies of individuals as well as peoples into a single groove. It was Motilal's fate to destroy, though he would have loved to build. His approach to politics, as to life in general, was severely practical. He did not have the imaginative sweep of his son; nor would he have vibrated enthusiastically to some of the trends in the present-day world. Yet few of his contemporaries had advanced faster and farther than he had done in his own time. His robust, rational, secular and fearless mind enabled him to bridge the gulf between the post-Mutiny and the pre-independence eras. During the hundred years since his birth, India has been able to break loose from the bonds of political subjection and social obscurantism. Motilal's life mirrored this struggle and contributed to its success in no small measure.

Chapter 5

The 'Relevance' of Gandhi

I

The question whether Gandhi was 'relevant' to his or our times is not so novel as it may seem. It was repeatedly asked during his lifetime from the day when, at the age of twenty-four, he plunged into the stormy politics of South Africa to the fateful evening fifty-five years later in New Delhi when three pistol shots posed this very question in the most tragic and dramatic manner possible. It was a question, which recurred during the twenty years of Gandhi's struggle in South Africa, in the course of which he evolved his technique of *Satyagraha* for righting wrongs and redressing injustice without hate and without violence. It was only natural that he should have appeared as a tenacious and dangerous adversary to his opponents, but there were not a few in his own camp, who chafed at his self-imposed restraints and discounted the possibility of changing the hearts of the dominant race.

Gandhi left South Africa in July 1914, and after spending a few months in England returned to India in January 1915. In the eyes of many of his countrymen he had the halo of a victorious campaigner around him, but he also seemed (in the words of J. B. Kripalani) an 'eccentric specimen of an England-returned Indian'.[1] Gokhale, whom Gandhi acknowledged as his political *guru*, laughed at some of his ideas and told him: 'After you have stayed in India, your views will correct themselves.' It had long been Gokhale's wish that Gandhi should join his Society – the Servants of India Society – but before long it became plain to Gandhi as well as to the members of that Society that he would be a square peg. Nor did Gandhi's political views fit in with those of the Moderates or the Extremists in the Indian National Congress. His advocacy, as a *Satyagrahi*, of unconditional support to the Government during the First World War, hardly carried conviction to the British, but it intrigued and exasperated fervent nationalists like Tilak and Mrs Besant, who wanted, on the Irish model, to turn England's difficulty into India's opportunity.

During these early years, Gandhi seemed to both European and Indian observers strangely unpolitical. In 1917, Edwin Montagu noted in his diary that Gandhi was 'a social reformer with a real desire to find grievances and to cure them . . . he dresses like a coolie, forswears all personal advancement, lives practically on the air and is a pure visionary'.[2] The Viceroy and his advisers watched Gandhi with mingled hope and anxiety. They wondered whether his energies would be drained off in harmless channels of religious and social reform, or whether he would repeat his South African performance. His denunciation of Western civilisation, industrialism and modern education grated on the ears of the Indian middle class which dominated the counsels of the Indian National Congress at that time. When he published his *Satyagraha* pledge as a protest against the Rowlatt Act in February 1919, the veteran politicians of India were shocked, almost horrified, and with a rare unanimity rushed to the press to give vent to their alarm and to warn their countrymen of the dangers ahead. Within the Congress organisation it took Gandhi nearly two years to have his ideas accepted. It was not until December 1920, after the Nagpur Congress that some of the sceptics such as C. R. Das were converted, and others like Jinnah walked off the Congress stage. Gandhi hastened to convert this sedate body of well-educated and well-dressed gentlemen into a mass organisation, and summoned the illiterate millions in towns and villages to direct action. The 'sober' politicians of the day had no doubt that the march to disaster had begun. 'What the consequences of this may be', Jinnah wrote, 'I shudder to contemplate.' Srinivasa Sastri, Gokhale's political heir, warned his countrymen against the perils of the course to which they were drifting by adopting 'an impracticable programme in unreasoning opposition to the government'. Rabindranath Tagore wrote in the *Modern Review*, criticising non-co-operation 'as a doctrine of negation, exclusiveness and despair which threatened to erect a Chinese Wall between India and the West'. These doubts and alarms found full expression in a book entitled *Gandhi and Anarchy*, by Sir Sankaran Nair, a former President of the Indian National Congress, who had also been a member of the Viceroy's Executive Council.

For the next eighteen months, the murmurs of dissent in the Congress were stilled by the roaring tide of non-co-operation which Gandhi had launched. But even during this period, some of his colleagues, such as C. R. Das and Motilal Nehru, were disturbed by the moral, almost mysterious aspects of the Mahatma's technique. When Gandhi refused to attend a round-table conference with Lord Reading, proposed by Pandit Madan Mohan Malaviya and other intermediaries, C. R. Das, who was in Alipore Central Gaol, is reported to have exclaimed that Gandhi was 'repeatedly bungling'.[3] A few months later, when Gandhi revoked his plans for civil disobedience after the Chauri Chaura tragedy, not only C. R. Das but a majority of the senior leaders of the Congress felt that the moral prepossessions of the Mahatma had reduced his political movement to a pious futility.

In the summer of 1922, soon after Gandhi had been sentenced to six years' imprisonment, an important part of his programme was challenged by an influential section of his own following, resulting in a split in the ranks of non-co-operators on the issue of contesting elections to the legislatures. A fierce struggle for the control of the party machine followed; it was resolved only when Gandhi gave in to the Swarajists and let them dominate the political stage.

During the mid-twenties, Gandhi retired from politics and buried himself in his *ashram* at Sabarmati, for 'constructive work': the propagation of *khadi*, the preaching of non-violence, communal unity and social reform. Neither the British Government nor the Indian political parties took these innocent activities seriously; they tended to regard 'the Saint of Sabarmati' as a spent force. It was only with the dramatic Salt *Satyagraha* in the spring of 1930 that Gandhi once again became a dominant factor in national politics. His pact with Lord Irwin revived doubts and criticisms in some of those who were close to him. And when the civil disobedience movement declined under the hammer blows of the government in 1932–3, and he called it off, he was again under fire. Subhas Chandra Bose and V. J. Patel, who were in Europe at that time, went so far as to issue a statement that Gandhi 'as a political leader has failed, that the time has come for a radical reorganisation of the Congress on a new principle and with a new method for which a new leader is essential'.[4]

The five years immediately preceding the Second World War found Gandhi engaged in the promotion of village handicrafts, sanitation, nutrition and basic education. Again, he was accused of side-tracking the 'main political issue of Indian freedom'. He replied:

'I do not see how thinking of these problems [of village uplift], finding a solution for them is of no political significance, and how any examination of the policy of the Government has necessarily a political bearing. What I am asking the masses to do is such as can be done by millions of people, whereas the work of examining the policy of the rulers will be beyond them. Let those few, who are qualified, do so; but until these leaders can bring great changes into being, why should not millions like me use the gifts that God has given them to the best advantage? Why should they not clean their doors and make of their bodies fitter instruments?'[5]

The Second World War revealed a conflict between Gandhi's doctrine of non-violence and his passion for Indian freedom. The proposition that India could defend herself with 'unadulterated' non-violence against foreign aggression was one which few of his adherents were prepared to accept. Gandhi felt, he himself could not give up his faith when it was being put to the hardest test: 'My position is confined to myself alone. I have to find whether I have any fellow-traveller along my lonely path. . . . Whether one or many, I must declare that it is better for India to discard violence altogether even for defending her borders.'[6] To the Government and people of Britain, locked in a desperate duel with Hitler's Germany, Gandhi's suggestion smacked of starry-eyed idealism, if not of deliberate sabotage. Many people in India feared that the Mahatma's idealism was outrunning his practical sense, that he was adopting the role of a prophet rather than that of a responsible politician. This fear found expression in Rajagopalachari's comment on the Quit India Movement: 'The withdrawal of the government without simultaneous replacement by another must involve the dissolution of the state and society itself.'[7]

We come now to the concluding stage of the Indo-British struggle: the Muslim League's agitation for Pakistan, the arrival of the Cabinet Mission, the celebration of the Direct Action Day by the Muslim League and the lighting of the fires of fanaticism at Calcutta, which were to spread over the land and torture the last days of Gandhi's life. He desperately tried to quench this conflagration by living and working in the riot-torn countryside of Bengal and Bihar. The Hindus blamed him for allowing himself to be outwitted by the Muslim League; the Muslim League

64 GOKHALE, GANDHI AND THE NEHRUS

proclaimed him 'Enemy Number One' of Islam. The growing
bitterness and bloodshed weighed heavily upon him. He had a
tragic sense of isolation during these last days; his fasts at Calcutta and Delhi shamed the Hindus and moved the Muslims, but
it was not until his final martyrdom that the futility and fatuity of
communal violence was seen in the sub-continent as if in a flash
of lightning.

The responsibility for Gandhi's murder rested not only on
Godse but on those – some of them quite respectable and well-
meaning men and women – who had given in to communal
hatred and thus contributed to the creation of that surcharged
atmosphere in which such a crime could be committed.

II

From this brief historical retrospect we may safely conclude that
January 1948 was not the water-shed in Gandhism as some of us
may have imagined. It would not be altogether correct to assume
that Indians adhered to Gandhi's teachings during his lifetime and
ceased to do so after his death. Even while he lived among us,
and tried to guide us, we followed him fitfully and with faltering
steps. His public life was not a triumphal procession; it had a
stormy passage; he had continually to reckon with misunderstanding, ridicule, opposition; his political movements had ups
and downs; he had more than his share of disappointments and
frustrations. Despite his undoubted magnetism and unrivalled
prestige he could command a mass following for his *Satyagraha*
campaigns only sporadically, in 1920–2, 1930–2 and 1940–2. The
educated class, the political elite of the day, was inclined to
discount his politics as romantic and his economics as unpractical.
It was too much to expect that the British would welcome the
idea of being evicted from India even non-violently. But there
were intelligent and patriotic Indians, who did not accept that the
patient, peaceful methods of *Satyagraha* were capable of producing
radical changes. Some left-wing critics indeed went so far as to
describe Gandhi a reactionary, and to suggest that he was not
serious about fighting the British, that his real game was to
harness the discontent of the peasantry, the lower middle and
working classes and to swell the profits of the tycoons of Bombay,
Ahmedabad and Calcutta.

The politically conscious classes wanted quick results; they
liked the spectacular side of *Satyagraha*, but were reluctant to

understand, much less to believe in the deeper motives and the long-term strategy of the Mahatma. In 1920 they had welcomed non-co-operation because he promised 'Swaraj within a year'. The promise was remembered, but not the conditions precedent to the fulfilment of that promise. Curiously enough, before Gandhi came on the scene, Indian political opinion was largely resigned to the idea of gradual political changes; but after he had sharpened the mass consciousness, *Swaraj* was seen, not as an inevitable reward of a long and hard struggle, but an immediate necessity. Gandhi knew only too well that his technique was not a magic wand; it required sustained effort and sacrifices which were forthcoming only intermittently in periods of intense political excitement. *Satyagraha* was seen, not as it appeared to Gandhi, a way of life, but something like a *coup*, capable of producing basic changes overnight. Too often the operation of *Satyagraha* was seen on the lines of a violent conflict; it was forgotten that in *Satyagraha* it is not a question of capturing a particular outpost, isolating and overwhelming any army corps, or bombing an industrial town or a military target out of existence. *Satyagraha* seeks to initiate certain psychological changes, first in those who offer it and then in those against whom it is directed. Gandhi's vegetarianism, Bernard Shaw once said, could not appeal to the tiger; Gandhi repudiated the suggestion that imperialism was all tiger, and not at all human or suseptible to change.

The changes which Gandhi sought to bring about in society and politics presupposed changes in the minds and hearts of men. We know that such changes operate consciously and unconsciously and at various levels, and success can be delayed or stimulated by imponderables. These changes cannot be accelerated or even anticipated beyond a point; in society, as in the human organism, there is a safe rate of change. Voluntary and peaceful changes may be slow, but they may be more enduring.

Critics are not wanting today to dismiss Gandhi as a 'traditionalist', an impossible idealist, even 'a peasant reactionary' whose virtues and limitations, useful to his country in the special context of the struggle against colonial rule, are no longer valid. It is argued that Gandhi was opposed to technology and scientific progress, that he glorified poverty, that he exaggerated the possibilities of non-violence in a harsh and cynical world, and that his economics do not make sense today.

It is important to remember that Gandhi was not a philosopher,

E

not even an economist; his ideas grew out of his own early experiences, and crystallised while he was in South Africa; they were
amplified, modified and refined by him later, but in essentials, they
remained intact. These ideas were not drawn from books. The
writings of Tolstoy and Ruskin served to confirm Gandhi's
inchoate convictions, rather than provide him with ready-made
formulae. *Hind Swaraj*, which may be described Gandhi's 'confession of faith', was published in 1909. That this book was
confiscated by the Government is not surprising;[8] no Government, and no foreign Government, could miss the social and
political dynamite it contained. Gandhi's position in this book,
approaching philosophic anarchism is an extreme one; his
rejection of materialism, industrialism and violence is almost
total; his judgements on the shams and equivocations of modern
society and state are sharp, penetrating, merciless. It was this
book which made many Indians and Europeans doubt whether
Gandhi would ever be able to make a practical contribution to
the country's public life. It is difficult to think of any prominent
politician or any established political party before the First
World War avowing the creed of *Hind Swaraj*. Neither Gokhale
nor Tilak, or indeed any politician of the day would have sub-
scribed to it.

Thus, very early in his career, Gandhi was faced with the not
unusual dilemma of an idealist in politics: on the one hand, he
had to discover and define his ideals for himself, and on the other
he had to discover the terms on which he could work with others
towards the realisation of these ideals. The first of these problems,
difficult as it was, Gandhi was able to solve before he had turned
forty. But the second problem of discovering the terms on which
he could co-operate with others, he could not solve to his own
satisfaction, though he went on trying till the end. The gulf
between himself and the men and women with whom his lot was
cast, was sometimes wide, sometimes narrow; it was rarely
bridged. It was open to him to adopt a lofty attitude, to offer a
compact and consistent political programme and to say 'take it
or leave it'. This may have made his own life more comfortable
and enhanced his reputation for consistency, but his sphere of
action would have been narrowed a great deal, and his ideas
would have made less impact than they actually did by being
practised even in a diluted form.

Gandhi's personal creed, as adumbrated in the *Hind Swaraj*,
was never tried by him in South Africa, much less in India, on

the political organisations through which he functioned from time to time. Indeed in 1920–1, when his opponents charged him with subversion of society and quoted *Hind Swaraj* to support their thesis, Gandhi wrote in *Young India*:

'I am individually working for the self-rule pictured therein. But today my corporate activity is undoubtedly devoted to the attainment of parliamentary *Swaraj* in accordance with the wishes of the people of India. I am not aiming at destroying railways or hospitals, though I would welcome their natural destruction. Nor am I aiming at a permanent destruction of the law courts, much as I regard it as a consummation devoutly to be wished for. Still less am I trying to destroy all machinery and mills. It requires a higher simplicity and renunciation than the people are prepared for. The only part of the programme which is now being carried out in its entirety is that of non-violence. But even that is not being carried out in the spirit of the book.'[9]

Gandhi's personal beliefs did not thus in their entirety become the operative principles of the political organisations which he led. For him an act was not moral, unless it was also voluntary. He knew too much about human nature and the facts of public life to fall a willing victim to the fallacy that to define a Utopia is to create it. He, who had spent his life battling against racial prejudice, religious dogmatism, social obscurantism and colonial domination knew that great changes could not be ordained at will and at short notice.

Gandhi was able to chart his own course with great clarity and confidence, but found it less easy to do so for masses of men. He seems to have adopted, both in his philosophy and technique, the principle of 'each according to his capacity'. His faith in *ahimsa* (non-violence) was boundless, but there were few who were prepared to go the whole hog with him. It was not opportunism, but a strong practical vein in the Mahatma which permitted the Congress to subscribe to non-violence as a 'policy' in the nationalist struggle; the majority of its members and leaders had no faith in non-violence as a 'creed'.

During the Second World War, Gandhi twice (in 1940 and 1941) found that most of the members of the Congress working committee did not believe in the possibility of India offering effective non-violent resistance to the Axis Powers. Rather than ram his ideas down the throats of his colleagues, he offered to retire from the political scene. If he had waited for ideal conditions and for colleagues who believed unreservedly in his philosophy and technique, he may have waited till the end of his life. He was therefore ready, within a fairly broad framework, to co-operate with others in order to promote the causes on which he had set his own heart. He once wrote:

'If I was a perfect man, I own I should not feel the miseries of life which I always do. As a perfect man I should take note of them, prescribe a remedy and compel its adoption . . . but as yet I see only through a glass darkly; and therefore, I have to carry conviction by a slow and laborious process and then, too, not always with success. Mine is a struggling, striving, erring, imperfect soul.'

The difficulty was not in Gandhi alone; it was inherent in the position of a national leader seeking to lead a mass movement peacefully. In 1942 as Gandhi looked back on the non-co-operation struggle of the twenties, he gave his reasons for having taken what he described as the 'maddest risk' a man can take.

'In South Africa . . . I introduced *Satyagraha* as an experiment. I was successful there, because resisters were a small number, in a compact area, and therefore easily controlled. Here [in India] we had numberless persons scattered over a huge country. The result was that they could not be easily controlled or trained. And yet it is a marvel the way they have responded. They might have responded much better and shown far better results. But I have no sense of disappointment in me over the results obtained. If I had started with men who accepted non-violence as a creed, I might have ended with myself.'

Tagore once described Gandhi as 'essentially a lover of men and not of ideas'.[10] The Mahatma himself disclaimed that he had discovered any new principle or doctrine; he was merely trying in his own way to apply eternal truths to the problems of daily life. But this application was in itself a highly original and radical process. Those who described Gandhi as a traditionalist or revivalist misread him as well as the political and social context of his activities. During the first five years after his return from South Africa, even before he had plunged into militant politics, Gandhi looked like a hurricane, shaking the cobwebs of make-believe spun by Indian politicians and social reformers and British bureaucrats. He was not an inconoclast by temperament, but his mind was too alert to accept anything as sacrosanct simply because it had the sanction of custom or authority. He would not accept every Hindu tenet or practice and insisted on applying 'the acid test of reason'. When scriptural sanction was cited for inhuman or unjust practices, his reaction was one of frank disbelief. The oft quoted text from Manu: 'For women there can be no freedom', he regarded as an 'interpolation'. If it was not an interpolation then he could only say that in Manu's time women did not receive the status they deserved. He lashed out at those who supported untouchability with verses from the Vedas. His Hinduism was ultimately reduced to a few fundamental beliefs: the supreme reality of God, belief in the unity of all life, and value of love (*ahimsa*) as a means of self-realisation. In this bedrock religion there was no scope for exclusiveness or narrowness. To Gandhi, true religion was more a matter of the heart then of the intellect; genuine beliefs were those which were literally lived. This was something beyond the grasp of those who had acquired, in the words of Swift, enough religion to hate one another, but not enough to love one another. In his lifetime Gandhi was variously labelled a Sanatanist Hindu, a renegade Hindu, a Buddhist, a Theosophist, a Christian and a Christian-Mohammedan. He was all these and more; he saw an underlying unity in the clash of doctrines and forms. 'God is not encased in a safe', he wrote to a correspondent who had urged him to save his soul by conversion to Christianity, 'to be approached only through a little hole in it, but He is open to be approached through billions of openings by those who are humble and pure of heart.'[11]

The fact that he was deeply religious did not prevent Gandhi from battling ceaselessly against excrescences on Hindu society. In this he achieved greater success than many of the earlier social reformers, partly because he did not let his campaigns develop into an assault on Hindu religion and culture, and partly because his own *bona fides* were beyond question in the eyes of the millions to whom he directed his teachings. If his message was to go home he had to communicate with these millions. He did not content himself with writing articles in newspapers and addressing meetings in the principal towns as the earlier reformers had done; he travelled from one end of the country to the other, penetrating into the interior of the Indian countryside which had been off the beaten track of national leaders. While speaking to these unsophisticated, wide-eyed, reverent multitudes, he did not quote from John Stuart Mill or Karl Marx, or even from Sankara; he talked to them in their own idiom. When he spoke of *Rama Rajya* he was not plotting a return to the social and political institutions of ancient India. Indeed, he thought of the epics as allegorical rather than historical writings; the battle between *Rama* and *Ravana*, good and evil, he argued, had not been fought long ago, but was waged daily in every human heart.

It is odd that a man who shook the British Empire, sounded the death knell of imperialism in Asia and Africa, fought relentlessly against social abuses sanctioned by immemorial tradition, should have been labelled as a traditionalist. Gandhi took a new, critical look at everything under the sun, from industrialism to ethics and from nature-cure to basic education. One may not always agree with him, but one cannot resist the impression that his was essentially an alive, creative mind, taking nothing for granted. He evolved his own code of ethics as a barrister, as a politician, as a journalist and as a social reformer. His ideas may not fit into the moulds to which many of us have become accustomed, but they were far from being those of a traditionalist; perhaps the misunderstanding was helped by Gandhi's habit of clothing the most radical ideas in the simplest and most unpretentious language. Far from being a traditionalist, he was the catalyst, if not the initiator, of three major revolutions of the twentieth century: against colonialism, against racism and against violence.

III

There are two crucial questions today to which the relevance of Gandhian techniques is often debated: one is the possibility of social and economic changes being brought about by non-violent methods, and the other is peace between nations.

Soon after Gandhi's death in 1948, a delegate, speaking at the United Nations, predicted that 'the greatest achievements of the Indian sage were yet to come'. 'Gandhi's times', said Vinoba Bhave, 'were the first pale dawn of the sun of *Satyagraha*'. This optimism was premature. The manner in which the Mahatma's techniques have been invoked even in his homeland in recent years would appear to be a travesty of his principles. And the world has been in the grip of a series of crises in Korea, the Congo, the Middle East and Vietnam, with a never-ending trail of blood and bitterness. A study of Gandhi's ideas and techniques may suggest a way out of this predicament. Unfortunately, however, his motives and methods have been misunderstood and misinterpreted, and not only by the mobs in the street. Not long ago, an eminent writer described Gandhi's attitude as one of 'passive submission to bayonetting and raping, to villages without sewage, septic childhoods and trachoma'. Such a judgement is, of course, completely wide of the mark. Gandhi never encouraged acquiescence in tyranny, nor in primitive and unhygienic living. He fought the evils which corroded Indian society with the same tenacity with which he battled against the British Raj. In the arena of social reform, he did not support the traditionalists, who were blind to the increasing irrelevance (under the impact of the West) of the outlook, norms and institutions of the traditional society. The 'liberal-rationalists', who spear-headed the fight for social reform in the nineteenth century and the early decades of the twentieth century, failed to resolve the tensions between outmoded values and institutions and the demands of a changing society. This failure was largely due to the inability of these reformers to offer an indigenous alternative to the traditionalist view of society. Advocacy of or even admiration for the western values had the effect of strengthening the traditionalists. The people were torn between the conflicting pulls of the past and the present. It was left to Gandhi, himself the epitome of traditional values in the eyes of the masses, to reinterpret tradition, and to assist in a relatively painless transition from the narrower loyalties of caste and village to the larger loyalties of the community and the nation. Gandhi's simple, old-world idiom helped him in his dialogue with the millions whose ignorance of the outside world was equalled only by their faith in him. The liberating influence which Gandhi exercised at the deeper levels of the Indian consciousness may have been slow, uneven and not always obvious, but there is no doubt that even in a diluted form it has been a force for change and progress.

Gandhi did not foster passivity among the Indian masses; he was not the kind of leader who makes religion the opiate of the people. 'A semi-starved nation', he wrote, 'can have neither religion, nor art, nor organisation.' No one was more haunted by the skeletons behind the ploughs in the Indian countryside; no one did more to make the upper crust of Indian society conscious of the mountain of misery and poverty on which it was sitting; no one did more to explore practical steps to alleviate that poverty. Functioning within the framework of colonial economics – with the government secretly suspicious or frankly hostile – Gandhi sought to add a few annas a day to the income of the underemployed peasant by promoting spinning, weaving and other village industries. He did not get his insights from official blue-books and statistics: his views on village sanitation, education, nutrition, housing, and fertilisers were based on personal observation and experiments. To him socialism was not an intellectual exercise, nor a Utopia to be brought into being by somebody else. Like his *swaraj* (self-rule), it was something which began, with oneself, here and now. We have on record an interesting interview he gave to a group of students, who professed to be Socialists. 'Now tell me', he asked, 'how many of you have servants in your own homes?' They said: 'A servant in each home.' 'And you call yourselves socialists, while you make others slave for you. The first step in the practice of socialism is to learn to use your own hands and feet.' He repudiated the idea that politics were a remote, complicated, or abstract business, which somehow could miraculously legislate a country into the golden age.

Gandhi's social philosophy came in for much ridicule in his own time, and not only by his political opponents. Even some of his closest colleagues considered his concept of a village-centred, decentralised economy as romantic. Indian experience in the post-independence period has, however, underscored the fact that through sheer intuition, Gandhi was able to recognise certain unique features of the Indian socio-economic situation which were not obvious to most of his contemporaries and which can be ignored only at our own peril. One of these features was – and still is – the predominance of the self-employed producer – agriculturist or artisan – engaged in productive activity for his basic requirements, and not for pursuit of wealth for its own sake. The mass of the small producers in India are thus a social category fundamentally different from either the medieval 'serfs' or the modern 'proletariat', which formed the basic argument for the Marxist model of a classless society. Nor does the small self-employed producer, working and living within the constraints of community life fit into the individual-based capitalist model propounded by the liberal-rationalist school. Both the liberal-rationalists and the Marxists have tended to identify economic development with the disintegration of the small peasant and artisan economy, and the growth of large-scale enterprises based on modern technology. Gandhi was perceptive enough to foresee the difficulties and dangers of rapid industrialisation of the

Western type in underdeveloped countries: it was bound to hit millions of small producers (who constituted the largest segment of the society), to alienate actual producers from the means of production, and to generate deep social tensions and political turmoil. Gandhi did not leave a precise blueprint for the reorganisation of the Indian economy, but some of his insights into Indian society and economy are as valid and valuable today as they were forty years ago. Indeed, Gunnar Myrdal, the Swedish economist, after his detailed survey of the social and economic problems of the underdeveloped world in the *Asian Drama* came to the conclusion that Gandhi was 'in practically all fields an enlightened Liberal'.

The charge that Gandhian economics were 'reactionary' was levelled against him even during his lifetime. In the 1930s and 1940s he was accused of favouring the *status quo* and supporting the vested interests of landlords, princes and businessmen. It is true that Gandhi did not call these classes the 'enemies of the people', but even while the struggle for national liberation continued, he generated or stimulated forces which were eventually to abolish landlordism, princely rule and to enforce social controls over private enterprise. In September 1931, he told a customs official in France: 'My earthly possessions consist of six spinning wheels, prison dishes, a can of goat's milk, six homespun loin cloths and towels and my reputation, which cannot be worth very much.' Property could have little personal significance for such a man. In fact, Gandhi put the debate on property in perspective when he wrote: 'Millions of men have no property to transmit to posterity. Let us learn from them that it is better for the few to have no ancestral property at all. The real property that a parent can transmit is equally in his or her character and educational facilities.'

IV

Gandhi did not think it possible to bring about radical changes in the structure of society overnight. Nor did he succumb to the illusion that the road to a new order could be paved merely with pious wishes and fine words. It was not enough to blame the adversary or bewail the times in which one's lot was cast. However heavy the odds, it was the *Satyagrahi*'s duty never to feel helpless. The least he could do was to make a beginning with himself. If he was crusading for a new deal for the peasantry, he could go to the village, and serve its inhabitants. If he wanted to bring peace to a riot-torn district, he could walk through it, entering into the minds and hearts of those who were going through the ordeal. If any age-old evil like untouchability was to be fought, what could be a more effective symbol of defiance for a reformer than to adopt an untouchable child? If the object was to challenge foreign rule, why not act on the assumption that the country was already free, ignore the alien government and build alternative institutions to harness the spontaneous, constructive and co-operative effort of the people? If the goal was world peace, why not begin today by acting peacefully towards the immediate neighbour, going more than half-way to understand and win him over?

Gandhi did not conceive *Satyagraha* only as a weapon in the armoury of Indian nationalism. He believed it could be used to end social injustice. He stressed the simple truth too often forgotten that there are two parties to every process of exploitation, that no tyranny can continue without the active support or passive acquiescence of the victim. Thus viewed, slavery is essentially a mental state. In 1946, when a group of university-educated students from West Africa called on Gandhi he told them: 'The first thing is to say to yourself: "I shall no longer accept the role of the slave", and tell your master, "I shall not work for your love or money." . . . This may mean suffering. Your readiness to suffer will light the torch of freedom which can never be put out.'[12] 'It may be through the Negroes', observed Gandhi, 'that the unadulterated message of non-violence will be delivered to the world.'

Gandhi had the courage and the vision to see beyond racialism, nationalism and militarism, even sixty years ago, when they were at a premium in a world which had not known the ravages of two global wars and the lengthening shadow of a third. As Gandhi tried his *Satyagraha* technique in India, he cherished the hope that he had a message for India, and India had a message for humanity. He knew that the best recommendation for non-violence was a successful demonstration of its application by millions of his own countrymen. That demonstration, alas, was not as satisfactory as he had hoped, but even the partial success he achieved was enough to suggest that his method could work. In any case, for Gandhi there was no other method. The problem of war and peace had to be tackled at the roots. Those who plotted war did so for a definite purpose – to exploit men and materials of the territories they set out to conquer. The aggressor's effort was to apply terrorism in a sufficient measure to bend the adversary to his will. Gandhi argued:

'But supposing a people make up their mind that they will never do the tyrants' will, nor retaliate with the tyrant's own method, the tyrant will not find it worthwhile to go on with his terrorism. If all the mice in the world held conference together and resolved that they would no more fear the cat, but all run into her mouth, the mice would live.'[13]

In the years immediately preceding the Second World War, when the tide of Nazi and Fascist aggression was relentlessly rolling forward, Gandhi reasserted his faith in non-violence and commended it to the smaller nations, which were living in daily dread of being overwhelmed by superior force. He expounded the non-violent approach to military aggression and political tyranny. He advised the weaker nations to defend themselves, not by increasing their fighting potential, but by non-violent resistence to the aggressor. When Czechoslovakia was being blackmailed into submission in 1938, Gandhi suggested to the unfortunate Czechs: 'There is no bravery greater than a resolute refusal to bend the knee to an earthly power, no matter how great, and that without bitterness of spirit, and in the fullness of faith that the spirit alone lives, nothing else does.'[14] Seven years later, when the first atomic bomb exploded over Hiroshima and Nagasaki, Gandhi's reaction was characteristic: 'I did not move a muscle. On the contrary, I said to myself that unless the world now adopts non-violence, it will spell certain suicide for mankind.'[15]

The irony of the very perfection of the weapons of war rendering them useless as arbiters between nations has become increasingly clear during the last twenty years. The atomic stockpiles, which the major nuclear powers have already built up, are capable of destroying civilisation, as we know it, several times over. The fact is that with these weapons of mass destruction, to attack another nation is tantamount to attacking oneself. This is a bitter truth which old habits of thought have prevented from going home. 'The splitting of the atom has changed everything', bewailed Einstein, 'save our modes of thinking and thus we drift towards unparalleled catastrophe.'

Gandhi knew that the creation of a heroic spirit of resistance in a whole nation was not easy. When he suggested non-violent resistance to the Axis Powers by India in 1940 and 1942, during the Second World War, he could not carry with him a majority of his colleagues in the Congress Working Committee. The task of instilling non-violent resistance into hundreds of millions of people is a gigantic task. But so is the task of mobilising the resources of a nation for armed resistance. Even the most brilliant general, with the best trained armies, requires the exertions of millions of men and women in fields and factories to win a modern war. There is nothing magical about *Satyagraha*: it would be an illusion to imagine that one man, a Gandhi or a Vinoba Bhave alone, without the allegiance of thousands of dedicated men, could transform a society and usher in the golden age. How long has it taken countless men and women in succeeding generations to pool their efforts in the laboratory, the staff college and the battle-field to perfect the science of war? How much 'dedication' has gone – if one may use the word – into the 'refinement' of nuclear weapons so as to make them progressively more powerful instruments of mass destruction during the last twenty years? As Joan Bondurant points out in her critique of Gandhi's techniques, applied non-violence is perhaps at present at the same stage of development 'as the invention of electricity was in the days of Edison and Marconi'.

The world trembles today, half in hope, half in fear, in the shadow of a precarious peace produced by the 'balance of atomic terror'. The perfection of technology and military might seems a standing refutation of Gandhi's vision of a brave, new, non-violent world. But perhaps this very fact adds greater relevance and urgency to that vision. Having reached the edge of the precipice, humanity may yet take a new turning along the road, to which Gandhi has beckoned it. His message was not for India only. Indeed, it is possible that Tagore's prophecy may come true: 'The West', Tagore wrote, 'will accept Gandhi before the East. For the West has gone through the cycle of dependence on force and other things for life and has become disillusioned. . . . The East hasn't yet gone through materialism and hence hasn't become disillusioned as yet.'[16]

Chapter 6

Gandhi and Jawaharlal Nehru

I

'Are we rivals?' Gandhi asked in the *Harijan* of 25 July 1936, and himself answered: 'I cannot think of myself as a rival to Jawaharlal or him to me. Or, if we are, we are rivals in making love to each other in the pursuit of the common goal.' It is doubtful if Gandhi's explanation carried conviction to the young socialists, who looked up to Nehru as the leader of the militant Left, or even to the British officials, who pinned their hopes on a split in the nationalist ranks.

The crisis in the Congress leadership in 1936 was a grave one – graver than the public knew – but this was not the first occasion when Gandhi and Nehru had differed. They had had serious differences in 1922 on the aftermath of Chauri Chaura tragedy, in 1928 on complete independence versus Dominion Status, in 1929 on the Viceroy's declaration, in 1931 on the Gandhi-Irwin Pact, in 1932 on the fast against separate electorates for untouchables, and in 1934 on the manner of the withdrawal of the civil disobedience movement.

The width of the intellectual gulf that divided them was revealed by Nehru himself in his autobiography which he wrote in 1934–5 in gaol. Among Nehru's colleagues were several who expected and even incited him to revolt against the Mahatma's dominance in the Congress. On 4 March 1936, just as he was leaving for India, Subhas Bose begged him not to consider his 'position to be weaker than it really is. Gandhi will never take a stand which will alienate you.'[1] Four years later, J. P. Narayan pleaded with Nehru to leave the Congress and form a new party 'to fulfil the remaining part of the political task and the main part of the social task of the Indian revolution'.[2]

Nehru did not heed these siren voices. He did not carry his differences with Gandhi to the breaking point: the clash of ideas between himself and Gandhi did not turn into a clash of wills. Nor did he encourage his followers to organise an opposition to Gandhi's leadership, or to plan a split in the Congress party. Despite differences of thought, temperament and style, Gandhi and Nehru stood together for more than a quarter of a century. It was one of the longest, most intriguing and fruitful partnerships in the history of nationalism.

How two men, divided not only by twenty years of age but by deep intellectual and temperamental differences, could work together for so long is an enigma to anyone who seriously studies their lives and the history of this period. The young aristocrat from Allahabad seemed to have little in common with the strange charismatic figure which burst upon the Indian political stage in 1919 with an almost elemental force. The primary school in Porbandar, where young Gandhi wrote the alphabet in dust with his fingers, or the Bhavnagar college where he painfully struggled with lectures in English, belonged altogether to a different world from that of European governesses and resident tutors in Allahabad, Harrow, Cambridge and the Inns of Court in England in which young Nehru grew up. True, Gandhi also went to England to study for the bar in the late 1880s. But young Gandhi poring over the Bible and the *Gita* and desperately fighting back the recurring temptation from 'wine, women and meat' was cast in an altogether different mould from that of the handsome, Savile Row-clad Kashmiri youth who prided himself on his agnosticism and Cyrenaicism, frequented the theatre, admired Oscar Wilde and Walter Pater and dabbled in Irish politics and Fabian economics. In the course of his twenty-odd years' stay in South Africa, Gandhi fashioned for himself a peculiar, almost unique philosophy of life which, though baffling to many of his contemporaries, was firmly grounded on deeply held convictions.

How could Jawaharlal Nehru with his enthusiasm for science and humanism take to a saint with prayers and fasts, inner voices and the spinning wheel? This is a question to which biographers, historians and political commentators will continue to seek answers. It has been suggested that Jawaharlal had a compulsive need to depend on someone, that at first the mentor was his father Motilal, and then Gandhi.[3] M. N. Roy suspected that Jawaharlal's mind was a slave to his heart, that he deliberately suppressed his own personality 'to purchase popularity' and become 'a hero of Indian nationalism . . . as the spiritual son of Gandhi'.[4] Hiren Mukerjee has hazarded the theory that Gandhi won over and astutely kept Jawaharlal on his side to expoit his charisma and influence with India's youth in the interest of the Congress party, which was really controlled by vested interests.[5] These interpretations have the merit of simplicity, but they do not fit the facts of a partnership which extended over nearly three decades. The story of this partnership, the strains to which it was subjected, and the factors which enabled it to survive show that it was not simply a case of domination of one by the other, that Jawaharlal needed Gandhi as much as Gandhi needed him, that political calculation no less than emotional affinity kept them together during these years.

II

When Gandhi returned to India at the age of forty-five early in 1915, his personality had already taken shape. To his Western-educated contemporaries he seemed a quaint figure on the political stage. His South African record had given him a halo, but in the shadow of the Great War, public opinion was worried less about the Indian minority in South Africa than about India's political future. Gandhi's view that unconditional support to the British war effort would earn its reward from a greateful Empire in the hour of victory, seemed to most of his contemporaries extraordinarily naive. And, as if this was not enough, Gandhi was also harping on the superiority of the Indian over the Western civilisation, denouncing industrialism and advocating village handicrafts. All this must have sounded strangely unpolitical and anachronistic, to Jawaharlal Nehru, who had returned to India in 1912 after a seven-year sojourn in England. Though he had seen Gandhi at the Bombay Congress in 1915, and again at Lucknow a year later, Jawaharlal was not really attracted to him until after the Champaran and Kaira campaigns and the anti-Rowlatt Bill agitation. There were good reasons why Gandhi's *Satyagraha* campaigns should have made an impact on Jawaharlal. Seven years at the Allahabad High Court, as his father's junior, had left Jawaharlal bored with the 'trivialities and technicalities' of the legal profession. The game of making money did not really excite him. He was groping for a new Weltanschauung. Political terrorism had little attraction for him. The annual session of the

Indian National Congress, and the armchair politics with which the elite of Allahabad amused itself seemed to him much too tame. He was drawn to Gokhale's Servants of India Society with its band of political *sanyasins*, but he was repelled by its association with 'moderate politics'. When Gandhi published the *Satyagraha* pledge and announced direct action to protest against the Rowlatt Bills, Jawaharlal was thrilled by the prospect of effective political action.

Motilal Nehru did not find it easy to reconcile himself to an extra-constitutional agitation, but Gandhi counselled patience on the son, and prevented him from taking an irrevocable step. Soon afterwards, in the wake of the tragedy of the martial law in the Punjab, Motilal came into closer contact with Gandhi, and was surprised to find in him not a starry-eyed saint but a politician with a keen practical sense.[6] Before long the whole Nehru family came under the Mahatma's spell, and learnt to seek solace and support from the saint of Sabarmati. This was an emotional bond independent of, but not without its influence upon politics: differences of ideology and tactics become a little less intractable if there is a reserve of mutual respect and affection.

III

Gandhi's first impact on young Nehru was strong indeed. Jawaharlal was, in his own words, 'simply bowled over by Gandhi straight off'.[7] The call to non-violent battle against the British Raj in 1919–20 struck a chord. 'I jumped at it. I did not care for the consequences.' His life underwent a metamorphosis. He turned his back on the legal profession, simplified his life, gave up smoking, turned vegetarian and began to read the *Gita* regularly, 'not from a philosophical or theological point of view', but because 'it had numerous parts which had a powerful effect upon me'.[8] He was fired by the missionary fervour of a new convert. 'Non-co-operation is to me', he wrote to the Chief Secretary to the UP Government, 'a sacred thing and its very basis is truth and non-violence.'[9] He was full of excitement, optimism and buoyant enthusiasm. He sensed 'the happiness of a person crusading for a cause'.[10]

From this ecstasy, a rude awakening occurred in February 1922. After a riot at Chauri Chaura in the United Provinces Gandhi called off civil disobedience. Jawaharlal, who was in prison at the time, received the news with 'amazement and consternation'.[11] He did not see how the violence of a stray mob of excited peasants in a remote village could justify the reversal of a national struggle for freedom. If perfect non-violence was to be regarded as a *sine qua non* for all the three hundred-odd millions of Indians, would it not reduce Gandhi's movement to a pious futility? A letter from Gandhi somewhat mollified Jawaharlal, but it was only much later, with the perspective that time gives, that he realised that Gandhi's decision was right, that 'he had to stop the rot and build anew'.[12]

The Chauri Chaura tragedy brought Jawaharlal down to earth. The exaltation of the non-co-operation days faded away. He had no stomach for the factional and communal politics of the mid-twenties. He served as Allahabad's Mayor and as General Secretary of the All India Congress Committee. These activities provided useful outlets for his boundless energy, but he did not recover his zest for politics, and indeed for life, until he visited Europe during 1926–7 for the treatment of his ailing wife. Under the stimulus of fresh reading and contacts with revolutionaries and radicals of three continents, the realisation dawned on him that Indian politics had been much too vague, narrow and parochial. He learnt to trace links not only between British imperialism in India and colonialism in other countries of Asia and Africa, but also between foreign domination and vested interests in his own country. The Brussels Congress of Oppressed Nationalities and the brief visit to the Soviet Union gave a tremendous impetus to these ideas. On return to the homeland in December 1927, he persuaded the Madras Congress to pass resolutions in favour of 'complete independence'. He denounced feudalism, capitalism and imperialism, and talked of organising workers, peasants and students.

Jawaharlal's performance at the Madras Congress deeply disturbed Gandhi. He wrote to Jawaharlal:

'You are going too fast, you should have taken time to think and become acclimatised. Most of the resolutions you prepared and got carried could have been delayed for one year. Your plunging into the "republican army" was a hasty step. But I do not mind these acts of yours so much as I mind your encouraging mischief-mongers and hooligans.... If ... careful observation of the country in the light of your European experiences convinces you of the errors of the current ways and means, by all means enforce your own views, but do please form a disciplined party.'[13]

F

Gandhi's objection was not so much to the radical views of the younger man, as to the light-hearted manner in which brave declarations were made without any serious effort to implement them. It was all very well to talk of 'complete independence', but did the Indian people have the will to enforce such a demand? 'We have almost sunk to the level of a school boys' debating society', the Mahatma told Jawaharlal. A few months later, he told Motilal Nehru, who headed the committee which was to draft an All-Parties Constitution (the Nehru Report) that 'unless we have created some force ourselves, we shall not advance beyond the position of beggars. . . . We are not ready for drawing up a constitution till we have developed a sanction for ourselves.'[14] The only sanction that Gandhi could forge was that provided by a non-violent struggle.

In December 1928, when the advocates of independence and Dominion Status clashed at the Calcutta Congress, Jawaharlal is reported to have told Gandhi: 'Bapu, the difference between you and me is this: You believe in gradualism; I stand for revolution.' 'My dear young man', Gandhi retorted, 'I have made revolutions while others have only shouted revolutions. When your lungs are exhausted and you really are serious about it you will come to me and I shall then show you how a revolution is made.'[15] After a long, heated argument, much vacillation and 'mental distress', Jawaharlal eventually fell into line with Gandhi's compromise formula. Dominion Status was accepted as the basis of the new constitution, provided the British Government conceded it before the end of 1929.

To many of his young admirers Jawaharlal's attitude at the Calcutta Congress smacked of political cowardice; to Subhas Bose and members of the Independence for India League it seemed an abject betrayal. But it was a sound instinct which kept Jawaharlal from breaking with the Congress Old Guard and the Mahatma. He seems to have sensed that if there were any conservatives at the Calcutta Congress, Gandhi was not one of them. As events were to prove, it was Jawaharlal, not the Old Guard who won at Calcutta. There were some apparent disappointments and setbacks, such as Congress leaders' reaction to Lord Irwin's declaration on Dominion Status in November 1929 and the peace parleys in Delhi just before the Lahore Congress. Nevertheless, the fact remained that within a year, 'complete independence', instead of being the catchword of a few young radicals, became the battle-cry of the Congress party, and Gandhi was back at its helm to direct, to Jawaharlal's delight, another *Satyagraha* struggle against the British Raj.

IV

After the Calcutta Congress the political atmosphere became electric. Gandhi abandoned a trip to Europe which he had been planning and called for a boycott of foreign cloth. There were rumours of Jawaharlal's imminent arrest as he threw himself into the organisational work of the Congress with redoubled vigour. Politics again acquired for him a sense of purpose, urgency and adventure. All the signs pointed to Gandhi's return to the active leadership of the party. A majority of the provincial congress committees voted for him to preside over the Lahore session in December 1929. Gandhi declined the honour, but persuaded the All India Congress Committee to confer it on Jawaharlal. The thought that he had come to the highest office in the Congress 'not by the main entrance or even a side entrance', but by a 'trap door' which had bewildered the audience into acceptance[16] was humiliating to Nehru. Nevertheless, the fact that it fell to him to preside over the momentous session at Lahore and to unfurl the flag of independence on the bank of the Ravi at midnight of 31 December 1929 rocketed his prestige overnight. The Lahore Congress gave a tremendous boost to Jawaharlal's popularity with the masses; it raised his stock with the intelligentsia and made him a hero of India's youth.

As the new year dawned, events moved fast. With the observance of the Independence Day and the launching of the *Salt Satyagraha*, the political scene began to be transformed under the magic touch of the Mahatma. And once again, in the midst of a struggle against the British Raj, Jawaharlal felt that sense of complete identification with Gandhi he had experienced ten years before. His mood found an eloquent expression in the tribute he paid to Gandhi as the Mahatma marched to Dandi on the western coast for breach of the Salt Laws:

'Today the pilgrim marches onward on his long trek, the fire of a great resolve is in him, and surpassing love of his miserable countrymen. And love of truth that scorches and love of freedom that inspires. And none that passes him can escape the spell, and men of common clay feel the spark of life.'[17]

The *Salt Satyagraha* drew the whole Nehru family into the arena. Jawaharlal was the first to be arrested; he was followed by

his father, his sisters and his wife. But once again history repeated
itself, and Gandhi called off the movement when it seemed to be
on the crest of a rising wave. Nehru was in Delhi in February
and March 1931 and in touch with the Mahatma during his talks
with the Viceroy. Nevertheless, the contents of the Gandhi-
Irwin Pact on 4 March and particularly its second clause concerning the safeguards in the new constitution, came as a great
shock to Jawaharlal:[18]

'So I lay and pondered on that March night and in my heart
there was a great emptiness as of something precious gone, almost
beyond recall. . . . The thing had been done, our leader had committed himself; and even if we disagreed with him, what could we
do? Throw him over? Break from him? Announce our disagree-
ment? That might bring some personal satisfaction to an individual, but it made no difference to the final decision.'[19]

Gandhi observed Jawaharlal's distress, took him out for a
walk, and tried to allay his fears. Jawaharlal was not convinced,
but at the Karachi Congress, a few days later, he swallowed his
dissent, and even sponsored the resolution supporting the Gandhi-
Irwin Pact. His motive in doing so was to prevent an open rift
in the party and to strengthen the hands of Gandhi who was to
represent the Congress at the Round-Table Conference in London.

V

In December 1931, when Gandhi returned from his abortive trip
to London, Jawaharlal was already in gaol. The Gandhi-Irwin
Pact went to pieces, civil disobedience was resumed, the Congress
was outlawed and more than sixty thousand people were convicted for civil disobedience. Jawaharlal had one of his longest
spells in gaol – a total of 1,170 days – between December 1931
and September 1935. It was towards the close of this period that
he wrote his autobiography. The author's preface referred to the
'mood of self-questioning', and the 'particularly distressful period'
of his life in which the book was written. The distress stemmed not
only from the anxiety about his wife, who was hovering between
life and death in Indian and Swiss sanatoria, but also from the
decline of the struggle against the British Raj. As he recalled the
story of his life and the course of the movement to which he had
given his all, Jawaharlal noted the conflicting pulls which Gandhi
exerted on him:

'For it was clear that this little man of poor physique had something of steel in him, something rocklike which did not yield to physical powers, however great they might be. And in spite of his unimpressive features, his loin-cloth and bare body, there was a royalty and kingliness in him which compelled a willing obeisance from others. . . . His calm, deep eyes would hold one and gently probe into the depths, his voice, clear and limpid would purr its way into the heart and evoke an emotional response. It was the utter sincerity of the man and his personality that gripped. He gave the impression of tremendous reserves of power.'[20]

Despite his admiration for the Mahatma, Nehru found much in Gandhi which puzzled and even infuriated him. When he learned about Gandhi's fast against separate electorates for the depressed classes he felt angry with the Mahatma 'at his religious and sentimental approach to a political question and his frequent references to God in connection with it. He even seemed to suggest that God had indicated the very day of the fast. What a terrible example to set.' As he thought of the tragic possibilities of the fast he was seized with despair. 'If Bapu died! What would India be like then? And how would her politics run? There seemed to be a dreary and dismal future ahead. So I thought and thought and confusion reigned in my head and anger and hopelessness and love for him who was the cause of this upheaval.'[21]

The untouchability fast was not the only occasion when Gandhi's religious idiom jarred on Nehru. In 1934, the Mahatma suggested that the terrible earthquake which Bihar had just suffered was a divine punishment for the sin of untouchability. It struck Nehru as a 'staggering remark . . . anything more opposed to scientific outlook it would be more difficult to imagine'.[22] A few months later Gandhi's statement, calling off civil disobedience because of the failure of a 'valued companion to perform his full prison task', left Jawaharlal gasping with its emotional irrelevance. Jawaharlal had

'. . . a sudden and intense feeling that something broke inside me, a bond that I had valued very greatly had snapped. I felt terribly lonely in this wide world. . . . Again I felt that sensation of spiritual isolation, of being a perfect stranger out of harmony, not only with the crowds that passed me, but also with those whom I had valued as dear and close colleagues.'[23]

On occasions Gandhi struck Jawaharlal as 'a medieval Catholic saint'.[24] Gandhi's philosophy of 'one step enough for me' seemed much too empirical, his political style too abrupt and unpredictable, his doctrine of non-violence too lofty for the common run of mankind. The autobiography reflects Nehru's doubts and self-questioning and mental conflict.[25] Was not non-violence already hardening into 'an inflexible dogma' and 'taking its place in the pigeonholes of faith and religion . . . [and] becoming a sheet anchor for vested interests'?[26] Was it not an illusion to imagine that a dominant imperialist power would give up its domination over a country, or a class would give up its superior position and privileges, unless effective pressure amounting to coercion was exercised?[27] Was it not romantic to hope for the conversion of princes, landlords and capitalists into trustees of their properties for the commonweal, or to expect *khadi* and village industries to solve the long-term problems of India's poverty? Was not Gandhi's emphasis on the spinning-wheel overdone and fore-doomed to failure in an industrialised world?[28]

These doubts assailed Jawaharlal as he wrote his autobiography. Some of them had found expression in his talks with Gandhi in 1933 when he was briefly out of gaol. There was a public exchange of letters, in the course of which the Mahatma had acknowledged with a typical understatement that while they agreed in 'the enunciation of ideals, there are temperamental differences between us'.[29] While Nehru was in gaol during the next two years, these differences grew sharper. His ideas were taken up by a band of young Congressmen who were disillusioned by the failure of civil disobedience, and were attracted to socialist doctrines. In the 1920s, the Congress leadership had been challenged by young radicals on political issues, such as dominion status versus independence. In the 1930s, the challenge was to be on economic as well as on political issues; the contest was to be more serious not only for the coherence of the Congress party, but for the relations between Nehru and Gandhi. It is impossible to understand their relations at this time without noting their diverse social philosophies.

VI

Though Jawaharlal had sampled Fabian literature and attended Bernard Shaw's lectures as a student in Cambridge and London, his enthusiasm for Marxism and the Russian Revolution was derived from reading and reflection in gaol, and the visit to Europe in 1926-7, which had included a four-day trip to Moscow. It is significant that one of the aims of the Independence for India League, which he and Subhas Bose had founded in 1928, was the revision of the economic structure of society on a socialist basis. In his presidential address at the Lahore Congress, Jawaharlal avowed himself a socialist and asserted that 'socialism had permeated the entire structure of society and the only point in dispute is the pace and methods of advance to this realisation'. A little earlier, he had presided over the All India Trade Union Congress and argued that, despite the bourgeois character of the Congress, it did represent the only effective force in the country. In March 1931, thanks largely to Gandhi's support, he was able to push through the Karachi Congress a resolution[30] on fundamental rights and economic policy, which envisaged, among other things, the state ownership of key industries and services, mineral resources, railways, waterways, shipping and other means of transport. It is true that this resolution was only mildly socialist, but socialist ideas had not yet gained much currency in the Congress party. What Acharya Narendra Deva told Nehru in 1929 about the UP Independence League was true of most protagonists of socialism in the Congress in 1931: 'We may all generally believe in the necessity of reconstructing our society on a new basis, but the ideas of most of us are vague and indefinite and most of us do not know how to proceed about the business.'[31]

Not until 1934 was the initiative for the formation of a socialist group in the Congress taken by a number of young Congressmen who happened to be in Nasik gaol and shared the disenchantment with Gandhi's leadership in the wake of his withdrawal of civil disobedience. Among them were Jayaprakash Narayan, Asoka Mehta, Achyut Patwardhan, Yusuf Meherally, and S. M. Joshi. They were later joined by Narendra Deva, Sri Prakasa, Sampurnananda, N. G. Ranga and others. They swore by Marxism, talked of the inevitability of class war, called for planned economic development on the Soviet model, discounted Gandhi's leadership and doubted the efficacy of non-violence in solving Indian political and social problems. Gandhi was their chosen target. Jayaprakash Narayan described him as 'autochthonism'.[32] He considered Gandhi was played out and could not carry the people further.[33] It was only by drawing in the masses, the peasants and the workers, that the Congress could broaden its base, rid itself of its defeatist mentality, 'socialise' the nationalist struggle and forge a massive imperialist front.[34]

Gandhi was not impressed by the political wisdom of these young men, whom he described as a body of 'men in a hurry'. The talk of class war, expropriation and violence was repugnant to him. Nevertheless – and this was characteristic of Gandhi – he refused to be a party to the muzzling of Congress Socialists. Indeed, he helped them to secure a larger representation in the All India Congress Committee by the introduction of a single transferable vote.[35] He also announced his own formal retirement from the Congress organisation, so that his critics, including the young socialists, should be able to express their views without being inhibited by his presence.

Nehru was in gaol when the Congress Socialist party was founded. He never became an office-bearer, or even a member of this party. But there is no doubt that he was its hero, from whom it derived its inspiration. Some of the leading lights of the party, such as Narendra Deva, Jayaprakash Narayan and Achyut Patwardhan were close to Nehru and shared his outlook on national and international issues. Nehru's socialism was, however, not doctrinaire. Nor did he plan 'to inoculate the masses with the virus of Communism', as the Goverment of India suspected.[36] 'I am certainly a socialist', he wrote in March 1938, 'I believe in the socialist theory and method of approach. I am not a Communist chiefly because I resist the Communist tendency to treat Communism as holy doctrine, and I do not like being told what to think and what to do.' He made no secret of his faith in scientific socialism. He believed in curbing the profit motive, in promoting public ownership of key industries, and in using the machinery of the state to regulate economic activity. Gandhi's approach was different.

When not yet forty, Gandhi had developed a social philosophy of his own, based on a faith in non-violence and a distrust of industrialism and the modern state. The India of Gandhi's dreams was 'a federation of small village republics', providing only for the essential needs of the community. Based on a thoroughgoing decentralisation of the economic and political structures, it was to reduce the temptation for exploitation from within and aggression from without. It was to imitate neither British nor Soviet models, but was to be tailored to Indian conditions. It was to be, in Gandhi's words, *Ram Rajya*, 'the sovereignty of the people based on pure moral authority'.[37] 'I tell my socialist friends', he said at Faizpur in December 1936, 'you are not talking anything new. Our ancestors always said, this is God's earth. It is neither of the capitalists nor of *zamindars* nor of anybody. It belongs to God.'[38]

Congress Socialists did not take the Mahatma's claim to be a socialist seriously. To them, as to Nehru, the Mahatma's socialism was a kind of 'muddled humanitarianism'.[39]

VII

Imprisonment and domestic affliction had kept Jawaharlal out of Indian politics for nearly four and a half years. Curiously enough, while he was behind the prison bars, his political stock had risen; his was a name to conjure with among the masses as well as the intelligentsia; his autobiography was soon to give him a world-wide reputation as a writer. Gandhi was aware of Nehru's popularity as well as his differences with the Congress leadership. Nevertheless, he secured his election to the Presidency of the 1936 Congress, which met at Lucknow a few days after Jawaharlal's return from Europe. Conscious of the fact that the socialists were a tiny minority in the party, Nehru included only three of them, Jayaprakash Narayan, Achyut Patwardhan and Narendra Deva, in the Congress Working Committee, and gave the remaining eleven seats to the Old Guard – the 'Gandhites'. The Committee found it hard to settle down as a happy family. The political temperature had risen before Nehru's return. His militant address at the Lucknow Congress raised it further. The Congress Socialists seemed anxious to drive their advantage home; the older leaders were suspicious and nervous; Nehru himself was on edge. 'Today I feel', he wrote to a friend on 3 May 1936, 'that there will be a tug-of-war in India between rival ideologies. . . . I feel myself very much on the side of one ideology and I am distressed at some of my colleagues going the other way.'[40] Two days later he wrote about his sense of intellectual isolation in the Congress Working Committee. 'The last dozen years have been years of hard and continuous work for me, of self-education and study and thought. . . . But others . . . have not taken the trouble to think or study and have remained vaguely where they were. But the world changes.'[41] By the end of June, the crisis, unknown to the public, came to a head when seven members of the Congress Working Committee sent their resignations to Nehru. A split in the party was on the cards.

It is tempting to dramatise the 1936 crisis as a tug-of-war between the Right and the Left in the Congress with Gandhi backing the Right. But could Gandhi, who had roused the Indian peasantry to a consciousness of its strength in Champaran, Kaira and Bardoli be fairly labelled a reactionary? Was it not Gandhi who had made the nationalist movement really conscious of its responsibility to the underdog and made poverty a live issue? The dispute, really, was not on the adoption or rejection of the socialist creed; the political issue still predominated. The members of the so-called Right wing in the Congress executive – Rajendra Prasad, Vallabhbhai Patel and others – looked askance at the Socialist group largely because of the threat it seemed to them to pose to the unity of the party, which had yet to recover from the hammer-blows inflicted upon it by the Willingdon regime. The party was still illegal in the whole of the North-West Frontier Province and parts of Bengal. Anti-Congress forces, encouraged by the Government, were raising their heads. A general election was due at the end of the year. And just when the party needed a united front, the Congress Socialists were embarrassing the leadership, talking of class war, frightening off potential supporters, and making new enemies. The slogans of class struggle against money-lenders and landlords by *Kisan Sabhas* and socialist conferences all over the country could prove costly to the Congress at a general election in which barely 10 per cent of the population was entitled to vote. A peasants' conference in Andhra had gone so far as to demand for Congress members of legislatures freedom to vote on issues concerning the peasants.[42] This was a demand which cut at the very root of party discipline; Nehru, who was the Congress President, rejected it out of hand. Nevertheless, it revealed a dangerous drift towards disintegration, which had to be checked, if the Congress was to survive as a strong and effective instrument for fighting British imperialism.

It was thus not only ideological differences, but conflicting readings of the political situation which brought on the crisis in the Congress executive. Perhaps, even more important was the mistrust between the Old Guard and the Congress Socialists. Each feared being edged out of the party. Nehru suspected that there was a conspiracy to destroy him politically. 'When I reached Bombay', he wrote to Gandhi on 5 July 1936, 'many people stared hard at me, hardly believing that I was still politically alive.' Gandhi was not, of course, a party to such a plot. He resolved the crisis with admirable speed, skill and firmness. He insisted on the withdrawal of the resignations, and vetoed the reference of the dispute to the All India Congress Committee on the grounds that a public discussion would only aggravate and distort the differences among the leaders, confuse and demoralise the rank and file, and ruin the party's chances at the election. 'I am firmly of opinion', the Mahatma wrote, 'that during the remainder of the year all wrangling should cease and no resignations should take place.' He played down the crisis, described it as a tragi-comedy,[43] and pulled up Nehru for his edginess: 'If they [the members of the Congress Working Committee] are guilty of intolerance, you have more than your share of it. The country should not be made to suffer for your mutual intolerance.'[44] Though as late as November 1936 Edward Thompson was predicting that the Congress would split and 'Nehru will lead a group into the wilderness'.[45] the crisis was really over.

Nehru was prudent enough not to heed the advice of the hot-heads among his admirers, who were urging him to extreme courses. If he had broken with Gandhi and the Congress in 1936, he would have dealt a blow not only to the Congress, but to his own political future. It was obvious that so long as Gandhi remained at the helm of the Congress, it was unlikely that any rival nationalist party could emerge or compete with it. The founding or even the running of a political party was not Nehru's *métier*. He could sway crowds, inspire intellectuals, reel off press statements and articles, run the AICC office, and travel from one end of the country to the other, but he was not cut out for the role of a party manager. He did not have Gandhi's gift for discovering, training, and harnessing to the national cause men and women of varying abilities and temperaments. 'I function individually', he told Subhas Bose, 'without any group or any second person to support me.'[46] This detachment, admirable in its own way, limited his room for manoeuvre within the party. When Bose reproached him for not backing him up against Gandhi, Nehru frankly said that a head-on collision with the Mahatma was likely to be suicidal. 'The Left', he warned Bose, 'was not strong enough to shoulder the burden by itself, and when a real contest came in the Congress, it would lose and then there would be a reaction against it.' Bose could win the election and become Congress President against Pattabhi Sitaramayya, but Nehru doubted whether Bose could carry the Congress in a clear contest with what was called Gandhism. Even if he won a majority within the Congress, it would not ensure Bose a sufficient backing in the country. And in any case a mass struggle against the Government without Gandhi was inconceivable. Finally, Nehru warned Bose that there were many 'disruptive tendencies' already in the country, and it was not right to add to them, and to weaken the national movement.[47]

What Nehru came to realise in 1938, after closer acquaintance with the balance of forces in the country and the party, Gandhi had seen two years earlier. An open rift in the Congress in 1936 would have crippled the Congress organisation at a critical juncture, and would have been a godsend to the British Government. It was not by seceding from the Congress, but by influencing it from within, that Nehru was to push it in the direction in which he desired it to go.

It was during this crisis that Gandhi, with remarkable candour, revealed his reasons for supporting Nehru's candidacy for the Congress Presidency in 1936, even though his ideas were in conflict with those of a majority of his colleagues in the party leadership. 'You are in office', wrote Gandhi to Jawaharlal on 15 July 1936, 'by their unanimous choice, but you are not in power yet. . . . To put you in office was an attempt to put you in power quicker than you would otherwise have been. Anyway that was at the back of my mind when I suggested your name for the crown of thorns.'[48] Thus it turns out that Nehru's elevation to the Congress Presidency in 1936 was not, as Hiren Mukerjee suggests, 'to imprison the socialist wave in a strong little reservoir of Gandhi's own making',[49] but to launch forth Nehru on a favourable wind on the wide and stormy ocean of Indian politics.

It is true that in 1936–7 Nehru could not have his way on two crucial issues: elections to the new legislature and the formation of Congress ministries. But, thanks to Nehru's influence, the decisions on these issues did not dampen Indian nationalism. The Congress election manifesto bore marks of Nehru's militant socialism and anti-imperialism. And the election campaign, largely because of the prominent part he took in it, had the effect of awakening the masses. Finally, when the Congress accepted office, it was on its own terms and not those of the British Government. The continual criticisms from Nehru and his socialist friends had the salutary effect of preventing the Congress ministries from sliding into bureaucratic grooves. Nehru's Presidency thus decidedly gave a radical twist to Congress politics in 1936–7. Even E. M. S. Namboodiripad acknowledges that the presence of a left-wing leader at the head of the Congress 'enormously strengthened the forces of the left; the ideas of socialism, of militant and uncompromising anti-imperialism, of anti-landlord and anti-capitalist struggles . . . began to grip the people on a scale never before thought possible'.[50]

In 1936, as in 1928, Nehru had stooped to Gandhi, but he had stooped to conquer. It is true that he was not able to get his views and programmes accepted immediately, or in their entirety, but he was able to influence the final decisions much more from within the party than he would have been able to do if – like Subhas Bose – he had left it to plough his own lonely furrow.

VIII

Thanks to Gandhi's intervention, the crisis in the Congress in 1936 was tided over. Jawaharlal continued to be the President and was in fact re-elected for another year. He was not, however, in tune with his colleagues in the Working Committee. Gandhi sensed Nehru's unhappiness and irascibility. 'Somehow or other, everything I say and even perhaps do', he wrote to Nehru, 'jars on you . . . you must bear with me till my understanding becomes clear or your fears are dispelled.'[51] 'I can't tell you', he wrote on another occasion, 'how positively lonely I feel to know that nowadays I can't carry you with me.'[52] Often the Mahatma would seek Nehru's approbation for whatever he was doing. When sending a copy of one of his articles in the *Harijan*, he told him on 15 July 1937 'When you see it you will please tell me if I may continue to write so. I do not want to interfere with your handling of the whole situation. For I want the maximum from you for the country. I would be doing distinct harm, if my writing disturbed you.' A note on Gandhi's talks with Jinnah was accompanied by the exhortation to Nehru, 'not to hesitate to summarily reject it, if it does not commend itself to you'.[53]

The differences between the two men during these years were often on current issues, representing a difference of approach or emphasis. Nehru, for instance, was not quite happy about Gandhi's interview with the Governor of Bengal on the release of the detenus, or about the embargo on Congress participation in popular agitation in the princely states. The slow implementation of the reforms by the Congress ministries vexed him, while most of his colleagues felt that he did not make a sufficient allowance for the limitations under which they worked. The activities of the Congress Socialists provided another cause for misunderstanding.[54] Some of them, who were close to Nehru, made no secret of their conviction that Gandhi was 'finished', that he was incapable of giving any further lead against the British Raj, that his technique of non-violence could not take the country to the final goal. After reading a book on the Russian Revolution, Rafi Ahmed Kidwai confided to Nehru: 'If we want to make further progress, we will have to make an attempt to destroy the mentality created by the CD (civil disobedience). . . . We will have to give up the present standards of scrupulousness, personal integrity, honesty and political amiability.'[55] Truth and non-violence, Narendra Deva told Nehru, were 'noble ideas. . . . But they are so much being misused today in India that the day is not far distant when they will stink in our nostrils.'[56] J. P. Narayan saw a real danger of the Congress being converted

'. . . from a democratic organisation of the millions of the down-trodden people into a hand-maid of Indian vested interests. A vulgarisation of Gandhism makes this transition easy, and gives this new Congress the requisite demagogic armour. . . . We are faced today with the real danger of Indian industry being made a synonym for Indian nationalism.'[57]

It is not unlikely that what his friends were saying reflected Nehru's own inner misgivings at this time. The intellectual hiatus between him and Gandhi tended to blow up even small tactical differences into minor crises. But there were also basic divergences between their reading of the political situation. During the two years preceding the war, Nehru was disconcerted by, what seemed to him, the tendency of the Congress ministries to slip into a compromise with the existing order. He was dismayed by the lack of intelligent interest on the part of his colleagues in the developments which were hastening the zero hour in Europe. And he was almost driven to despair by their inability to grasp the significance of the National Planning Committee and its many sub-committees, which had under his guidance held as many as seventy-two meetings in twenty months. 'I have never been able to understand or appreciate the labours of the Committee', Gandhi blandly told Jawaharlal on 11 August 1939, 'I have not understood the purpose of the numerous sub-committees. It has appeared to me that much labour and money are being wasted on an effort which will bring forth little or no fruit.'[58]

Because of all these differences with Gandhi and most of the Congress leaders, Nehru felt 'out of place and a misfit', and welcomed an opportunity in 1938 to visit Europe for a few months 'to freshen up' his tired and puzzled mind.[59]

IX

The outbreak of war in September 1939 added yet another strand to a complex situation. It set into motion forces which were to transform not only party alignments in India, but the structure of power in the world. It was also to reveal a fundamental cleavage between Gandhi and Nehru in their attitudes towards the war. 'Perhaps this is the most critical period in our history', Gandhi wrote to Nehru on 26 October 1939, 'I hold very strong views on the most important questions which occupy our attention. I know you too hold strong views on them, but different from mine. Your mode of expression is different from mine.'[60]

Nehru had been publicly hailed by Gandhi as his 'guide' on international affairs. It was at Nehru's instance that the Indian National Congress had denounced every act of aggression by the fascist powers in Manchuria, Abyssinia, Spain or Czechoslovakia and taken the Western powers to task for their policy of 'appeasement' towards the dictators. Nevertheless, Nehru had a lurking feeling that Gandhi had often accepted his viewpoint on international affairs 'without wholly agreeing with it'.[61] The Mahatma was second to none in his hatred of the tyrannies set up by the Fascist and Nazi regimes. He defined Hitlerism as 'naked ruthless force reduced to an exact science worked with scientific precision'. Gandhi regarded Nazism and Fascism as symptoms of a deep-seated disease – the cult of violence. He did not, however, believe that violence could be neutralised with counter-violence. Through the pages of his weekly paper, the *Harijan*, he exhorted the victims of aggression, the Abyssinians, the Czechs and the Poles to defend themselves with non-violent resistance. 'There is no bravery', he argued, 'greater than a resolute refusal to bend the knee to an earthly power.' Even after Hitler had swiftly overrun Poland in 1939, and Europe was gripped by fear and foreboding, the Mahatma continued to affirm that non-violence could serve as an effective shield against aggression.

Neither Nehru, nor the majority of the members of the Congress

Working Committee, nor indeed the rank and file of the party shared Gandhi's boundless faith in the efficacy of non-violence. Clearly, Nehru did not view the war as an occasion for asserting the efficacy of non-violence; the really important point was how the monstrous war-machine built by Hitler was to be stopped and destroyed before it could enslave mankind. Nehru had never accepted non-violence as a method for all situations or all times:

'The Congress had long ago accepted the principle and practice of non-violence in its application to our struggle for freedom and in building up unity in the nation. At no time had it gone beyond that position or applied the principle to defence from external aggression or internal disorder.'[62]

It soon became obvious that behind the facade of unity, the Congress leaders had serious differences in their approach to the war. The primary motivation of radicals like Jayaprakash Narayan was anti-British, of Nehru anti-Fascist, and of Gandhi anti-war. These differences would have come sharply into focus, if the British Government under the influence of Churchill and Linlithgow had not short-sightedly tried to 'freeze' the constitutional position for the duration of the war. So long as there was no question of effective Congress participation in the central government, the question of whether India's support of the Allies was to be moral (as Gandhi advocated), or military (as Nehru proposed), remained purely academic. There were two occasions, however, when the vicissitudes of war seemed to bring a rapprochement between the Congress and the Government within the realm of practical politics: in 1940 after the French collapse and in 1941–2 after the Japanese triumph in South-East Asia. On both these occasions Gandhi found that the majority of his colleagues were ready to switch from a pacifist stand to a whole-hearted participation in the Allied war effort in return for a reciprocal gesture by the British Government. The Congress parleys with Sir Stafford Cripps finally broke down not on the issue of violence versus non-violence, but on constitutional and administrative details of a provisional government for the effective prosecution of the war.

The period immediately preceding and following the Cripps Mission in 1942 was a testing time for Jawaharlal. He had little love for the British Government, but he was dismayed by its obstinate refusal to read the writing on the wall. Meanwhile,

Indian public opinion was reaching the height of frustration. Between British folly and Indian frustration, the Allied cause, and particularly the future of the hard-pressed Chinese and the Russians, was trembling in the balance. In the aftermath of the Cripps Mission, Gandhi's decision to launch a mass struggle created a further painful dilemma for Nehru. The idea of launching a mass civil disobedience, when the war was on India's doorstep at first seemed to him fantastic. His mind was full of thoughts of citizen armies, home guards and guerilla warfare to beat off the Japanese invaders. Deep heart-searching and anguish led him even to think of deviating from the Congress policy towards the war. It was with some difficulty that he was persuaded not to strike out his own line on co-operation with the Allies.[63] During the months of May and June, he had long talks with Gandhi, who wrote later to the Viceroy: 'I argued with him [Jawaharlal] for days together. He fought against my position with a passion which I have no words to describe.'[64] Eventually, Nehru fell into line with the 'Quit India' stand, even though he was conscious that it 'gave second place to logic and reason' and 'was not a politician's approach but of a people grown desperate and reckless of consequences.'[65] Nehru agreed to support the 'Quit India' policy, but before he did so he had persuaded Gandhi to agree that Allied troops would remain on Indian soil during the war, and the 'provisional' government of free India would throw all its resources into the struggle against Fascism. For Gandhi, with his passionate commitment to non-violence, this was, as Nehru noted, 'a bitter pill'.[66] Nehru's decision to support the Mahatma on the 'Quit India' movement was thus not really the one-sided compromise it was made out to be by some of his critics. M. N. Roy wrote:

'Godly power of the Mahatma has overpowered the human wish of the romantic politician [Nehru]. . . . In vain has he dilated upon his differences and final agreement on fundamentals with Mr Gandhi, for throughout his whole career he has blindly followed Mr Gandhi. In fact he has no independence of thought or action.'[67]

What M. N. Roy failed to see was that in reaching a compromise Nehru did not make all the concessions. If the internationalist had given in to the nationalist in Nehru, the pacifist had given in to the patriot in Gandhi.

G

X

After spending nearly three years in gaol, Nehru was released in June 1945 just before the Simla Conference convened by the Viceroy, Lord Wavell. This was the starting point for a series of triangular negotiations between the British Government, the Congress and the Muslim League which culminated in the transfer of power and partition of India two years later. In these negotiations, the leading part was played by Nehru, Vallabhbhai Patel and Abul Kalam Azad, but they remained in touch with Gandhi and took his advice. Only in the last phase of the negotiations, towards the end of 1946 and the beginning of 1947, when Gandhi was busy touring the riot-torn countryside of East Bengal and Bihar, did his influence on events become minimal. This may have been due partly to his absence from Delhi – the hub of political activity – and partly to the swiftness with which the political landscape changed during this period owing to the eagerness of the Muslim League to cash in on the British decision to quit India, and the anxiety of the Congress for a speedy and smooth transfer of power. In the aftermath of the Muslim League's 'Direct Action Day' at Calcutta in August 1946, communal violence spread like a prairie fire, and threatened to engulf the whole country. At the centre the conflict between the Congress and Muslim League members paralysed the Interim Government. As the danger of a civil war loomed on the horizon, Nehru, Vallabhbhai Patel and most of the Congress leaders came to the painful conclusion that the partition of the country was a lesser evil than a forced and fragile union, that it was a worthwhile attempt to salvage three-quarters of India from the chaos that threatened the whole. Against this background the Congress Working Committee mooted the partition of the provinces of the Punjab and Bengal in March, and accepted the Mountbatten Plan for the transfer of power (and the partition of the country as its corollary) in June. The final decision was taken against Gandhi's advice.

Michael Brecher has suggested that Nehru and Patel opted for the partition of the country because they were tempted by 'the prize of power'.[68] Human motives are rarely unmixed, but in the summer of 1947 partition seemed the lesser evil not only to Nehru and Patel, but to the entire Congress leadership, with a few exceptions such as those of Abdul Ghaffar Khan and Jayaprakash Narayan. Gandhi's eleventh hour proposal that the

Viceroy call upon Jinnah to form an exclusively Muslim League Government was a bold gesture, but the Congress leaders, after their experience of association with Muslim League ministers in the Interim Government, were in no mood to endorse it. Nor did Gandhi's alternative of a mass struggle appeal to them. Struggle against whom? The British were in any case going, and the Muslim League with its calculated mixture of bluster and bullying was hardly susceptible to the moral nuances of *Satyagraha*. J. B. Kripalani explained the predicament of even those who prided themselves on being Gandhi's blind followers. 'Today also I feel that he [Gandhi] by his supreme fearlessness is correct and my stand is defective. Why then am I not with him? It is because I feel that he has as yet found no way of tackling the [Hindu-Muslim] problem on a mass basis.'[69]

To Nehru and Patel it seemed in the spring and summer of 1947 that the Mahatma's idealism had outrun the needs of a critical and developing crisis, that the intransigence of the Muslim League and the mounting chaos in the country really left no alternative to partition, that to insist on unity under such circumstances was to court an even greater disaster.

Gandhi's rocklike faith in non-violence was admirable, but to most of his colleagues he seemed at the time an uncompromising prophet rather than a practical statesman. It was not for the first time that Gandhi found himself isolated. In 1940, the Congress had declined to accept non-violence as a shield against external danger; seven years later, it refused to embrace it as a shield against internal disorder.

Gandhi seems to have had a lingering regret that in the final stages of the negotiations with the British Government, he had been by-passed by Nehru and Patel.[70] Nevertheless, he lent them his powerful support at the crucial meetings of the Working Committee and the All India Congress Committee.[71] During the five and a half months which remained to him, he wore himself out in an effort to heal the wounds inflicted by the partition, and became in the words of Mountbatten, a 'one-man boundary force for keeping the peace in disturbed areas'. Gandhi was not the man to nurse a grievance, and there is no evidence to show that the events leading to the partition created any permanent estrangement between him and Nehru.

As Prime Minister, Nehru continued to lean on Gandhi for advice and moral support during the latter half of 1947. A tragic reminder of this dependence came to Nehru within a few hours of the tragedy on 30 January 1948: 'I was sitting in my chair . . . worried about Bapu's funeral. The colossal problem that it presented baffled me. Suddenly, I said, let me go and consult Bapu.'[72]

Gandhi's death sublimated Nehru's relationship with him. The heroic fight of the Mahatma against fanaticism and violence in his last months, and finally his martydom burnt themselves into Nehru's soul. The memory of 'the Master'– as Nehru loved to recall him – suffused with a fresh glow, and nourished by mingled feelings of love, gratitude and guilt remained with him till the last. He told a correspondent in 1957 that he could not write at length on Gandhi as 'I get emotionally worked up and that is no mood to write. If I was a poet, which I am not, perhaps that mood might help.'[73] The awesome responsibility of running the party and the government perhaps gave him a fresh retrospective insight into the methods of the Mahatma, who had borne the burden of conducting the movement for nearly thirty years. The process of intellectual reconciliation had indeed begun in Gandhi's lifetime; this can be seen by comparing the *Autobiography* with the *Discovery of India*, in which the criticism of Gandhi's ideas have been considerably toned down. In the intervening decade, Nehru had gone a long way towards rediscovering not only India, but Gandhi.

XI

The political equation between Gandhi and Nehru, extending as it did over a quarter of a century, was not static. It was continually evolving, and seeking a new equilibrium in response not only to the inner drives of two men of exceptional energy and integrity, but to the realities of the changing political scene in India. During the first ten years, the partnership was really between Gandhi and Motilal, young Nehru's role being that of a favourite and earnest disciple of the Mahatma. The Lahore Congress brought Jawaharlal to the forefront of national politics, but it was not until the late thirties that he really became a factor to reckon with in the counsels of the Congress. It is an indication of his rising political stature that while in the twenties his dissent was merely an inconvenience to the Congress establishment, in 1936 it brought the party to the verge of a split. He owed his position in the party and the country in a great measure to his own qualities: his high idealism and dynamism, tireless energy and robust optimism, infectious faith in the destiny of his party and his country, his glamour for youth and charisma for the masses. Nevertheless, it is doubtful if he could have reached the apex of party leadership so early and decisively, if Gandhi had not catapulted him into it at critical junctures in 1929 and 1936.

Gandhi knew that Jawaharlal was not a 'blind follower' and had a mind of his own. Their philosophies of life diverged widely, but they were at one in their desire to rid the country of foreign rule and its gross poverty and social and economic inequalities. Gandhi wanted to harness Nehru's great talents and energies and was confident of containing his impetuous and rebellious spirit. 'He is undoubtedly an extremist', Gandhi wrote soon after Nehru's election to the Congress Presidency in 1929, 'thinking far ahead of his surroundings. But he is humble enough and practical enough not to force the pace to the breaking point.'[74] Seven years later, on the eve of a serious crisis in the party, the Mahatma assured an English correspondent: 'But though Jawaharlal is extreme in his presentation of his methods, he is sober in action. So far as I know him, he will not precipitate a conflict. . . . My own feeling is that Jawaharlal will accept the decision of the majority of his colleagues.'[75]

To the question why two men with such diverse backgrounds, and temperament remained together, the simple answer is that they needed each other. In 1919, young Nehru needed Gandhi to provide an outlet to his passionate but pent-up nationalism, and Gandhi, about to enter the Indian political stage, was on the look-out for able lieutenants. He had already enlisted Mahadev Desai, Vallabhbhai Patel and Rajendra Prasad. It is not surprising that young Jawaharlal should have caught the Mahatma's perceptive eye and evoked from the outset a special consideration. Jawaharlal was to become Gandhi's link with the younger generation and his window on the world. Informed by study and travel, he became Gandhi's mentor on international affairs. His passion for clarity and logic often clashed with the Mahatma's intuitive and pragmatic approach, but he discovered before long that the Mahatma had an uncanny sense of the mood of the Indian masses, their potential and their limitations, and that his political decisions were in fact sounder than the explanations with which he clothed them. Nehru realised the indispensability of Gandhi's leadership, and, therefore, never pressed his differences to an open breach with him. Whatever his inner doubts about the possibilities of non-violence for changing the hearts of those who wielded political and economic power, Jawaharlal felt certain that Gandhi was leading the country in the right direction. Indeed, realising Gandhi's receptivity, flexibility and unpredictability, Nehru continued to hope that eventually the Mahatma's weight would be thrown in favour of radicalising India's politics and economy.

Whatever their political differences, it is important to remember, that Gandhi's link with Jawaharlal Nehru transcended the political nexus. The Mahatma's extraordinary capacity to love and be loved was experienced by many of his colleagues and their families, but for the Nehru family he seems to have had a special corner in his heart. With Motilal his equation was that of a colleague rather than that of a mentor. Jawaharlal was doubtless a disciple, but a favourite one: the Mahatma's face shone with pleasure and pride in the company of young Nehru, whom he hailed as his son long before he described him his 'heir'. Intellectual and political differences did not diminish Gandhi's affection, which was deeply reciprocated by Jawaharlal. There was hardly a major domestic decision – whether it was the treatment of his ailing wife, the education of his daughter, or the marriage of his sister – on which Jawaharlal did not seek the Mahatma's advice and blessing. It was to 'Bapu' that the family instinctively turned for solace in moments of grief. When Kamala Nehru was dying in Switzerland, Jawaharlal was cabling her condition daily not only to her mother in India but to Gandhi as well.

Gandhi had much less difficulty in understanding Nehru than Nehru had in understanding Gandhi. The Mahatma seems to have sensed almost immediately the deep loneliness, idealism and restless energy of young Nehru even better than Motilal had done. Indeed, in the earlier years, Gandhi acted as a bridge between father and son. For Gandhi, the crucial test came when, after his visit to Europe in 1927, Jawaharlal suddenly seemed to have outgrown the political and economic framework of the party. Gandhi's reaction to young Nehru's rebellion was characteristic. He did not attempt to muzzle him. On the contrary he encouraged him to be candid about the differences: 'I suggest a dignified way of unfurling your banner. Write to me a letter for publication showing your differences. I will print it in *Young India* and write a brief reply.'[76] Subsequently when Jawaharlal was straining at the leash after signing the Delhi Manifesto, welcoming Lord Irwin's declaration on Dominion Status for

India, Gandhi told him: 'Let this incident be a lesson. Resist me always when my suggestion does not appeal to your head or heart. I shall not love you the less for that resistance.'[77]

Gandhi's refusal to impose his ideas on Nehru could not but have a moderating influence on Jawaharlal. The lack of resistance from the Mahatma reduced the incentive for an open revolt. Repeatedly Gandhi offered to step off the political stage altogether, and to leave the field to Nehru and others. Since Gandhi did not owe his influence in the party to any office, it made him the less vulnerable: it was pointless to seek to throw out a leader who was always willing to retire voluntarily.

It was not without much inner conflict and anguish that Nehru was able to reconcile the conflict between his mind and heart, between his own convictions and loyalty to Gandhi and the party. Yet nobody knew more than Nehru how much he owed to Gandhi. It was from the Mahatma that he imbibed an ethical outlook, a concern for the 'naked hungry mass' of India, and faith in peaceful and patient methods, and in good means as a lever for good ends, in argument and persuasion rather than in coercion.

The working partnership between Nehru and Gandhi lasted till the end, but their philosophies of life never really converged. In October 1945, a few months before the negotiations for the final demission of British power began, Gandhi wrote to Nehru: 'I am now an old man . . . I have, therefore, named you as my heir. I must, however, understand my heir and my heir should understand me. Then alone shall I be content.' The Mahatma went on to express his conviction that truth and non-violence could only be realised in the simplicity of village life and to envisage independent India, as was his wont, as a federation of self-reliant village republics. Nehru replied,

'The question before us is not one of truth versus untruth and non-violence versus violence. One assumes as one must, that true co-operation and peaceful methods must be aimed at, and a society which encourages these must be our objective. The whole question is how to achieve this society and what its content should be. I do not understand why a village should necessarily embody truth and non-violence. A village, normally, speaking, is backward intellectually and culturally and no progress can be made from a backward environment. Narrow-minded people are much more likely to be untruthful and violent. . . .'[78]

This scepticism about the feasibility of the rural Utopia, as outlined in the *Hind Swaraj*, was not confined to Nehru; it was shared by almost the entire Congress leadership, and the intelligentsia, who never learned to appreciate Gandhi's philosophic anarchism, unqualified commitment to non-violence, and criticism of science and technology, industrialism and institutions of the West.

The argument between Gandhi and Nehru in 1945 on what constituted the good society remained inconclusive, but Nehru adhered to the line he had always taken in public and private. 'We cannot stop the river of change', he had written in his autobiography, 'or cut ourselves adrift from it, and psychologically, we who have eaten the apple of Eden cannot forget the taste and go back to primitiveness.'[79] Hardly anyone affected surprise when, in Gandhi's lifetime, the Constituent Assembly set itself to the task of framing a constitution for a strong nation-state, based on parliamentary democracy, with all the paraphernalia of a civil service, army, navy and air-force, along with an infrastructure of modern industry. For Nehru and his colleagues the question in 1947, as a shrewd critic recently pointed out, was not that of 'personal loyalty' to Gandhi, but 'a matter of social perspective and principles . . . a choice between a strong industrial (and military) state versus a commonwealth of barely self-sufficient agricultural communities'.[80] Nehru chose the first, as indeed he had even said in the Mahatma's lifetime that he would.

Nehru would have been the last person to profess that he was following Gandhi's blueprint for an independent India during his years in power. Even if it had been possible to recognise such a blueprint, it could hardly have been adapted to the mechanism of the modern state. *Sarvodaya*, unlike socialism, cannot be legislated into existence. The changes it postulates in the minds and hearts of men can be better attempted through voluntary efforts and the example of devoted men, rather than through the authority of parliaments, cabinets, civil services, courts and the police. In fairness to Nehru, it must, however, be acknowledged that he applied Gandhi as far as he could to the needs of a modern nation-state. In that process 'something of Gandhi was knocked out, everything could not be absorbed. But nobody absorbed so much of Gandhi as Nehru did or incorporated so much of him in the inexorable working of statehood.'[81] The spirit of Gandhi may be seen in Nehru's consistent respect for individual liberty and secularism, his rejection of violence and regimentation, and his determination to find a national consensus within the parliamentary system. Like Gandhi, Nehru had a deep concern for the small peasant, the landless labourer and the industrial worker. The concept of Five Year Plans, though far removed from Gandhian economics, stressed the uplift of rural India and included programmes for community development, village self-government and cottage industries. Indeed, the point has recently been made that the Planning Commission in India gave away hundreds of crores to subsidise village handicrafts, 'as a form of rural unemployment relief and as a tribute to Gandhi's sacred memory'.[82]

In foreign policy Nehru was not Gandhian enough to advocate unilateral disarmament of India, nor did he turn the other cheek to Pakistan and China. Nevertheless, throughout his years of office, he threw his weight in favour of non-alignment with military blocs, conciliation, peaceful negotiation of differences between nations, and the widening of the area of peace. The deep conviction with which, despite difficulties and rebuffs, he pursued these aims doubtless stemmed from his long association with Gandhi. During his twilight years, in a world darkened by growing cynicism, violence and ruthlessness, Nehru was speaking more and more in Gandhian accents, pleading for the linking of 'scientific approach' and the 'spiritualistic approach',[83] and warning the Planning Commission against the dangers of 'giganticism'.[84] And almost the last thing he wrote pointed out that while progress in science, technology and production were desirable, 'we must not forget that the essential objective to be aimed at is the quality of the individual and the concept of *Dharma* underlying it'.[85]

Chapter 7

Jawaharlal Nehru and Socialism: The Early Phase

I

The growth of Indian socialism during the two crowded decades which span the First and the Second World Wars can best be studied in the political and social context of the time. This growth was not, however, in a straight line; it suffered from false starts and set-backs; it was affected by the hostility of the British authorities, recurrent economic crises, the changing international scene, and the rather violent shifts in the attitudes of the Communist International towards the nationalist struggle in India. The organisation of 'Left Politics' took place in the face of official opposition and Congress suspicion. The periods favourable to socialist ideas were those which formed the troughs of the Gandhian waves of *Satyagraha* struggles.

There is no doubt that socialist ideas and parties gave a certain social content and occasionally a sharper edge to Indian nationalism, as represented by the Indian National Congress. That they could not achieve more was due to the internal contradictions of the parties of the Left, the limitations imposed by their grasp of the political realities, and the charismatic, but dynamic and skilful leadership of the Indian National Congress by Mahatma Gandhi throughout this period.

It is a curious fact that even though Marx was a contemporary of Keshub Chunder Sen and Dadabhai Naoroji, and Lenin of Gokhale and Tilak, socialist ideas hardly figured in the Indian imagination in the period before the First World War, when politics constituted probably the only hobby of the educated classes. Some of the Indian leaders had contacts with socialists in Britain: Dadabhai was friendly with Hyndman, Gokhale with the Webbs, Tilak with Lansbury, Lajpat Rai with Col. Wedgwood.

It would seem, however, that British socialists and the Labour Party were viewed by Indian leaders not so much as champions of the British working class as possible allies in extracting constitutional reforms from Britain.

Indian politicians, Extremists as well as Moderates, seem to have been too preoccupied with the Herculean task of making a dent in the armour of the British bureaucratic machine to think of reconstructing the Indian economy. Such a reconstruction was indeed an idle dream so long as all political and economic power rested in an alien agency. There was also a built-in fear of drastic changes. Memories of the civil disorder and instability in the eighteenth century, doubtless exaggerated by British writers, conditioned the first generation of Indian nationalists against root-and-branch reforms. The agrarian disturbances in the Deccan in the 1870s and 1890s struck the Indian intelligentsia not as the welcome stirrings of an oppressed peasantry, but danger signals of a possible relapse into anarchy. The Congress leaders wanted gradual changes towards a rational, secular, progressive society and an administration at first responsive and ultimately responsible to public opinion.

The Indian educated class constituted a small minority, but it was not merely the mouthpiece of the upper and middle classes. That it did not neglect the interests of the masses is shown by its persistent and persuasive advocacy of increase in the minimum limit for income-tax, the abolition of the salt tax, the extension of local self-government, the establishment of the village *panchayats*, the reduction of land revenue and the institution of free and compulsory elementary education – reforms which would benefit the poorer sections of the community. It is true that leaders of the pre-war Congress did not idealise the masses – nobody did before 1917 – but they had a deep concern for the well-being of the peasantry and the weaker sections of the community. They were of course far from being socialists. Indeed the word had a bad odour about it, just as a hundred years earlier the word 'Liberal' was looked down upon as a term of abuse by 'respectable' people in Europe.[1]

II

It was the Russian Revolution which was to make socialism a word to conjure with. It was only natural that Indian nationalists, engaged in a continual debate with the British Government, should have seen in the fall of Tsarist autocracy the confirmation of their hope that British autocracy in India would also crumble one day. The annulment of the partition of Persia and Turkey by the revolutionary government in Russia was well received in India; it was a practical token of the renunciation of imperialism by a European power. But the other important aspect of the Russian Revolution, the fashioning of a new socio-economic system – seems curiously to have made relatively little immediate impact on the Indian imagination. This may have been due to the fact that Marxist literature had enjoyed little vogue in this country and the news from Russia filtered through the British press, tended to produce a dark picture of disorder and bloodshed, wholesale executions of political opponents, expropriation of property, censorship and regimentation. 'Russia indeed has hinted a moral', Lord Chelmsford told the Imperial Council, 'which it would do us all good to take to heart.'[2] That the revolution and anarchy were considered synonymous is indicated by Gandhi's comment that India 'did not want Bolshevism. The people are too peaceful to stand anarchy'.[3]

The Russian Revolution seems to have stimulated the organisation of labour and the formation of trade unions in India. In April 1918, Wadia formed a trade union in Madras, and in the same year, Bombay saw the emergence of the Indian Seamen's Union. The GIP Railway Union came into existence in 1919, the Ahmedabad Textile Workers' Union, and the All India Trade Union Congress in 1920. The success of the proletarian revolution in Russia powerfully affected a few individuals such as the poet Nazrul Islam, who wrote his *Byathar Dan* in 1919 and young men like A. K. Fazlul Huq and Muzaffar Ahmed[4] who brought out a new Bengali paper, the *Navayug* in 1920 in Calcutta, and S. A. Dange who published *Gandhi and Lenin* in 1921. The effect on established political parties and its leaders was however hardly perceptible. Raja Mahendra Pratap, Barkatullah and other romantic revolutionaries, who assured Lenin in Moscow that India was ripe for revolution in 1919,[5] had been so long in the terrorist underground or in exile that they had little knowledge of the real conditions in India. The brilliant M. N. Roy who had arrived in Moscow via the USA and Mexico, was perhaps in no better position. He impressed Lenin as one of the best representatives of colonial revolutionism and was catapulted into the counsels of Communist International, but he tended to generalise from his limited experience as a hunted Bengali terrorist. He misjudged the Indian situation, the emergence of Gandhi and the non-violent non-co-operation movement. Curiously enough, at the meeting of the Second Communist International in 1920, it was not Roy, the expert on Asian colonialism but Lenin who was nearer the mark in assessing the revolutionary potentialities of the national liberation movements in colonial countries.

Communist ideas, and the news from the Soviet Union did not immediately influence major political parties and well-known leaders, but it inspired some young men who were to become the founding fathers of the Communist Party in India. One of them, Muzaffar Ahmed recalls the enthusiasm of the first converts when they were a mere handful and possessed only a 'superficial knowledge of Marxism', but felt an 'unquestioned loyalty to the directives of the Communist International'.[6] These directives were changed somewhat arbitrarily from time to time according to the reading of the Indian or world situation from Moscow.

The First Communist International in 1919 had expected that the imminent downfall of capitalism in the imperialist countries themselves would ensure the liberation of the colonies. As imperialism did not crumble so easily, the Second Communist International in 1920 tackled the problem in dead earnest, and received two theses, one from Lenin himself advocating alliance with 'bourgeois democratic liberation movements'; the other from M. N. Roy advocating independent action through the setting up of a proletarian party, untrammelled by restrictions as to means. Roy came to be recognised as the expert on India and largely moulded the thinking of the Soviet leaders in the twenties. The Indian military school which he set up at Tashkent with Russian money and arms to recruit and train an army of Indian ex-patriates for liberation of India was still-born. It encountered unexpected difficulties. The Afghan Government was reluctant to allow infiltration through its territory, and the Kremlin itself, anxious to conclude a trade agreement with Britain, could hardly reject British representations for disbandment of the Tashkent School.[7] The hopes that the road to Bombay and Calcutta would lie via Kabul were thus dashed.[8] Henceforth, Roy operated from European capitals with an unending stream of journals, leaflets and letters aimed at potential and actual sympathisers of the revolution in India.

Roy's propaganda and emissaries did not make much headway in India so long as the non-co-operation movement was on the crest of a rising wave. His chance came in the wake of the Chauri

Chaura tragedy and the demoralisation following the revoca-
tion of civil disobedience. Deviating somewhat from his own
thesis at the Second Congress, he made a bid to cultivate support
within the Indian National Congress and even to transfer leadership into Communist hands.[9] He tried to win over C. R. Das,
who was known to be in favour of simultaneously promoting the
economic welfare of the masses as well as the struggle for political
liberation. Das was too shrewd a politician to play Roy's game
and to challenge Gandhi's leadership on non-violence as well as
on Council entry at the Gaya Congress (December 1922). To
Roy's discomfiture, Das included an anti-Bolshevik broadside
in his presidential address. 'History has proved over and over
again', said Das, 'the utter futility of revolutions brought about
by force and violence. I am one of those who hold to non-violence
on principle.'[10]

Roy did not give up all hopes of redeeming the National
Congress, but henceforth his efforts were largely directed to the
building up of a Communist party in India. These efforts received
a check in 1924 when the Government hauled up the more important Communist workers in the Kanpur Conspiracy case.
Nevertheless he had achieved a measure of success. A number of
devoted Communists were enlisted in Bombay, Calcutta, Kanpur,
Lahore and other towns, though it was not possible for them to
function in the open. In 1927 Jawaharlal Nehru attended the
Congress of Oppressed Nationalities at Brussels, and was elected
to the executive committee of the League against Imperialism –
a Comintern sponsored body. There was a great deal of discontent in the countryside and in industrial towns. There was a
no-tax campaign in Gujarat in 1928 and strikes in industrial
towns. A strong leftist group within the Indian National Congress
was also emerging under Jawaharlal Nehru and Subhas Bose.
However, just when the climate seemed ideal for the growth of
Communist influence in the nationalist movement, the Communist International executed a *volte face*. The Sixth Congress
meeting in 1928, on the basis of the recent experience in China,
where the *Kuomintang* had turned upon its Communist allies,
came to the conclusion that the national bourgeoisie in all
colonial countries had turned counter-revolutionary. The Communists in India were thus enjoined to 'unmask', and oppose 'all
talk of Swarajists, Gandhists, etc., about passive resistance', and
to advance 'the irreconcilable slogan of armed struggle for the
emancipation of the country and expulsion of the imperialists'.[11]

This was a return to Roy's thesis at the Second Congress, but eight years later, Roy with better knowledge of Indian conditions thought differently, and preferred a united front with the National Congress. He was expelled from the Communist International in 1929.

The result of the new directive was that in the early thirties, as in the early twenties, in the heyday of Gandhi's campaigns against the Raj, the Communists were cut off from the mainstream of Indian nationalism. In fact, the official Communist line was that the Indian bourgeoisie, as represented in the Congress, were counter-revolutionary. The eighteen accused in the Meerut Conspiracy case, who included some of the founding fathers of the Indian Communist Party, in their long statement before the court declared that, 'to the ordinary Congress leader independence was a phrase with which to keep the rank-and-file contented and perhaps to threaten the Government', that civil disobedience was a means of 'sabotaging revolutionary movements', that the Congress deliberately eschewed violence, as it did not really want to overthrow British rule, and that Gandhi, Jawaharlal Nehru and Subhas Chandra Bose were working for a compromise with imperialism in accordance with the interests of the bourgeoisie.[12] With such a reading of Gandhi's movements against the Raj, it was obvious that the Communist International and its adherents in India could have no place in it.

III

One reason why the Russian Revolution initially failed to make a great impact on India was that from 1917 onwards the Indian political cauldron itself had begun to boil. The Home Rule Movement, Edwin Montagu's declaration and visit to India in 1917, the publication of the Montagu-Chelmsford Report, the secession of the Moderates from the Indian National Congress, the Rowlatt Act, the Khilafat and the emergence of Gandhi raised the political temperature. Not only the large presidency towns and provincial headquarters, but small towns and villages vibrated to Gandhi's call to non-violent resistance. The Khilafat issue sucked the Muslim middle and lower middle classes into the political arena.

To M. N. Roy and his friends in Moscow, as they looked through the telescope of the Communist International, Gandhi may have seemed a petty bourgeois 'reactionary',[13] who was restraining the revolutionary stirrings of the masses. The people and the Government of India had reasons to feel differently. The appeal that Roy sent – with the approval of Lenin and Stalin – to Gandhi at the Ahmedabad Congress in December 1921 to broaden the base of his struggle with the help of peasants and workers went unheeded, almost unnoticed. But Roy had hardly any idea of the burdens and anxieties Gandhi bore in leading a mass movement. In South Africa, his *Satyagraha* struggles had been waged in a compact area and involved a few thousand Indian immigrants whom he could directly influence. In India the canvas was much larger, almost continental in scale; the people to be controlled were not in thousands but in millions. How to rouse the patriotic fervour of these millions and still maintain a semblance of discipline was Gandhi's critical problem. In the very first week of the *Satyagraha* against the Rowlatt Act in April 1919, riots had broken out in Delhi, Ahmedabad, Nadiad and Bombay. Gandhi discovered with a shock that he had underrated the forces of violence in the country; this was his miscalculation, what he penitentially described as his 'Himalayan blunder'. Soon afterwards, the Punjab went through the tragedy at Jallianwala Bagh and the horrors of martial law.

During the next three years, even as Gandhi led the non-co-operation movement, he was reluctant to launch mass civil disobedience without adequate preparation. In February 1922, he succumbed to pressure from within the Congress for launching mass civil disobedience in selected areas, but immediately afterwards, when he heard of the riot at Chauri Chaura, he applied the reverse gear. There is little evidence to show that the reasons which Gandhi gave for cancelling the aggressive phase of his movement were not honest. He knew the outbreak in Chauri Chaura was no revolutionary up-rising of the peasantry,[14] but another manifestation of the mob violence that had been creeping into his movement. The occasional communal riots culminating in the fanatical Moplah outbreak in Malabar and the riots at Bombay on the occasion of the visit of the Prince of Wales had disconcerted him. For Gandhi, the Chauri Chaura incident was, as he wrote to Jawaharlal Nehru, 'the last straw . . . I assure you that if the thing [civil disobedience] had not been suspended, we would have been leading not a non-violent struggle, but essentially a violent struggle. The movement had unconsciously drifted from the right path'.[15]

IV

As we have already seen, M. N. Roy had failed to win over C. R. Das or any other important nationalist leader. Neither Das nor Lajpat Rai, who had presided over the first All India Trade Union Congress in 1920, was destined to introduce socialist ideas into the Congress. That task was to be performed by one of the younger leaders in the mid-twenties, Jawaharlal Nehru, the son of the veteran Motilal Nehru and the favourite disciple of the Mahatma. In his student days in England Jawaharlal had sampled Fabian literature and in 1907 heard George Bernard Shaw speak on 'Socialism and the University Man'.[16] Young Nehru's main driving force at this time was a passionate nationalism which was fanned on return to India by the Home Rule Movement and then by the coming of Gandhi. The contact with the Mahatma rubbed off some of his anglicism and aloofness, but he owed his first encounter with 'the naked hungry mass' of India to an accidental visit to the Oudh countryside in June 1920. His interest in economic and social questions developed in the enforced leisure of the prison in 1922–3 when he delved into the history of the Russian Revolution. In 1926–7 he visited Europe for the treatment of his ailing wife and came into closer contact with the anti-colonial as well as the anti-capitalist crusaders from Asia, Africa, Europe and America, particularly at the Brussels Congress of Oppressed Nationalities. Already a student of Marx and an admirer of Lenin, he was deeply impressed by his brief visit to Moscow in November 1927 and returned to his homeland just in time to attend the Madras Congress where he piloted resolutions with a radical slant. In the following year he clashed with the Congress Establishment on the issue of Dominion Status versus Independence. As a gesture of defiance, he joined hands with Subhas Bose to found the Independence League, vowed to the severance of all relations with Britain and to 'a socialistic revision of the economic structure of society'. The Independence League did not last long, but at least one of its goals, that of complete independence, was indirectly conceded at the Calcutta Congress, and embodied in the Congress creed at Lahore, the following year when Nehru, as Congress President, unfurled the banner of 'complete independence' on the banks of the Ravi.

Nehru's presidential address at the Lahore Congress was at once an onslaught on British imperialism, Indian feudalism and capitalism. He frankly avowed himself as 'a socialist and a

H

republican and . . . no believer in kings and princes, or in the order which produces the modern kings of industry'.[17] The philosophy of socialism, he asserted, had permeated the entire structure of society the world over, and 'the only point in dispute was the pace and methods of advance to its realisation'. He questioned the proposition that the Congress should hold the balance fairly between capital and labour, and landlord and tenant. The balance was, said Nehru, 'terribly weighted on one side'; to maintain the *status quo* 'was to maintain injustice and exploitation'. He called for changes in land laws, a minimum wage for every worker in the field or factory, organisation of industry on a co-operative basis and effective liaison between the Congress and the labour movement. That all this was not merely a verbal exercise became evident fifteen months later when under his pressure, but with the backing of Gandhi, the Karachi Congress embodied some of his ideas in a catalogue of fundamental rights and economic principles, including a living wage, imposition of death duties, and state ownership or control of basic industries. These may seem 'mildly socialist' today; in 1931 they sounded revolutionary.

Nehru's admiration for Marx and Lenin, evident in his books, *Soviet Russia, Glimpses of World History* and *An Autobiography* was, however, never uncritical or unqualified. Marxism was neither the first nor the most important ingredient in his make-up. In his student days, he had been exposed to Fabian ideas and savoured the Western humanism and liberalism with its rational, aesthetic and human approach to life. From Gandhi, he had imbibed an ethical framework, respect for human dignity, compassion for the underdog, and the importance of truth as a guiding principle in personal as well as in public life. Certain aspects of Gandhi's philosophy jarred upon him; he did not like the Mahatma's idealisation of the simple life, 'his glorification of poverty', or antipathy to industrialism. The mysterious, almost mystical overtones of the *Satyagraha* movements disconcerted him. Jawaharlal was shocked and bewildered by the Gandhi-Irwin Pact in 1931, and the untouchability fast in 1932. The withdrawal of the civil disobedience in 1934 came when he was in Alipore jail. He felt (he wrote in his *Autobiography*) with 'a stab of pain' that 'the chords of allegiance that had bound me to him [Gandhi] for many years had snapped'.[18]

V

In another gaol in Nasik in western India, hundreds of miles away, a group of young Congressmen, who were admirers of Nehru, felt a similar disenchantment with Gandhi's leadership. The members of this group, Jayaprakash Narayan, Asoka Mehta, Achyut Patwardhan, Yusuf Meherally, N. G. Goray and S. M. Joshi, were ardent nationalists as well as ardent socialists. They felt that a new orientation to the Congress was necessary, and drew up the blueprint of a new political party which was to function within the Congress. They were later joined by some of the senior Congressmen in the UP – Acharya Narendra Deva, Sampurnanand and Sri Prakasa – all from the Kashi Vidya-peeth. The foundations of the Congress Socialist party were laid at Patna in May 1934 when a meeting of the AICC was held there. A few months later, the party had its first conference at Bombay and adopted a fifteen-point programme which included the repudiation of the public debt of India, 'transfer of all power to producing masses', planned development of the economic life of the country by the State, socialisation of key industries, State monopoly of foreign trade, co-operative and collective farming, organisation of co-operatives for production, distribution and credit, and elimination of princes and landlords without compensation. This was a thoroughgoing socialist programme, which the Communist Party could well have included in its manifesto. Indeed the leaders of the new party were avowed Marxists, and believed that planned economic development on the Soviet model was the answer to the problem of Indian poverty and backwardness. They criticised the leadership of the Congress, but professed loyalty to the organisation. Their object (in the words of their most respected leader, Narendra Deva) was 'to resuscitate and reinvigorate the Congress',[19] and to draw into it the mass of workers and peasants, in order to widen the base of the anti-imperialist front. They were critical of Gandhi, of his self-imposed limitations on the score of non-violence, of his ethical approach to politics, and of his theory of 'trusteeship'.

The new party with its demands for an alternative programme and a new leadership for the Congress was bound to clash with the Old Guard. There was no dearth of issues on which differences arose: the approach to the Act of 1935, the formation of ministries in 1937, the organisation of *kisan sabhas* and agitation for agrarian reforms, the release of political detenus and agitation in the

Indian states. There was the curious spectacle during these years of Congressmen leading agitation against Congress ministries in the provinces. There were prolonged and bitter controversies in which the Congress leadership was continually under fire. 'Gandhism has played its part', declared J. P. Narayan. 'It cannot carry us further and hence we must march and be guided by the ideology of socialism.'[20] The socialist leaders did not realise the predicament of the Congress executive, harassed as it was by a ceaseless cold war with the Muslim League and a never-ending battle of wits with the British Government. Without a minimum discipline in the party and stability in the country, the Congress could hardly speak effectively on behalf of nationalist India.

In the Congress executive, Nehru was ideologically the closest to the Congress Socialist Party; he was in gaol when the party was formed, but his support, moral and perhaps financial, was available to its founders in the early years of the party. With some members, such as J. P. Narayan, Narendra Deva and Achyut Patwardhan, whom he included in the Working Committee formed by him as Congress President, he was on particularly cordial terms. Nehru was sympathetic to the CSP, but he could not hold a brief for it in the Working Committee for the verbal barrages and acts of defiance on the part of its ebullient members. This may account for Nehru's somewhat querulous equation with them, and the 'public rebukes', which, according to Sampurnanand,[21] he was occasionally administering to them.

Gandhi had frankly avowed his differences with the Congress socialists in 1934 and gone so far as to say that if they gained ascendancy in the Congress, he could not remain in it.[22] The talk of class war, expropriation and violence grated on his ears. The gulf between Gandhi and the Congress Socialists was not really as wide as it seemed at the time. He did not want too many fissures in the national front, while the battle with the British remained unresolved, but he was no supporter of the *status quo*, or of vested interests. Indeed, he was not unwilling to be pushed in the direction in which the socialists desired him to go. He had given his powerful backing to the adoption of the resolution on fundamental rights and economic policy at Karachi in 1931; it was his support which had brought the Congress 'Crown' to Nehru in 1936 and 1937, and enabled him to spell out his socialist programme from the presidential chair of the Congress.

Gandhi seems to have hoped that, in 1936, as in 1929, responsibility of office would have a mellowing effect upon Jawaharlal. Subhas Chandra Bose urged Nehru to be firm with the Congress establishment. 'I earnestly hope', he wrote, 'that you will utilise the strength of your public position in making decisions. . . . Your position is unique and I think that even Mahatma Gandhi will be more accommodating towards you than towards anyone else.'[23] Much as his left-wing colleagues wanted him to, Nehru did not, during these difficult years before the war, defy Gandhi or break away from the Congress. Besides the emotional bond between the two men ('My dear Bapu', this is how Jawaharlal started his letters to Gandhi), it is important to remember that Gandhi owed his influence not to any position he held in the Congress, but to his moral authority. Again and again he offered to step off the stage altogether, if his ideas were unacceptable to the Working Committee or the All-India Congress Committee. 'I must not lead', he wrote to Nehru in October 1939, 'if I cannot carry all with me. There should be no divided counsels among the members of the WC [Working Committee]. I feel you should take full charge and lead the country, leaving me free to voice my opinion.'[24]

Gandhi's departure from the political scene was the last thing Nehru could envisage with equanimity. He was not unaware of his own limitations and those of the left wing in the Congress organisation. He could rouse the masses and inspire the intelligentsia, and slog at the desk, but he was not an expert in party management. His aloofness from party politics limited his room for manoeuvre within the organisation.

There is evidence that with closer acquaintance with the balance of forces in the country and within the Congress party during the years 1937–9, his approach to the socialist revolution was changing; it became less doctrinaire and more pragmatic. This was the time when Nehru's thinking on socialism, as applied to Indian conditions, was crystallising, thanks to his association with the National Planning Committee. He began to visualise the actual process of modernising the Indian economy. Socialism was to be attained not in a single forward leap, but gradually, by measured steps. It was to be a pattern of development which would 'inevitably lead us towards establishing some of the fundamentals of the socialist structure'. He was already groping towards the concept of, what came to be known later, as a 'mixed economy' and democratic socialism through planned economic development formulated in Five Year Plans of the post-independence era.

VI

Whatever the differences of the Congress Socialists with the leadership of the National Congress, and however violent the language they used, they had no intention of carrying their opposition to the breaking point. Their socialist blueprint could not be implemented without ousting the British, and they realised that this task, under Indian conditions, could only be performed by the Indian National Congress. The Congress Socialist Party won a great deal of support among the youth, the industrial labour and the peasantry, but it was still a minority, albeit a vocal minority. It was not a homogeneous group, consisting as it did of Marxists like J. P. Narayan and Narendra Deva, Social Democrats like Asoka Mehta and M. R. Masani, Gandhians like Patwardhan, and populists like Ram Manohar Lohia. The CSP could not have its own way on several important issues; nevertheless it succeeded in giving, to a limited extent, a radical orientation to Congress policies. On the rejection of the federal part of the Act of 1935, the release of the political detenus, the introduction of agrarian reforms, or the resignation of the Congress ministries in 1939, the Socialists' pressure within the Congress organisation doubtless made some contribution to the final result. The Second World War and the breach with the Government brought the Congress Socialists nearer to Gandhi and the Congress leadership. The bitter dose of repression in 1942 and the process of political re-education provided by the conduct of other left groups during the war led to a shift in the positions the Congress Socialists had adopted in 1934–8. Gandhism which they had rejected so contemptuously in the thirties was to strike them as relevant in the forties and the fifties, not only to a political but a social revolution.

The Congress Socialists had always been keen to consolidate all leftist forces in the country. When the Nazi menace led to a change in the stance of the Communist International in favour of 'popular fronts', the Congress Socialist Party opened its doors to Communists in 1936. The Communist Party was still illegal; its leaders were glad to get a chance of functioning openly through the CSP and the Indian National Congress. In retrospect, the experiment seemed disastrous to the Congress Socialist Party;[25] at its Lahore Congress in 1938, even its control of the party executive was challenged.[26] In 1940 the Communists were expelled, but they took with them the southern branches of the CSP. The 'Popular Front' phase brought solid gains to the

Communist Party, and gave it a foothold in the Congress organisation. But before long, Hitler's invasion of Russia caused another reversal of the party line; the Communists now felt bound to support Britain against the Axis Powers. When the 'Quit India' movement brought on the clash between the Congress and the Government in 1942, they found themselves on the wrong side of the battleline.

When we see these two decades in historical perspective, the progress of socialist ideas and organisation seems to have been affected by a series of events on the national and world stage, and by a complex interplay of personalities and politics. It is difficult to say what the results would have been if the Second Communist International had endorsed only Lenin's thesis on colonialism; if M. N. Roy had not been the chief guide of the International in the twenties, and Indian Communists had been allowed to function within the national movement during this period; if Nehru and other leaders of the Left had joined hands in the pre-war years and revolted against the Congress establishment; if Gandhi, the most charismatic as well as the most tolerant, receptive, and creative leader of nationalism in history had not been at the helm of the Indian National Congress; if Nehru's bonds with the Mahatma had not been as strong as they actually were, and he had chosen to lead the Congress Socialists; and, finally, if the British had not skilfully alternated reform with repression, and in 1947 confounded the theoreticians of revolutions by deciding to go while the going was good.

Chapter 8

Jawaharlal Nehru as a Writer

'At the present moment I can imagine nothing more terrifying', Jawaharlal wrote to his father from London in 1911, 'than having to speak in public.'[1] The sensitive, shy, young botanist-cum-barrister could have imagined himself no more in the role of an author than that of a speaker. It is a curious but significant fact that Nehru, one of the most distinguished and successful writers of our time, made his debut into the world of letters not only comparatively late in life, but unwittingly, almost unconsciously.

Young Jawaharlal had early imbibed a love of reading and his letters from Harrow to Allahabad were marked by a fluency, elegance and (in political matters) a maturity beyond his years. After he had given up the project of taking the ICS examination, his reading did not have to be channelled along fixed grooves. He read widely, browsing happily and discursively on science and law, fiction and poetry, politics and economics. His intellectual zest does not, however, seem to have spilled into a magazine article, or even a letter to the editor of a newspaper.

The years which followed his return from England were taken up by professional and domestic preoccupations, and the little leisure that was available was taken up by local and provincial politics. His intellectual curiosity remained, but his reading lagged. In 1917, came the internment of Mrs Besant and the Home Rule agitation. Two years later came the Mahatma and the intoxication of the struggle against the British Raj, when Jawaharlal 'gave up all my other associations and contacts, old friends, books, even newspapers, except in so far as they dealt with the work in hand. . . . I almost forgot my family, my wife my daughter. . . .'[2] It was during these ecstatic years that he had his first taste of journalism. Early in 1919, he helped his father in starting the *Independent*, to offset the influence of the *Leader*, the local Moderate paper. The *Independent* soon ran into difficulties, and became a great drain on the bank balance of his father, but it provided a useful outlet for Jawaharlal's political and literary enthusiasms. Of one article, Motilal wrote that it was excellent: 'I smelt Jawahar in every word and sentence.'[3] Newspaper articles are notoriously ephemeral; almost every politician in those days was a journalist, and every journalist a politician.

1922 was a year of ecstasy as well as agony for Jawaharlal. The Chauri Chaura tragedy and the withdrawal of civil disobedience dashed his hopes of an immediate, massive and successful blow to imperialism. It was a critical test for Jawaharlal; he had to keep up his faith and courage while his world – his political world – crashed around him. Unlike many of his colleagues in gaol, he did not delve into the scriptures, or seek comfort in metaphysical speculation. He confided his plans to his father in a letter dated 1 September 1922:

'My mind is full of books I ought to read and it is with great difficulty that I refrain from sending you even longer lists than I have done so far. . . .

'. . . Ever since my return from England I had done little reading, and I shudder to think, what I was gradually becoming, before politics and NCO [non-co-operation] snatched me away from the doom that befalls many of us. . . .

'Many years ago Colonel Haksar told me that, after he had finished his academic career, he gave a year or two to reading and thinking and did nothing else during that period. I envied him that year or two, And now the chance has been given to me. Shall I not rejoice? . . .'[4]

The British Government was generous enough to give Jawaharlal enforced leisure of not one but nine years – suitably spaced – in prison. He put it to good use, embarking on one of the longest and most fruitful courses of adult self-education that a prisoner has ever undertaken. Obviously, prison is not an ideal place for such a venture. The Naini gaol library in 1922 could boast of little, besides prison manuals, and the prison Superintendent, an English Colonel of the Indian Medical Service, who confessed to Jawaharlal that he had finished his reading at the age of twelve, was not untypical of his class. The library in Anand Bhawan was well stocked, but gaol regulations prescribed that a prisoner could not keep more than six books at a time, even if they included copies of the *Gita* and a couple of dictionaries.

Jawaharlal's studies were abruptly interrupted by his release from prison early in 1923. They were not to be resumed in full vigour until 1926, when he accompanied his ailing wife to Europe for treatment, and could take some time off for reading and reflection. In November 1927, he paid a four-day visit to Moscow, and on return to India summed up his impressions in a few articles in the *Hindu* and *Young India*. In 1928 he issued them in a volume entitled, *Soviet Russia*, 'with considerable hesitation', describing them as 'disjointed and sketchy'. It required, he wrote, 'a person of considerable knowledge and some courage to write about the complex and everchanging conditions of Soviet Russia. I claim no such knowledge . . . though I may possess the habit of rushing in where wiser people fear to tread.'[5]

Jawaharlal was no less apologetic about his second book. The *Letters from a Father to His Daughter*, were addressed to the ten-year-old Indira in the summer of 1928 when she was in Mussoorie and her father in Allahabad. They dealt with rocks, plants and the first living things, of the struggle of early man against the forces of nature and of the races, religions and languages of mankind. The letters were meant only for his daughter, but when he was persuaded to publish them, he expressed the hope 'though with diffidence', that other boys and girls would find in the reading of them 'a fraction of the pleasure that I had in the writing of them'.[6]

In April 1930, the Salt Satyagraha brought Jawaharlal back to gaol. He was released in October, rearrested after a week, and convicted for sedition. This was his sixth term. As he braced himself to face another two and half years in prison, he thought of occupying himself by writing a new series of letters to his daughter. She was nearly thirteen and needed more solid fare than what he had given her two years before in his *Letters from a Father to His Daughter*. The new series of letters, which was intended to be a broad survey of world history, began on 26 October 1930, but was interrupted by Jawaharlal's sudden release in January 1931 in that unexpected chain of events which culminated in the Gandhi-Irwin Pact.

Jawaharlal did not resume his *Letters to Indu* (as he tentatively entitled them), until after the resumption of civil disobedience and his return to gaol a year later. Between 26 March and 9

August 1933, he wrote 176 letters, running to no less than 1,000 pages. It was an enterprise which might well have daunted a professional historian. Jawaharlal, who had studied natural sciences at Cambridge, had never had any training as a historian. True, he had been a voracious reader, especially in prison, and had enjoyed reading historical works. His reading was eclectic but random. If he read Rene Grousset's *Civilisation of the East*, Spengler's *Decline of the West*, Motley's *Rise of the Dutch Republic*, Trotsky's *History of the Russian Revolution*, R. H. Tawney's *Religion and the Rise of Capitalism*, K. T. Shah's *The Splendour that was 'Ind'*, Babar's *Memoirs*, and Emil Ludwig's *Napoleon*, he also read Bertrand Russell's *The ABC of Relativity*, Tolstoy's *War and Peace*, Swinburne's poems and *How to Keep Fit at Forty*. Since the prison regulations did not permit him – even as a Class A prisoner – to retain more than six books at a time, he made copious notes as he read – usually fifteen to twenty books a month. He did not have ready access to archives and libraries, and most of the books he could lay his hands on were secondary works. The epistolary form was not ideally suited to the writing of history. These were formidable handicaps, and it is doubtful if Jawaharlal would have been able to overcome them if it had not been for a powerful double impulse: to seek an antidote to the monotony and solitude of gaol life, and to feel closer to his only child from whom the prison walls had cut him off.

Academic historians, who have struggled with masses of source materials and experienced the excitement as well as the frustrations of painstaking research are suspicious of universal histories, and the theoretical pegs on which they are usually hung. Oswald Spengler's *Decline of the West*, published in 1915, affirming that there were seasonal phases in the historical cycle, and that Western civilisation was entering the long winter of decay, had been useful to Hitler in creating the mythology of Nazism. Similarly, Vilfredo Pareto's *Mind and Society* by distinguishing between rational and non-rational elements in history, and suggesting a recurrent alternation of liberty with authority came to be exploited as an intellectual justification by the theoreticians of Italian Fascism. H. G. Wells's *Outline of History*, which became a best-seller in western Europe, was permeated by the author's faith in reason, science and the educability of mankind. Jawaharlal Nehru shared this faith, but as an Indian nationalist, he saw what Wells, and indeed most European writers, had failed to see clearly: that their image of the past was excessively centred on Europe and America, that it did less than justice to Asia and Africa, and that Western domination of these latter continents was not going to be a permanent phenomenon. Such was Nehru's passionate commitment to India's struggle for freedom that his preoccupation with her present and future could not but intrude into his survey of the past. He did not deprecate the achievements of Europe or the heritage of Greece and Rome, but he gave an equal emphasis to the contributions made by Persia, Arabia, India and China, and by the great non-Christian religions, Hinduism, Buddhism and Islam. With his deep humanism, nourished by his contact with Gandhi, he made no secret of his hatred of violence, racial discrimination, religious fanaticism and authoritarian rule. As one reads his account of the French Revolution, the American War of Independence or the Russian Revolution, one has little doubt as to where his own sympathies lie. It is significant that more than a third of his history of mankind is taken up by the twentieth century – a period he had himself intensely lived through. Some of the most interesting chapters in the book concern the political and economic cross-currents in the world as it was moving to the brink of the Armageddon in the 1930s.

'These letters of mine', Jawaharlal told his daughter in his last letter (9 August 1933), 'are but superficial sketches joined together by a thin thread.' He had written, not history but 'fleeting glimpses of our long past'.[7] This was disarming but excessive modesty. When such a wide-ranging work as the *Glimpses of World History*, running to nearly half a million words, is subjected to critical scrutiny under the microscope of historical scholarship, it is not difficult to pick out errors of facts and argument. But such errors are to be found in the *Outline of History* by H. G. Wells, even though he had successive drafts of his chapters revised by specialists, and in the *History of the English Speaking Peoples* by Churchill, even though he had the proofs vetted by a small army of historians under the guidance of Alan Hodge, the editor of *History Today*. Nehru of course had no such facilities in prison.

Nevertheless *Glimpses of World History*, remains even today, forty years after it was written, a good, if somewhat discursive introduction to world history – and not only for children. J. F. Horrabin, who read it in December 1935, and agreed to illustrate the English edition with maps, found it 'absolutely exciting reading'.[8] The book requires scarcely more effort from the reader than a good novel. Doubtless, there are other surveys of world history which may be more compact and scholarly than the *Glimpses*, but there is scarcely any which is more direct, vivid and humane, better portrays the creative thrust of mankind, and more effectively constitutes, in the words of Norman Cousins, 'a liberal university education'.[9]

Not until June 1934, when he was in his mid-forties did Jawaharlal embark on his first real literary venture, his autobiography. 'The primary object in writing these pages', he explained in the preface, 'was to occupy myself with a definite task which was necessary in the long solitudes of daily life, as well as to review past events in India with which I have been concerned, to enable me to think clearly about them.' There were reasons enough for this self-questioning mood. The civil disobedience movement started with such high hopes in 1930 had languished; public enthusiasm had ebbed; the Congress leadership was unsure and divided; the rank-and-file seemed confused or apathetic. Jawaharlal himself was tortured with doubts. He felt if he could take a critical look at his own past, he might be able to see the future in clearer perspective. The book was less a chronicle of his life than of the national movement. There are fascinating glimpses of his childhood, of his father whom he admired, loved and feared, of his delicate and doting mother, and of Ferdinand T. Brooks the resident tutor in Anand Bhawan who introduced him to the joys of reading and the thrills of science. But the bulk of the book is devoted to the story of the national struggle, the coming of Gandhi, the course of *Satyagraha*, the changing national and international scene. We see Nehru in varying moods, as he reacts to the vicissitudes of politics. We see the blend of admiration, affection and bewilderment with which he follows Gandhi, and the anger and sorrow he feels at the obscurantism, the divisions and narrowness rampant in his country. He confesses he is 'lonely, homeless, unable to enter into the spirit and ways of thinking of my countrymen'. The black moods do not last. He reasons his way out of his dilemmas; his spirits are buoyed up by the sight of a floating monsoon cloud, a flowering tree, a flitting squirrel, and most of all, by the discipline of reading and writing of which the *Autobiography* was itself a product.

'I was not writing deliberately for an audience', Nehru wrote in his preface to his *Autobiography*, 'but if I thought of an audience, it was one of my own countrymen and countrywomen.' He gave

126 GOKHALE, GANDHI AND THE NEHRUS

no quarter to the apologists of the Raj whether they were Britons
or Indians. He was hardest on the Indian Liberals, and provoked
strong reactions from them. The review published in the *Leader*,
the Liberal paper of Allahabad, was headlined: 'Bad Politics and
Worse History'.[10] N. C. Kelkar of the *Mahratta*,[11] once the right-
hand man of Tilak, and B. S. Moonje of the Hindu Mahasabha,
charged Nehru with misrepresenting them. But, on the whole,
the Indian press hailed the book as a contribution both to
literature and politics.

What was astonishing was the reception Nehru's *Autobiography*
had in England. His earlier books, *Soviet Russia, Letters from
a Father to His Daughter* and *Glimpses of World History*, had
been published in India. It is not quite clear why he decided to
publish the *Autobiography* (which was initially entitled *In and
Out of Prison*) in England. He had not been too happy with the
production of the Indian edition of *Glimpses of World History*,
published during 1934–5, and since he was in any case going to
Europe to join his ailing wife, he may have decided to take the
manuscript with him. The fact that there was a lesser risk of the
book being banned in England may have also weighed with him.

The mystique of best-sellers has often baffled publishers and
authors alike. Even that shrewd publisher Stanley Unwin failed
to see the makings of a best-seller, and allowed the book to slip
from his hands to The Bodley Head. The book had not been
tailored to the British reader, and in any case, it was too much
to expect that the British public would relish trenchant criticisms
of imperial rule by an avowed rebel against the Raj. 'Mr Nehru',
wrote *The Sunday Times*, 'is a good hater and seems to enjoy the
procedures of verbal flagellations'.[12] This view was not, however,
shared by most other critics. The Marquess of Lothian, while
reviewing the book on the BBC, paid a tribute to Nehru's 'astonishing philosophic detachment and unflinching honesty, in the most
admirable, terse English about persons and nations'.[13] The
Spectator wrote that 'bitterness and rancour were absent from
the book'.[14] *The Economist* noted that Nehru was 'not anti-
British – he himself, in many ways, is a product of British education – but he is opposed to the rule of nation by nation or class
by class'.[15]

The book ran through ten printings in 1936. It turned out to
be the most influential of Nehru's books. It was translated into
thirty-one languages. It made the first dent in the psychological
barrier between the British intelligentsia and Indian nationalists

since the emergence of Gandhi on the political scene in 1920. Nehru had written in an idiom which the British could begin to understand. A few months before the book was published, C. F. Andrews, a friend of Gandhi, Tagore and the Nehrus had written to Jawaharlal: 'You are the only one outstanding person who seems instinctively to know what the West can understand and follow easily. Bapu's [Gandhi's] writings had to be condensed and explained over and over again. Even Gurudev [Tagore] is very difficult when he gets away from poetry to prose.'[16]

The *Autobiography* thrilled the young intellectuals in India, who were not satisfied with the Gandhian programme as expounded in the *Harijan*, and hungered for a more coherent and forward-looking ideology, which took account of the challenges of nationalism, science, technology and industrialisation confronting India in the twentieth century. It was this wider context of Nehru's *Autobiography*, which also fascinated and inspired young intellectuals of Asia and Africa, who were growing up in the late 1930s and were to lead the anti-colonial revolutions twenty years later.

The sensational success of the *Autobiography* established Nehru's reputation as a writer. Allen & Unwin, with whom Horace Alexander had negotiated a contract for reprinting some of Nehru's articles,[17] expressed a wish to commission Nehru to write another book on India. But once out of gaol, Nehru could not find time to revise what he had written, or even to read the proofs. During the next five years, he occasionally contributed articles to newspapers and journals. Some of them were collected and published in India and England.[18] These occasional writings were the utterances of a journalist and politician. 'They are', in the words of a competent critic, 'the little berries plucked hastily from the thorny and tangled bushes of an extraordinarily strenuous public life. But they are not for all that carelessly plucked and they taste uncommonly fresh.'[19]

If we do not take into account the slim volume, *India Today and Tomorrow*, which was hastily dictated for the first Azad Memorial Lectures in 1959, Nehru's last book, *Discovery of India*, was written in 1944 in the Ahmednagar Fort prison. Once again he had felt an irresistible urge to explore the past – the past of his own country. 'What is my inheritance', he asked himself, 'To what am I heir?' He did not set out to cut up the past of India and to present it as ancient, medieval and modern periods, with dates and dynasties, and causes and consequences of wars.

We get something more exciting in *Discovery of India*: a pageant of India's past unfolds itself on a screen, as it were. *Discovery* did not provide new facts, but it gave valuable new insights; it was a useful corrective to the pride and prejudice of those Hindu, Muslim and British historians who had been grinding their own sectarian or racial axes.

Jawaharlal's interest in the past of his country was not for its own sake, but 'in relation to the present'. Indeed, it seemed to him that the nationalist movement in India was a culmination of a historical process, which had been working itself out over the centuries. The political, social and economic issues facing India in the 1940s were very much on his mind, as also were the potentialities and the limitations of his own people. *Discovery of India* gives an intimate peep into the mind of its author, which had considerably mellowed since he wrote the *Autobiography*. When Nehru wrote *Discovery of India* in Ahmednagar Fort Prison, he could hardly have imagined that within a couple of years he would be heading the government of independent India. The subjective blend of the past and the present, the personal and the political in this book, while it might detract from its 'architectural' proportion as a historical work, illuminates the personality and philosophy of one of the leading statesmen of the twentieth century on the eve of his assumption of office. Only in rare cases (such as that of Churchill) do we have such an intimate glimpse. That we should have a history of India by Jawaharlal Nehru is something to be thankful for. 'What would we not give', J. H. Plumb asks, 'for Roosevelt's *History of America*, Stalin's *History of Russia*, and Mao's *History of China*?'[20]

It is dangerous for a writer, says W. Somerset Maugham, 'to let the public behind the scenes'. The danger is the greater if the writer happens to be a politician. For Nehru, with his natural reserve and innate loneliness, it must have been a tremendous effort of will to lay bare his intellectual processes and the conflicting pulls on his mind and soul. His candour made his books deeply human documents, but it also helped to foster the myth that he was a man of thought and not a man of action. When Lord Lothian, the British Liberal leader, confided to Sir Thomas Jones in 1936 that Jawaharlal Nehru 'has probably given up action for philosophic meditation for the rest of his life',[21] the wish may have been the father to the thought. But not a few critics of Nehru have called him a starry-eyed idealist, a poet, a professor who had strayed into the political arena. Some of his admirers, even, lamented that he should have given to politics what was meant for literature. This was a complete misreading of the man and his motives. Without his passionate commitment to politics it is doubtful if Jawaharlal would ever have become an author. It is true he had great gifts: a penetrating mind, a tenacious memory, a fertile imagination and a facile pen. Nevertheless the fact remains that he wrote hardly anything before his plunge into politics. Once he had cast in his lot with Gandhi, he felt an irresistible urge to act. He travelled from one end of the country to the other, dividing his time between railway trains and public meetings, reeling off speeches and press statements, organising, exhorting, admonishing, inspiring. He needed all this ceaseless action to abate the fever in his brain; in gaol, his action took the form of writing about the struggle which raged outside. Jawaharlal's books were thus not only personal, but political testaments; an indictment of imperialism, and an outline of the new order he envisaged for India and the world.

Discovery of India, published in 1946 was Jawaharlal's last important book. In 1947, he became the Prime Minister of independent India. He continued to write and dictate interminably: letters, press statements, memoranda. He knew the excruciating delights of creative writing, but personal predilections had to give way to the claims of office. A few minutes' reading before retiring at night, or an occasional hour in an aeroplane journey – this was all he could snatch from his relentless schedule. He was 'condemned', to use his own words, 'to hard labour'. One wonders if the thought ever occurred to him that the spacious Teen Murti House in New Delhi was in some ways a worse prison than the barracks of Naini, Almora, and Dehradun gaols. Till the last day of his life, he continued to toil at his desk, to plod through protocol, to suffer bores and self-seekers who proverbially hang about in the corridors of power, to do his duty to the party and parliament, and to manfully cope with the never-ending crises in India and abroad. Meanwhile, the world waited in vain for that unwritten masterpiece: *Memoirs of Prime Minister Nehru.*

I

Chapter 9

Jawaharlal Nehru and the Partition of India

I

During the twelve years preceding the partition of India Jawaharlal Nehru was one of the foremost leaders of the Indian National Congress, a member of its executive (the Working Committee) and presided at three of its annual sessions. He exercised a considerable influence on the politics of the organisation, but he did not by any means dictate them. In spite of the allegations of its political opponents at the time, the Congress organisation was not monolithic, but collective in its leadership. No one individual, not even Gandhi, could bend the Congress to his will without carrying conviction to its leadership and educating its rank-and-file. The Congress Working Committee included members who diverged widely in temperament and political convictions, who argued, differed and even quarrelled, but finally made up under the force of events or the benign influence of Gandhi.

Nehru's views on the communal problem were clearly thought out and strongly held, but they cannot be explained except with reference to the changing pattern of Indian politics, the pressures operating within and on the Congress and the state of almost continual conflict between the Congress and the Government. Nehru did not see the communal problem and the challenge of the Muslim League as a thing apart; the communal issue seemed to him one aspect of the total situation with which nationalist India had to reckon. In this essay an attempt has, therefore, been made to interpret the attitudes and actions of Nehru – and the Congress leadership – to the challenge of Muslim separatism in the context of not only the Congress-Muslim League equation, but of the Congress-Government equation; the latter influenced, aggravated and distorted the former.

II

When the Government of India Bill was being piloted through the House of Commons during the winter of 1934–5, Jawaharlal Nehru was in gaol and writing his autobiography. 'It is an illusion to imagine', he wrote in this book which was as much a personal chronicle as a political manifesto, 'that a dominant imperialist Power will give up its superior position and privileges unless effective pressure amounting to coercion is exercised.'[1] He quoted with approval the words of Reinhold Niebuhr: 'Since reason is always to some degree the servant of necessity in a social situation, social justice cannot be resolved by moral or rational suasion alone.'[2] In a country without a democratic constitution, 'constitutional' activity had little meaning: it was synonymous with what was 'legal', which in practice meant the will of the all-powerful executive. Nehru did not therefore set much store by the Government of India Act 1935: it was hedged with too many 'safeguards', checks and balances: it was as if a motor vehicle was to be set in motion in low gear with the brakes on. In the federal legislature, the Princely States were to be allotted nearly one third of the total seats; in the absence of elective bodies, the States' representatives were to be nominees of the Princes. Apart from this built-in conservatism of the federal legislature, its powers were severely circumscribed: matters relating to the military, the services and the interest charges, for example, were outside its purview. In the Provinces, a wider field had been permitted to ministers responsible to elected legislatures, but even there the Governors were invested with overriding and preventive authority in financial and other matters.

These limitations led Nehru to describe the Act of 1935 as 'a Charter of Slavery'.[3] In his presidential address to the Lucknow session of the Indian National Congress in March 1936, he declared that the new constitution offered India only responsibility without power, and therefore, deserved to be rejected 'in its entirety'. Sensing the mood of the party, he did not oppose Congress participation in the elections. But he left his audience in no doubt that he did not expect India's salvation through the new constitution. On the other hand, he pinned his hopes on a:

'Constituent Assembly elected on adult franchise and a mass basis. . . . That Assembly will not come into existence till at least a semi-revolutionary situation has been created in the country and the actual relationships of power, apart from paper constitutions, are such that the people of India can make their will felt.'

When this was to happen he could not predict, but the world seemed to him in 1936 'too much in the grip of dynamic forces today to admit of static conditions in India or elsewhere for long'.[4]

Though Nehru had agreed that the Congress should contest the elections to prevent politically reactionary elements from capturing the new legislatures, the idea of his party holding office under the new constitution seemed unthinkable to him. He warned,

'It is always dangerous to assume responsibility without power even in democratic countries; it will be far worse with this undemocratic constitution, hedged in with safeguards and reserved powers and mortgaged funds where we have to follow the rules and regulations of our opponents' making. . . . The big things for which we stand, will fade into the background and petty issues will absorb our attention and we shall lose ourselves in compromises and communal tangles and disillusion with us will spread over the land.'[5]

Nehru's distrust of the Act of 1935 and of British intentions stemmed not only from the clauses of that Act, but from what he and the Congress had gone through at the hands of the Government. The Government of India under Lord Willingdon had waged a total war on the Congress, gaoled its members by the thousand, sealed its offices, frozen its funds, choked its publicity media, and tried to crush it once and for all.[6] All this could not but leave a bitter taste in Nehru's mouth. Early in 1936 he confessed to Lord Lothian:

'I feel a certain hesitation in meeting people who have been officially associated with the Government of India during the past nightmare years. That period is full of horror to us and it is very difficult for me to understand how any sensitive person could tolerate it, much less give his approval to it. It is not so much the repression and suppression of much that was best in India that I refer to, but the manner of it. There was, and is, in it an indecency and vulgarity that I could hardly have conceived. And the wonder of it is that hardly anyone in England realises this or has any idea of what is happening in India's mind and heart.'[7]

III

'The real problem before us', Jawaharlal Nehru had told the Lahore Congress in December, 1929, 'is the conquest of power; and the withdrawal of the army of occupation and economic control by Britain.'[8] Seven years later, he held the same opinion. He was convinced that the communal problem had been over-rated and overemphasised both by the Government and vested interests in the two countries.[9] He himself was remarkably free from religious passion and prejudice. His father, Pandit Motilal Nehru had defied Hindu orthodoxy, employed Muslim clerks and servants, and avowed his love of Persian classics and Urdu poetry. Both father and son cherished Muslim friends and colleagues. Indeed they were often accused of being objectionably pro-Muslim. A Hindu Mahasabha leader went so far as to describe Jawaharlal Nehru as 'English by education, Muslim by culture and Hindu by an accident of birth'.[10] The fact is that Jawaharlal was a rationalist and a humanist, and did not view cultural conflict in twentieth-century India in the same way as the leaders of communal parties did. The real struggle seemed to him not between Hindu and Muslim cultures, but between these two cultures and the conquering scientific culture of modern civilisa-tion. 'I have no doubt personally', he added, 'that all efforts, Hindu or Muslim, to oppose modern scientific and industrial civilisation are doomed to failure and I shall watch this failure without regret.'[11] 'The communalism of today,' he told an English correspondent, 'is essentially political, economic and middle class.'[12] Of this communalism he had a good glimpse in 1928 when he helped his father in drafting the report of the All-Parties Committee, which came to be known as the Nehru Report. He saw how upper-class politicians both Hindu and Muslim, with little contact with the masses, or appreciation of the social and economic issues, wrangled endlessly over the distribution of seats in legislatures and jobs under the Government, which in any case could benefit only a tiny minority. It was a crazy political puzzle in which majorities in legislatures (such as in the Punjab and Bengal) wanted to be protected, minorities asked for weight-ages, and rival claims of Muslims, Sikhs, Scheduled Castes and others were irreconcilable. The protagonists of these claims had one eye on the unity conference they were attending, and the other on Whitehall or the Viceregal Lodge, the repositories of real power and patronage. This had led Motilal Nehru to lament at the Calcutta Congress in December 1928: 'It is difficult to stand against the foreigner without offering him a united front. It is not easy to offer a united front while the foreigner is in our midst domineering over us.'

Jawaharlal had thought deeply on the causes of the communal deadlock that frustrated the Nehru Report and blocked the Round-Table Conference, and came to the conclusion that the political bargaining and haggling could not take the country far, because 'whatever offer we make, however high our bid might be, there is always a third party which can bid higher and, what is more, give substance to its words. The third and controlling party inevitably plays the dominant role and hands out its gifts to the prize boys of its choice.'[13] It was only by visualising a political structure without the British, and an economic structure orientated to the needs of the masses rather than to those of the upper and middle classes, that the communal problem could be lifted out of the grooves in which it had been stuck. This was the reason why Nehru was attracted to the idea of a Constituent Assembly elected on adult franchise to draw up the constitution of free India. By 1936 he had won over Gandhi and the Congress to this solution of both the political and communal problems. The demand for the Constituent Assembly figured prominently in the Congress election manifesto.

IV

After the Lucknow Congress, Nehru was intimately concerned with the preparations for the election campaign. There was not much time to lose. The Congress Working Committee constituted a Parliamentary Board consisting of a number of national leaders and of presidents of all the provincial Congress committees. The Parliamentary Board met on 1 July 1936 and elected an Executive Committee of eleven members with Vallabhbhai Patel as President and Rajendra Prasad and G. B. Pant as secretaries. The burden of planning the election campaign and guiding the provincial committees fell on this executive committee.

Though most of the restrictions on its activities had been withdrawn, the Congress organisation was still illegal in the whole of the North-West Frontier Province, and in parts of Bengal. Elsewhere, it was not difficult to see that official sympathy – if not active support – went to parties opposing the Congress. In Nehru's home province, the United Provinces, the Governor and

high British officials had encouraged the formation of the National
Agriculturist Party in which Hindu and Muslim landlords com-
bined to oppose the Congress.[14] In December 1936, the Chief
Secretary to the UP Government reported to the Government of
India:

'Though the National Agriculturist Party do not appear to be
functioning very effectively . . . they are concentrating on, and
strengthening, their personal influence, relying on friendly visits
and the feudal tie. The latter still seems fairly powerful and the
Congress are not likely, even in districts where their forces are
strongest, to have a walk-over.'[15]

Nehru was aware of the fact that the Congress was anathema
to the official world. In September 1936, he came across a copy
of a circular letter from the Secretary of the Court of Wards,
Allahabad, to all district officers advising them that it was

'essential, in the interests of the class which the Court of Wards
represents, and of agricultural interests generally, to inflict as
crushing a defeat as possible on the Congress with its avowed
socialistic principles. To this end, it is of the utmost importance
to avoid to the greatest extent practicable, a split in the landlord
vote, and a consequent dissipation of the voting power of the
elements opposed to the Congress.'[16]

It was after reading this letter that Nehru issued a statement to
the press on 18 September 1936:

'The real contest is between the two forces – the Congress as
representing the will to freedom of the nation, and the British
Government of India and its supporters who oppose this urge
and try to suppress it. . . . Let this position be clearly understood
by our people as it has been understood and acted upon by the
Government. For the Government, there is only one principal
opponent – the Congress.'

This statement was directed not against the Muslim League –
which later was to make much play with it – but against the
Government. It is noteworthy that Nehru had described the
contest as between 'two forces', not between 'two parties'. What
he was stating was the obvious truth: the Congress represented
the main anti-imperialist force in India.

It was in this election that Nehru revealed for the first time his
tremendous stamina and ability as a campaigner. During the

eight months preceding the election, he covered over 50,000 miles by train, car and aeroplane, addressed thousands of meetings and came into direct contact with about ten million people.

His labours and those of his colleagues were well rewarded. The Congress won clear majorities in Bihar, United Provinces, Central Provinces, Madras and Orissa. In Bombay it came out as the largest party; in Assam and NWFP, it gave a very good account of itself. Nehru's own assessment of the election results was given in a letter to Sir Stafford Cripps on 22 February 1937:

'Remarkable as this election victory has been the really significant feature of the election campaign has been the shaking up of the masses. We carried our message not only to the thirty million and odd voters, but to the hundreds of millions of non-voters also. The whole campaign and the election itself have been a revelation of the widespread anti-imperialist spirit prevailing throughout the country. It has made clear the class cleavages among the people. The big landlord class and other vested interests were ranged against us. They were swept away in the flood, their most determined opponents being their own tenants. This class cleavage is very apparent in the comparison between the elections for the Provincial Assemblies [Lower Houses] and the Provincial Councils [Upper Houses]. In the former, the franchise was low and the electorates were large, the average constituency having as many as forty to sixty thousand voters. In the latter, the franchise was a high property one and the electorate was very small, usually some hundreds. In the Assembly elections we carried all before us and our majorities were prodigious. . . . In the Council elections we fared badly (though even here we won a few seats). The election made it perfectly clear that the wider the mass appeal, the greater was our success.'

Nehru acknowledged that the Congress had not done so well in Muslim constituencies:

'Partly, this is due to our own timidity as we ran few Muslim candidates. The burden of running over a thousand candidates (in the general constituencies) was great and we did not wish to add to it. If we had run more Muslim candidates, I trust we could have had a fair measure of success, especially in the rural areas. . . . It is true that the Muslim masses are more apathetic. They have been too long fed with communal cries. . . . Even these Muslim masses are getting out of the rut of communalism and are thinking along economic lines. Equally significant is the change that is coming over the younger generation of Muslims. These young people are definitely cutting themselves away from the old communal ways of thought. On the whole I think that the communal position is definitely brighter. The Hindu communalists have been largely swept away by the Congress and they count for little.[17] The Muslim communal leaders still function, but their position weakens, for they have no reply to the question of poverty, hunger and unemployment and independence that their own people put to them. They can only think in terms of jobs for the upper classes.'

In the light of later history, it may seem that Nehru's optimism was premature, but early in 1937, he had good reasons to hope that the Muslim intelligentsia and masses were acquiring keener consciousness of economic issues: he himself had done much to sharpen this consciousness.

The UP Government had indeed been alarmed by the impression that Nehru was beginning to make on the Muslim community and even on avowedly loyal elements. Commenting on Nehru's tour of the western districts, which had a sizeable Muhammadan population, the UP Government reported to the Government of India in September 1936:

'What the tour makes evident for the first time in this province is the remarkable hold that Mr Nehru has obtained on the popular imagination. He has in fact become Mr Gandhi's successor as the popular leader. That the Municipal Board, Cawnpore, constituted of what was regarded as a strong anti-Congress majority, should have taken the lead in presenting him with an address was not perhaps extraordinary in view of Hindu feeling in urban areas; but it is remarkable that the Muslim Chairman of the Meerut District Board, a leader of the National Agriculturist Party, who was justifiably proud of his success in routing the Congress party at the local elections, should find it necessary to read an address to the arch-enemy of his party and class. Lawyers and businessmen who would be the first to suffer if Mr Nehru achieves his objects, which he makes but little attempt to disguise, joined in doing him honour. . . .'[18]

In his 1,500-word survey of the election results to Cripps, Nehru did not so much as mention the Muslim League. Evidently in February 1937, Nehru had a low opinion of the League, but his opinion was not different from that Jinnah himself is reported to have expressed a year earlier. According to Khaliquzzaman, Jinnah told him in February 1936 that the Muslim League 'consisted mostly of big landlords, title-holders and selfish people who looked to their class and personal interests more than to communal and national interests and who had always been ready to sacrifice them to suit British policies'.[19] It is true that Jinnah had promised Khaliquzzaman that he would reform the League, of which he had been virtually a permanent president for twenty years. To the average observer in 1937 the composition of the League did not, however, seem to have changed much: the titled gentry, the Khan Bahadurs, the Nawabs and the gallant knights still occupied important positions in it; former Congressmen like Khaliquzzaman, who had recently switched their allegiance to the League, were in a small minority and regarded with a little suspicion by their colleagues as well as by the Government. It is true that the League manifesto in 1936 had expressed some progressive views; but so did almost every other party. Neither the composition nor the past history of the League raised hopes of its capacity to pursue a radical course on political and economic issues.

After the elections the question of office acceptance was fiercely debated in the Congress party. It was argued that if the Congress abstained from forming ministries, conservative elements, favoured by the Government would step in. Gandhi's opinion seems to have tilted the scales in favour of office acceptance. The Mahatma himself had no ambition to be a legislator or a minister, but he wondered whether, with all its limitations, the new constitution could not be used to improve the lot of the people in India's villages: to encourage village industries, ensure a clean water supply, and a cheap and nutritious diet, reduce the burdens on the peasantry, promote the use of homespun cloth and extend education. Those who opposed office acceptance – and Nehru was one of them – felt that nothing much could be got out of the new constitution, and that the Congress would have to bear the odium for the apparatus of imperialism without securing a real relief to the people. As a compromise between the two opposing groups it was decided by a convention of Congress members of the provincial legislatures, and members of the All India Congress Committee held on 18 March 1937, that the Congress should form ministries, provided the leader of the Congress party in the provincial legislatures was satisfied and was able to state publicly that the Governor would not use his special powers of interference or set aside the advice of ministers 'in regard to their constitutional activities'. This assurance the Governors seemed unwilling to give. Official spokesmen took the line that the Governors could not contract themselves out of the terms of an Act of Parliament or 'Instrument of Instructions' issued to them. The Government called upon other parties in the legislature to form interim ministries. 'It is clear now', Patel wrote to Nehru on 29 March 1937, 'that there is going to be no Congress ministry anywhere.'

Not until 22 June 1937 did the Viceroy issue the statement which became the basis for acceptance of office by the Congress. The 'assurances' given by the Government were not very explicit, but it was evident that much would depend upon the strength and discipline of the Congress parties. The political situation was fraught with a great deal of uncertainty. No one could say in the summer of 1937 how the Congress would hit it off with the British bureaucracy, which until recently had been its arch enemy. The long record of antagonism between the two was not likely to be erased overnight. The Congress approach to office acceptance was, therefore, marked by a measure of caution and reserve. Nehru and his colleagues were apprehensive that, in the peculiar conditions of India, 'parliamentary activities' could lead to demoralisation and division in nationalist ranks. In the 1920s, Motilal Nehru, his tremendous personality and prestige notwithstanding, had been unable to stop the rot in the Swaraj Party; some of his adherents had succumbed to official blandishments and communal pressures. Strong and disciplined parties in the provincial legislatures were therefore, a necessity if the Congress was not to lose its character as a militant national party.

It is important to remember this background when reviewing the negotiations between the Congress and the Muslim League in the UP for the representation of the latter in the provincial cabinet. The crucial question in these negotiations was not whether the UP cabinet should have one or two representatives of the Muslim League,[20] but whether the provincial cabinet, after the induction of the League members, would be able to maintain its cohesion. Nehru's own part in these negotiations was small. Soon after the elections he had one of his rare spells of ill-health which made him less active than usual. He was of course consulted by Abul Kalam Azad (who conducted the negotiations on behalf of the Congress) but the decision did not really rest with Nehru. Indeed G. B. Pant, Rafi Ahmed Kidwai, K. M. Ashraf,

P. D. Tandon and other members of the UP legislature exercised as much influence, if not more, on the ultimate result of the negotiations. The most important consideration with the provincial Congress leaders, as with Nehru, was that if the Muslim League with its landlord support came into the provincial cabinet, the Congress programme for agrarian reform, particularly the abolition of *zamindari*, would be jeopardised.[21] That this fear was not groundless is proved by the stubborn opposition of the Muslim League to land reforms in the UP during the years 1937–46.[22]

Khaliquzzaman and Nawab Ismail Khan may have honestly felt that they could co-operate with the Congress in 1937; but it is doubtful if they would have been permitted to do so by the League leadership. On 25 April 1937, Khaliquzzaman and his friends were taken to task by the Working Committee of the UP Muslim League Parliamentary Board for their flirtations with the Congress.[23] Early in May, the Committee of the Bombay Provincial Muslim League, with Jinnah in the chair, appealed 'to the Muslim members of the UP Legislative Assembly who had been elected on the League ticket not to act in such a way as to cause disunion among Muslims of India by arranging sectional or provincial settlements with the Congress'.[24] 'We shall face the challenge of the Congress', Jinnah declared, 'if they think that the Muslims will accept their policy and programme, because our policy and programmes are different in vital respects.'[25]

A couple of days later, Jinnah visited Lucknow to assert his authority over the provincial party. He was reported to have rebuked Leaguers, who 'talked loosely of co-operating with the Congress', and affirmed that 'for the time being they would join hands neither with the Congress nor with the Government, but wait till they had gained strength by organising the Muslims.'[26]

Such a minatory posture on the part of the League leader was not calculated to reassure Congress leaders that a coalition with the League was workable. Indeed, in the negotiations for an understanding between the League and the Congress in Bombay, the Congress was willing to let Jinnah nominate two members of the provincial cabinet. But his conditions were such as the Congress could not accept. According to K. M. Munshi (with whom Vallabhbhai Patel and Abul Kalam Azad were staying in Poona when Jinnah's terms were received) the 'position would have been that Mr Jinnah would have dictated the whole policy (of the Bombay cabinet) through one or two of his nominees who would threaten to resign at any moment they chose. . . . Such terms would have imposed the dictatorship of Mr Jinnah over every Congress Government in the country.'[27]

The Congress could not afford to make its first experiment in ministry-making vulnerable at the very outset. The party position in the UP legislature did not suggest any urgent need for or the inevitability of a coalition with the Muslim League.[28] In 1937 it was difficult for the Congress to foresee how the equation with the Government would work out. For nearly four months (March–June 1937) there seemed little prospect of the Congress being able to form ministries. Indeed in April 1937 – after the introduction of the new constitution – the Government of India at the highest level was considering the prosecution of Jawaharlal Nehru for the speeches he had delivered during the election campaign.[29] Even after the formation of the ministries in July, the Congress was not sure how far it would be allowed to carry out its programme, in such matters as release of political prisoners and radical economic reforms. In these circumstances it is not difficult to see why the Congress should have been reluctant to admit the Muslim League (whose leader emphasised fundamental differences in outlook and programmes between the two organisations) into partnership in the UP without ensuring that the cohesion of the cabinet would be maintained.

V

Whatever the merits of the coalition controversy in UP, there is no doubt that the events of 1937 had a tremendous, almost a traumatic effect upon Jinnah. The tide of provincial autonomy had come and gone, and left him high and dry. The real tragedy was not the failure of his party to secure two seats on its own terms in the UP cabinet, but the collapse like a house of cards of the assumptions on which he had conducted his politics for twenty years. He had pinned his hopes on separate electorates and on organising Muslims on a separate political platform, on the formation of as many Muslim majority provinces as possible by 'redrawing provincial boundaries', and on weighted representation for Muslims in provinces where they were in a minority. His 'Fourteen Points' had been practically conceded in the new constitution. But all these safeguards had not yielded the fruits he had hoped from them. In the Muslim majority provinces, where indeed the Muslim League could legitimately have hoped to be voted to office, it had met with an electoral disaster of the first magnitude. In the Sind Legislative Assembly the League had won three seats, in the Punjab only one, and in the North-West Frontier Province none at all. In Bengal it had won a third of the Muslim (and one-sixth of the total) seats in the Legislative Assembly, but it did not occupy a commanding position even in that province. Party alignments in Muslim majority provinces had cut across religion; Sir Sikandar Hyat Khan in the Punjab, Fazl-ul-Huq in Bengal, and Sir Ghulam Husain Hidayatullah in Sind had not responded to Jinnah's appeal for 'Muslim unity', and seemed to be swayed by personal and class interests rather than by religious affiliations. The Muslim electorate had failed to vote the League to office in the Muslim majority provinces; in the Muslim minority provinces the League's performance was hardly less disappointing. It did not win a single seat in the Lower Houses of three provinces, Bihar, the Central Provinces and Orissa. Only in two provinces did it do well, winning 27 out of 64 Muslim seats in the UP and 20 out of 29 Muslim seats in Bombay. And it was only in these two provinces that the possibility of a coalition was seriously explored.

In the summer of 1937 Jinnah was faced with the stark fact that his party scarcely figured on the political map of India under the new constitution. While Gandhi and Nehru and the Congress leaders would guide and control six (and later eight) provincial ministries, there was not one ministry he could call his own, or in the formation of which he had a say. And it may have seemed that Jinnah could do little about this situation until the next round of elections. He was however not the man to let history pass over his head. 'In politics', he once said, 'one has to play one's game on the chess board.'[30] He made a masterly move calculated to achieve through a propaganda blast what the ballot box had denied him.

The by-election to the Jhansi-Jalaun-Hamirpur Muslim seat in the UP gave an inkling of the new strategy. In this by-election the Muslim League simply raised the cry of 'religion in danger'. Nehru was shocked by this unabashed exploitation of religious feeling; even the appeal issued by Jinnah in support of the League candidate did not contain a single reference to political and economic issues. Nehru begged Jinnah not to import religious emotion into politics:

'The leaders of the Muslim League have issued many . . . leaflets and appeals. I have read some of these, but in none of them have

I found any reference to a political and economic issue. The cry raised is that Islam is in danger, that non-Muslim organisations have dared to put up candidates against the Muslim League. . . . Mr Jinnah has capped the sheaf of Muslim League leaflets and statements by his appeal in his capacity as the President of the Muslim League. He appeals in the name of Allah and the Holy Koran for support of the Muslim League candidate. Mr. Jinnah knows well that many eminent Muslims, including leaders of the Jamiat-ul-Ulema like Maulana Hussain Ahmed, are supporting the Congress candidate. Have they ceased to be Muslims because of this? . . . To exploit the name of God and religion in an election contest is an extraordinary thing . . . even for a humble canvasser. For Mr Jinnah to do so is inexplicable. I would beg him to consider this aspect of the question. . . . It means rousing religious and communal passions in political matters; it means working for the Dark Age in India. Does not Mr Jinnah realise where this kind of communalism will lead us to?'[31]

Nehru wrote to Khaliquzzaman, the UP League leader who was once his fellow-prisoner during the non-co-operation movement, protesting against the electioneering tactics of the League. Khaliquzzaman in his reply deplored these occurrences but explained how candidates had to proclaim themselves 'to be as good and pious Muslims as their opponents . . . and all the religious zeal of the belligerents must be brought into play to carry the electorate with them'.[32] This was an eloquent commentary on the effect of separate electorates on Muslim politics, particularly at election time, and on the difficulty of posing concrete political and economic issues to the electorate. The by-election was a pointer to the new strategy which unfolded itself at the Lucknow session of the All India Muslim League in October 1937. Not even three months had passed since the Congress had formed ministries, but Jinnah was already proclaiming that Muslims could 'not expect any justice or fair play at their hands'.[33] The majority community had clearly shown their hand by saying that 'Hindustan is for the Hindus. The result of the present Congress party policy will be, I venture to say, class bitterness and communal war.' There had not yet been time to circulate 'atrocity stories', but the League leader was warning his co-religionists: 'There are forces which may bully you, tyrannise over you and intimidate you . . . but it is by going through this crucible of fire of persecution which may be levelled against you . . . a nation will emerge worthy of its past glory. . . .'[34] Writing in the British-owned *Pioneer*, a Muslim observer noted the heated atmosphere at the Lucknow meeting of the League.

'The doctrine of aloofness was preached *ad nauseam* in a most unrestrained and irresponsible language. Out of the clouds of circumlocution and confusion arose the cry of "Islam in danger". The Muslims were told that they were disunited and about to be crucified by the Hindus. Religious fervour was raised to a degree when it exhibited itself in blind fanaticism. In the name of Muslim solidarity Mr Jinnah wants to divide India into Muslim India and Hindu India.'[35]

Conscious humility had rarely characterised Jinnah's public utterances, but from the summer of 1937, they acquired a new edge of bitterness. Referring to Nehru in a press statement on 26 July he said: 'What can I say to that busybody President [of the Congress]. . . . He seems to carry the responsibility of the whole world on his shoulders and must poke his nose in every-thing except minding his own business.'[36] Commenting on a statement by Gandhi, he said: 'A more disingenuous statement it would be difficult to find, coming from Mr Gandhi, and it is a pity it comes from one who is a votary of truth!'[37] The Mahatma, Jinnah jeered on another occasion, was the 'oracle of Delphi'.[38] Light had not dawned upon Sevagram. Mr Gandhi was groping in the dark; he had designs to 'subjugate and vassalise the Muslims under a Hindu Raj'.[39] The Congress was trying to 'encircle' and 'annihilate' the 'Muslim nation'. For Muslim nationalists, who did not follow Jinnah's lead, the harshest epithets were reserved. Abul Kalam Azad was denounced as a 'puppet president' of the Congress.[40] Muslims differing with League programmes or policies were guilty of the 'grossest treachery' and 'betrayal' and stabbing their co-religionists in the back. Indian Muslims were warned to beware of 'Muslim agents of the Hindus' and 'Muslim agents of the British'. In spite of the not too recent discomfiture of his party at the polls, Jinnah was arrogating to himself the right to speak on behalf of the 100 million Muslims of India: 'When I say 100 million I mean that 99 per cent of them are with us – leaving aside some who are traitors, cranks, supermen or lunatics. . . .'[41]

When Nehru returned after a brief visit to Europe in 1938, he was struck by the similarity between the propaganda methods of the League in India and of the Nazis in Germany: 'The League

leaders had begun to echo the Fascist tirade against democracy.
. . . Nazis were wedded to a negative policy. So also was the
League. The League was anti-Hindu, anti-Congress, anti-national.
. . . The Nazis raised the cry of hatred against the Jews, the League
[had] raised [its] cry against the Hindus.'[42] The denunciation of
democracy as a form of government, the right of a racial minority
to blackmail and disrupt the State, the claim by sub-national
groups to self-determination, the reiteration of wildly exaggerated
and usually fictitious 'atrocity stories'– all these were the common
coinage of German propaganda in 1937–8, and to all appearances
the Nazis were earning good dividends from this propaganda.
If the Sudetan Germans could embarrass the Czech majority and
dismember the state of Czechoslovakia, could not the Muslim
minority do the same to the Hindus in India? At a meeting of the
Sind Muslim League Provincial Conference in October 1938,
Abdulla Haroon, the Chairman of the Reception Committee,
warned the Hindus that if the League's demand was not conceded, 'Czechoslovakian happenings would find an echo in India
as well'.[43] The warning was repeated by Jinnah. Syed Wazir
Hasan (a former Chief Judge of the Oudh Chief Court, who
had presided over the 1936 session of the All-India Muslim League)
warned Nehru of 'the propaganda of misrepresentation, lies and
religious and communal hatred, not only between Mussalmans
and Hindus, but also between Mussalmans and Mussalmans'
which had been started at the Lucknow session of the League.[44]

VI

Nehru was shocked by the propaganda of the League, but he did
not take long to realise its explosive possibilities. When riots
broke out in Allahabad in April 1938, he rushed to his home-
town and helped to restore peace. He urged the UP Premier
Pant not to spare any official, high or low, who was guilty of
partiality in communal riots. Nehru knew that the communal
temperature had risen not because of local grievances, but through
the political heat generated by the League. He tried to remove
the misunderstanding by opening correspondence with Jinnah
and explaining to him Congress attitudes and policies. Jinnah's
response was cold, formal, legalistic. At the same time Nehru
wrote at great length to Nawab Mahomed Ismail, a League
leader of UP to clear doubts on such general questions as the
'mass-contact movement', the national anthem and the national

K

flag which had become the targets of League criticism.[45] The Congress 'mass-contact movement', he told the Nawab, was not directed against the Muslim League; it had never been thought of in terms of Muslims alone, nor was it confined to them. The Congress had worked among the Hindu masses and 'disabled the Hindu Mahasabha politically'; it had done effective and success-ful work among the Christian masses of the South, the Parsis, the Jews and the Sikhs. The *Bande Mataram* song, Nehru recalled, had first become popular during the agitation against the parti-tion of Bengal, when it came to be regarded by the British as a symbol of sedition. From 1905 to 1920, the song had been sung at innumerable meetings at some of which Jinnah himself was present. The Congress flag had been born during the days of the Khilafat Movement, and its colours had been determined to represent the various communities: saffron for Hindus, green for Muslims and white for other minorities. Had not Maulana Muhammad Ali, the Khilafat leader, delivered scores of speeches on the 'national flag' as representing the unity of India? As for the Wardha Scheme of basic education, it was no diabolical plot against Muslim children; it had been devised by two eminent Muslim educationists, Zakir Husain and K. G. Saiyidain, to substitute a co-ordinated training in the use of the hand and the eye for a notoriously bookish and volatile learning which village children unlearned after leaving school.

The Congress leaders were distressed by the widening of the communal rift and discussed all aspects of it from the choice of Muslim ministers to that of a national anthem. How far the Congress leadership was prepared to go to soothe Muslim feelings is shown by the fact that a sub-committee went into the question of national anthem and, on its recommendation, it was decided that, out of deference to Muslim susceptibilities, only the first two stanzas should be sung on ceremonial occasions.

Not content with making general allegations, the Muslim League brought forward charges of cruelty and tyranny against Congress ministries: the *Pirpur Report* and *Shareef Report* listed these charges in highly coloured language. Some of the allega-tions in these reports were discussed in provincial legislatures; some were inquired into by British officers and refuted in press communiqués. The Bihar Government issued a detailed and (as Professor Coupland described it)[46] a reasoned reply to the *Pirpur Report*. Nevertheless, the charges continued to be repeated against the Congress ministries by Muslim League politicians and newspapers. Nehru vainly appealed to Jinnah to agree to an impartial inquiry. Rajendra Prasad suggested an inquiry by Sir Maurice Gwyer, the Chief Justice of the Federal Court: this suggestion was not accepted by Jinnah on the ground that the matter was under His Excellency the Viceroy's consideration. Later, in December 1939, Jinnah called for a Royal Commission, a demand which the British Government were hardly likely to concede in war-time and for raking up such a controversy.

'It has been our misfortune', Nehru wrote to Jinnah on 14 December 1939, 'that charges are made in a one-sided way and they are never inquired into or disposed of. You will appreciate that it is very easy to make complaints and very unsafe to rely upon them without inquiry.'

While isolated acts of petty tyranny by local officials may have occurred in remote villages and towns in Congress (as well as in non-Congress) provinces, the theory of a concerted tyranny directed against the Muslim community in the Congress provinces in 1937–9 would be difficult to sustain. It is important to recall that during these years nearly half of the members of the ICS were still British.[47] They occupied almost all the key appointments in the secretariat besides holding charge of important districts. Almost all the Inspectors-General of Police were British,[48] and so were most of the police superintendents. There was a fair sprinkling of Muslims and Christians in the ICS and in the Indian Police, and Muslims were well represented in the middle and lower ranks of the police. It is also a significant fact that there is hardly any evidence in the records of the Home Department of the Government of India to support the theory of a Hindu Raj in Congress-governed provinces. Law and order was of course a provincial subject, but the channels of communication between the Viceroy and his colleagues in the Executive Council on the one hand, and the British Governors and Chief Secretaries on the other, had not dried up.[49] It is impossible to believe that deliberate ill-treatment of the Muslim minority could have gone unnoticed and unrecorded by the representatives of the Raj even in their confidential correspondence.

That the Muslim League should have thrown cold water on proposals for holding judicial inquiries into its allegations against the Congress ministries is understandable. The League was not trying to convince the British or the Hindus: its propaganda was meant for 'home consumption', for the Muslim community: in this aim it attained a remarkable success. The spectre of a Hindu

Raj roused the deepest fears of the Muslim intelligentsia; religious emotion was worked up to a high pitch; political and economic issues receded to the background. The effect of this propaganda was felt not only in the Hindu majority provinces, but in the Muslim majority provinces where the Muslim League had cut no ice in the 1937 elections.

At the Patna session of the Muslim League (December 1938) a threat of direct action was held out against the Congress and even the soft-spoken Sir Sikandar Hayat Khan, the Premier of the Punjab, offered to join this agitation. 'Such an offer', Nehru wrote to Sir Sikandar, 'by a Prime Minister of a provincial government is unusual and if seriously meant, likely to lead to grave consequences'.[50] In adopting this heroic posture, Sir Sikandar may have been swept off his feet by the overheated atmosphere at Patna, but it is not unlikely that he was acting under the impulse of self-preservation. He was aware of the deep religious feeling which was being roused among his co-religionists, and of the fact that with its help the Muslim League could cut the ground from under his feet in the Punjab. Sir Sikandar had therefore no objection to joining in the tirade against the Congress if in return he was left alone in his own province. Similar considerations seem to have influenced Fazl-ul-Huq, the Prime Minister of Bengal, who had been at first unresponsive to Jinnah's overtures.

Nehru and his colleagues in the Congress Working Committee were distressed by the League's propaganda which was bound to provoke a reaction from Hindu communal groups. As President of the Congress Nehru had tried, and so had Subhas Chandra Bose after him, to open negotiations with Jinnah. Neither of them could proceed beyond the preliminary stage. Jinnah insisted that before the dialogue started, the Muslim League must be recognised as the sole authoritative organisation of Muslims. This was a novel demand; it had not been raised earlier, when Jinnah had discussed the Communal Award with Rajendra Prasad, who was Congress President in 1935. At that time he had insisted that the agreement with the Congress should also be endorsed by the Hindu Mahasabha.[51] From 1937 onwards, Jinnah branded the Congress as a Hindu organisation and denied its right to speak for any other community. The Congress was of course not a homogeneous organisation and included in its ranks members of different communities as well as different schools of thought. The divisions in the Congress, however, were not along religious lines. If the Congress was to accept Jinnah's condition and accept the status of a communal body, what was it to do with the hundred thousand Muslim members on its rolls, with the Christians, the Jews, the Sikhs and the Parsis who had served it devotedly for many years? And what was to be done about trade unions, peasant unions, chambers of commerce, employers' associations and others which cut across communal lines, and looked up to the Congress for political leadership?

In retrospect it would seem as if this precondition for the recognition of the Muslim League as the one and only organisation of Muslims was laid down by Jinnah to avoid coming to the negotiating table. In March 1938 when Nehru had urged the League leader to spell out the demands of the League, all that he could do was to refer Nehru to the Fourteen Points and to an anonymous article in the *Statesman* dated 12 February 1938, another article in the *New Times* of 1 March 1938 and to a statement by M. S. Aney, the Nationalist Party leader. The fact is that almost all the political demands of the Muslim community embodied in the Fourteen Points had been practically conceded in the constitution which had come into force in 1937, and Jinnah had no concrete demands to make. This interpretation is supported by the confession of Khaliquzzaman that if the negotiations between the Congress and the League had really got off the ground during the years 1938–9, he (Khaliquzzaman) 'wondered what positive demands we could have then made. The Communal Award had been conceded. There was no demand by the Hindu community for its abrogation after 1936. . . . Both Nawab Ismail Khan and I were at a loss to find any substantial radical demand on the Congress to satisfy us and our community.'

So the interesting fact emerges that during the years 1937–9 while the Congress ministries offered the handiest peg on which the Muslim League could hang its grievances, it had really no political demands to make on the Congress.

VII

The brief partnership between the Congress and the Government which the installation of Congress ministries in eight provinces had begun, ended with the outbreak of World War in September 1939.

Thanks to the lead given by Nehru, the Indian National Congress had consistently and emphatically expressed its sympathy in favour of the Allies and denounced every act of aggression by Japan, Italy and Germany. Nehru, who had visited Europe in 1936 and 1938, had reacted strongly against the make-believe policy of the 'appeasement' period. When the war broke out, he was touring China. He hurried back to India and declared that in the conflict between democracy and freedom on the one hand, and Fascism and aggression on the other, 'our sympathies must inevitably be on the side of the democracy . . . I should like India to play her full part and throw all her resources into the struggle for a new order'.[52]

The Congress Working Committee met soon afterwards and offered its co-operation in the struggle against Fascism, but it was to be 'a co-operation between equals by mutual consent for a cause which both considered to be worthy'. This was in Nehru's view, the only honourable course for the Congress to adopt. How could India hold aloft the banner of freedom and democracy in Czechoslovakia or Poland while she was herself in bondage? Apart from the moral aspect, there was an important and practical consideration. Wars were no longer bouts between professional armies in distant battlefields; whole nations had to be mobilised as workers or soldiers; unless Britain could release India's energies by treating her as an equal partner in a common struggle, it was hardly possible for her to play her full part in the world struggle.

What was required in the autumn of 1939 was a little imagination and a little courage: these qualities were not forthcoming from the Government of India headed by Lord Linlithgow and the British Government headed by Neville Chamberlain. The Viceroy had made the blunder of issuing a declaration of war on behalf of India without any kind of consultation with Indian opinion. He tried to make up for this omission by inviting Indian leaders to meet him, but he had precious little to tell them. During the early weeks of the war, Linlithgow was extraordinarily cautious; he seems to have been lulled into a false sense of security by the 'phoney war'. In his assessment of the political implications of the war, he lagged behind even the India Office. He under-rated the gravity of the international situation and misread the mood of the Congress. The Congress plea for a declaration that after the war Britain would concede Indians 'the right of self-determination by framing their own constitution through a Constituent Assembly', left him cold. Nor was he willing to let the Congress and other political parties have an effective partici-pation in the administration at the centre. It had never been the

British policy in the past (he told the Secretary of State) 'to expedite in India constitutional changes for their own sake or gratuitously to hurry the handing over of controls to Indian hands'.[53] The continuing discords between the communities, he thought, would strengthen Britain's hold on India for many years.[54] Among the minorities and special interests which stood in the way of accepting the Congress demand, the Viceroy listed not only 'the great communities of India' but European business interests and the Indian Princes.[55] As he went through the interminable negotiations with numerous parties and individuals, it was obvious that he was finding arguments for maintaining the political *status quo*.

'The same old game is played again', Nehru wrote to Gandhi, 'the background is the same, the various epithets are the same, and the actors are the same, and the results must be the same.'

Having failed to receive a response from the Government, the Congress decided to withdraw its ministries in eight provinces. The suspension of the provincial part of the constitution was a serious step, but to the British officials in Delhi it may not have been entirely unwelcome; unhampered by the politicians they could now concentrate upon beating the Germans.

The Congress had realised at an early stage of the war that it could flare up at any time and envelop India. The old issues had suddenly become outdated. The crisis called for new initiatives. It was this feeling which had led the Congress Working Committee to invite Jinnah to attend its first meeting after the outbreak of the war in September 1939. Jinnah did not of course avail himself of the invitation, but Nehru wrote to him on 18 October after learning from a common friend (Raghunandan Saran) that the Muslim League leader seemed to be in a co-operative mood. Nehru made as cordial an overture as he could:

'I entirely agree with you that it is a tragedy that the Hindu-Muslim problem has not been settled in a satisfactory way. . . . With your goodwill and commanding position in the Muslim League a solution should not be as difficult as people imagine . . . for after all the actual matters under dispute should be, and indeed are, easily capable of adjustment.'

He begged Jinnah to join the Congress in protesting against India being plunged into the war, without her consent. He appealed to Jinnah's patriotism: 'Our dignity and self-respect as Indians has been insulted.' For once Jinnah seemed interested and even cordial, but he did not commit himself to any course of action, and agreed to continue the conversations.

There were good reasons for Jinnah to adopt this position. The war had created a new situation; the Congress and Government were drifting apart, but there was still a possibility of a *modus vivendi* between them. It was only when the talks between the Government and the Congress broke down that he showed his hand. In December 1939, just when Nehru was preparing to leave for Bombay to meet him, the League leader called upon Indian Muslims to observe 22 December as a 'Day of Deliverance' from the Congress Ministries, 'from tyranny, oppression and injustice during the last two and a half years'. The aggressiveness of this gesture left Nehru gasping, but it took many people including members of the League by surprise. Some observers felt that Jinnah had overshot his bolt, and that his extreme tactics might even cause a split in the League.[56]

Jinnah's statement on Deliverance Day was a vitriolic attack on the Congress party; after reading it Nehru could not bring himself to meet the League leader. He began to wonder if there was any common ground between them at all. Nehru's heart was set on political independence and a socialist society, and the instrument of the new order was to be a Constituent Assembly elected by the people on the basis of adult franchise.

To Jinnah, the proposal for the Constituent Assembly seemed wholly utopian. 'It is puerile', he said 'to ask the British Government to call a Constituent Assembly of another nation and afterwards to have the honour and privilege of placing the Constitution framed by this supreme assembly of India on the Statute Book of the British Government.'[57] On social and economic problems Jinnah spoke rarely, but he had no sympathy with Nehru's radical economics: 'All talk of hunger and poverty', he declared, 'is intended to lead the people to socialistic and communistic ideas for which India is far from prepared.'[58]

VIII

By December 1939 it was clear to Nehru that Jinnah would neither settle with the Congress nor embroil himself with the Government. What Nehru did not quite foresee was Jinnah's ability to turn to his advantage the growing rift between the Congress and the Government. The observance of Deliverance Day had created a new gulf between the League and the Congress.

Three months later, the Lahore session of the League in March 1940 made the gulf wider. It was at this session that the League resolved that:

'... no constitutional plan will be workable in the country or acceptable to the Muslims unless it is designed on the following basic principles, viz., that geographically contiguous units are demarcated into regions which should be so constituted, with such territorial readjustments as may be necessary, that the areas in which the Muslims are numerically in the majority as the north-western and eastern zones of India should be grouped to constitute "Independent States" in which the constituent assemblies are autonomous and sovereign.'

The 'Pakistan resolution', as it came to be known, gave a new twist to the communal problem. All the solutions hitherto thought of – separate electorates, composite cabinets, reservation of posts – suddenly became out of date.

Thirty-three years after the passage of this resolution and twenty-six years after the emergence of Pakistan as an independent State, it is difficult to realise that it came as a bombshell not only to the Congressmen, but to almost everyone outside the inner circles of the Muslim League.

Nehru's immediate reaction was that

'all the old problems . . . pale into insignificance before the latest stand taken by the Muslim League leaders at Lahore. The whole problem has taken a new complexion and there is no question of settlement or negotiations now.'

Nehru was not alone in reacting sharply to the League's new stand. Gandhi described the two-nation theory as 'an untruth'. the strongest word in his dictionary. Rajagopalachari called it 'a medieval conception';[59] Abul Kalam Azad described it as 'meaningless and absurd'.[60] Sir Sikander Hyat Khan, Premier of the Punjab[61] and Sir Ghulam Husain Hidayatullah, Premier of Sind,[62] rejected the idea of partition of India outright. Abdul Qaiyum Khan, who was later to be a lieutenant of Jinnah, declared that 'the Frontier Province will resist [partition of India] with its blood'.[63] Syed Habibul Rahman, a leader of the Bengal Krishak Proja Party, said that the proposal was not only absurd, chimerical and visionary, but

'. . . will for ever remain a castle in the air . . . Indians, both Hindus and Muslims, live in a common motherland, use the offshoots of a common language and literature, and are proud of the noble heritage of a common Hindu and Muslim culture, developed through centuries of residence in a common land. There is no one among the Hindus and Muslims who will be prepared to sacrifice all this in order to accept what is demanded by Mr Jinnah.'[64]

'For the moment', wrote the *Manchester Guardian*, 'Mr Jinnah has re-established the reign of chaos in India.'[65]

In the spring of 1940, most serious observers of the Indian scene would have described the Pakistan plan as 'chimerical and impractical', words used by prominent Muslim witnesses before the Joint Parliamentary Committee in August 1933.[66] Even after the Pakistan proposal had been embodied in a resolution of the All India Muslim League, it was no more than a political phantom. It was left to the spokesmen of the British Government to give it body and soul.

We know now that in March 1939, two Muslim League politicians, Khaliquzzaman and Abdul Rahman Siddiqui, met Lieutenant Colonel Muirhead, the Under-Secretary of State, and Lord Zetland, the Secretary of State for India, and got the impression that if the proposal for a separate Muslim State in the north-west and east of India was put forward the British would 'ultimately concede'[67] it. This impression was conveyed to Jinnah and may have influenced him in formulating the Pakistan demand in 1940. There is also evidence to show that Jinnah took the Viceroy into confidence and mentioned the Pakistan resolution to him several weeks before the League held its Lahore session.[68] In private the Viceroy may have described the Pakistan proposal as an extreme and 'preposterous claim', which had been put forward for 'bargaining purposes', but he did more than any other person to lend to it the air of feasibility which was needed before it could gather support even among the Muslims. In his long-awaited public statement of 8 August 1940, the Viceroy included a remarkable passage:

'It goes without saying that they [His Majesty's Government] could not contemplate the transfer of their present responsibilities for the peace and welfare of India to any system of government whose authority is directly denied by large and powerful elements in the Indian national life, nor could be a party to the coercion of such elements into submission to such a government.'

Evidently this passage had been included out of deference to Jinnah.

It is a curious fact that the Indian National Congress had to agitate for thirty-two years before securing Edwin Montagu's declaration of 1917 about 'responsible government' being the goal of British policy in India. Another twelve years had to elapse before the phrase Dominion Status was used with reference to India. But it took the Muslim League exactly four and half months to secure an indirect endorsement of a novel and – in the light of Indian constitutional evolution until 1940 – drastic doctrine for the solution of the Indian constitutional problem.

A further encouragement to the Pakistan proposal came in a speech delivered by Amery, the Secretary of State in the House of Commons:

'The foremost among these elements stands the great Muslim community, ninety million strong and constituting a majority both in north-western and north-eastern India, but scattered as a minority over the whole sub-continent. In religious and social outlook, in historic tradition and culture, the difference between them and their Hindu fellow countrymen goes as deep, if not deeper than any similar difference in Europe. . . .'

These two statements by the Viceroy and the Secretary of State were later cited by Jinnah as 'solemn declarations' on the part of the British Government endorsing the two-nation theory and Pakistan.[69] The Viceroy and the Secretary of State could not have been unaware of the implications of the League's demand. But they had their own reasons for not antagonising the Muslim League. On the very day the August offer was announced by Lord Linlithgow, he had signed a secret letter to the Governors informing them of the plans which had been perfected in the Home Department of the Government of India for a knock-out blow at the Congress, 'a declared determination to crush that organisation as a whole'.[70] Having written off the Congress, the Viceroy and his advisers could hardly resist the temptation of backing up its principal opponent. 'Some British officials', says Tinker, 'welcomed this [Pakistan] plan as a means of checkmating Congress demands.'[71] Testimony has been borne by at least one League leader to the support received from senior British officers:[72] it is difficult to say how far this support was due to their affinity with the Muslim Leaguers, whose loyalty had never been in doubt, and with whom they could meet on friendly terms, and how far to their antipathy to the *khadi*-clad, vegetarian, gaol-going Congressmen who were the avowed enemies of the British Raj. In 1940 many of these British officers may not have troubled themselves about the merits of the proposal for the partition of India; it was enough for them that there was little chance of other parties accepting the proposal, that the political deadlock was likely to last indefinitely, and that the only alternative was the continuance of British rule.

IX

The circle of mistrust between the Congress and the Government which had begun with Linlithgow's declaration of war in September 1939 was to be completed with the passage of the 'Quit India' resolution by the All India Congress Committee in August 1942. It was borne in upon the Congress leaders during the first two years of the war that the British Government, headed by Winston Churchill in Britain and by Linlithgow in India, was reluctant to pledge itself to Indian freedom after the war, or to take the Congress and other political parties into effective partnership during the war. All that the Indian National Congress was offered was membership of advisory committees and seats in the Viceroy's Executive Council without effective voice in the administration. This was a passive role which a militant nationalist party, with twenty years of struggle behind it, could not accept. It could hardly sit back with folded hands, and be a spectator of events while the future of nations was in the melting pot. Pressures began to build up within the Congress for a mass civil disobedience movement. Gandhi resisted these pressures as long as he could, and then diverted them into the relatively innocuous channels of 'individual *satyagraha*'. This was conceived as a token protest without seriously embarrassing the war-effort, but nearly 30,000 prominent Congressmen courted imprisonment during the years 1940–1. A certain complication arose at this time because of Gandhi's firm faith in non-violence and his refusal to countenance anything but non-violence even against external aggression. Gandhi's pacifism was not, however, shared by Nehru and indeed the majority in the Congress Working Committee. On two occasions, after the fall of France and the entry of Japan in the war, when a National Government for vigorously prosecuting the war seemed to be on the cards, Gandhi did not stand in the way of his colleagues and stepped aside to let them co-operate with the Government, if honourable terms were forthcoming. At the beginning of 1942, as the Japanese swept everything before them in South-East Asia, and eastern India came perilously close to the theatre of war, a section in the Congress, led by Nehru, Azad and Rajagopalachari, felt that it was time to mobilise national resources to the utmost for defence against Japan.

The critical war situation had also its impact on the British War Cabinet, and resulted in the despatch of Sir Stafford Cripps to India. His Draft Declaration was a great step forward in so far as it recognised India's right after the war to frame a constitution through a Constituent Assembly. The basic demand of the Congress had been conceded, but vitiated by certain provisions introduced out of deference to the Muslim League, the Indian princes and perhaps the British Tories. This clause in the Draft Declaration laid down that any province or provinces, which did not acquiesce in the new constitution, would be entitled to frame a constitution of their own, giving them 'the same full status as the Indian Union'. This clause threatened to convert India into a political chequerboard, containing scores of princely states and independent provinces, or groups of provinces, which could make short work of India as a political and economic entity. This was a prospect which made every Indian nationalist shudder. Gandhi, who had been specially invited from Wardha to see Cripps, after reading the proposals, advised him to take the first plane home. Nehru's feelings on 'balkanisation' were equally strong; in a telegram to Krishna Menon in England he criticised the 'whole conception [of] leading [to] break up India with British forces guarding States interfering [with] freedom [of the] Union, encouraging disruptive tendencies'.

In his press conferences and broadcasts, Cripps defended the provision for non-accession of provinces on the ground that it would, by reassuring Muslims, make the drastic step of secession superfluous. 'The door must be left open', Cripps said in one of his broadcasts. 'If you want to persuade a number of people who are inclined to be antagonistic to enter the same room, it is unwise to tell them that once they go in, there is no way out.'[73] Cripps failed to foresee that this approach would have a contrary effect upon the Muslim League. Jinnah welcomed the non-accession clause as a 'recognition given to the principle of partition'. His only grievance was that it was a 'veiled recognition', and in equivocal terms.[74] He demanded amendments in the details of the constitution-making process, which would ensure beyond doubt the secession of the provinces he claimed for Pakistan. In the event, Cripps succeeded not in weaning Jinnah from his secessionist aims, but in encouraging him in the belief that the partition of India would be conceded by Britain, if the League persisted in its campaign.

In its resolution of 2 April 1942, on the Cripps proposals, the Congress Working Committee criticised the 'novel principle of non-accession for a Province', but affirmed 'nevertheless the Committee cannot think in terms of compelling the people of any territorial unit to remain in an Indian Union against their declared and established will'. As an organisation pledged to democratic principles and non-violent methods, the Congress may have felt justified in making such a declaration, but it was an indirect endorsement of the possibility of secession by a territorial unit, which could not but be a source of encouragement to the Muslim League. The immediate effect of the Cripps Mission was therefore to give a boost to the movement for Pakistan and to lower the morale of those particularly nationalist Muslims, who had stood against it.

For Jawaharlal Nehru, as for his colleagues in the Working Committee, the long-term proposals of Sir Stafford Cripps had serious snags, but he was prepared to shelve the constitutional issue and to concentrate on the formation of a National Government to resist the Japanese, who were battering at the gates of India. Nehru's mind was full of plans for raising national militias to fight the invader if he got a foothold on Indian soil. No agreement could, however, be reached on the formation of a National Government owing to the basic hostility of not only the Viceroy, but also of Prime Minister Churchill, to bringing the Congress or, as he had frankly described it, 'hostile elements into the defence machine'. While the British Government was unwilling to admit the Congress as a partner in the defence against Japan, the Muslim League maintained its hostility to the Congress despite the immediate peril from Japan. When Nehru suggested that the Muslim League would have joined a 'national government' if it had been possible to form one, Jinnah immediately refuted the statement. 'I assert', he said, 'that if the Congress demand [for national government] had been accepted, it would have been the death-knell to the Mussalmans of India'.[75] We know now that there was a school of thought in the Muslim League Council which opposed participation in a national government at the centre even during the war lest this participation in a unitary government should prejudice the demand for Pakistan.[76]

In the weeks following the failure of the Cripps Mission, Gandhi was driven to the conclusion that something had to be done to save India from going the way of Malaya and Burma, by giving to the Indian people a stake in the defence of their country. He became convinced that no solution of the communal problem was possible so long as Hindus and Muslims had a third party – the British – to look up to. These convictions provided the main impulse behind the 'Quit India' resolution which the All India Congress Committee passed at its Bombay meeting on 8 August 1942. This meeting was preceded by hectic political activity. The Congress leaders felt that their organisation faced the greatest crisis in its long history. In this crisis they were prepared to review relations not only with the British Government, but with other political parties, particularly the Muslim League. They were clapped into prison immediately after the 'Quit India' resolution was passed, but there is evidence to show that if they had been allowed time to do so, they would have tried to reach an agreement with the League. Testimony to this is borne by Dr Abdul Latif of Hyderabad who had been meeting and corresponding with Nehru and Azad at this time. In a letter dated 6 August 1942, Nehru explained his views on the Pakistan issue to Dr Latif:

'India, as it is, contains nearly all the important elements and resources that can make her a strong and more or less self-sufficient nation. To cut her up will be, from the economic point of view as well as others, a fatal thing, breaking up that national economic unity and weakening each part.

'All these arguments are reinforced by recent world history, and in fact by the course of the war itself.

'This has shown that small nations have no future before them, except as hangers-on of larger nations. We do not want India or any part of India to be such a hanger-on or a kind of semi-dependency, political or economic, of any other nation. . . . In fact the tendency in the world is for large federations to come into existence.'

The All India Congress Committee's main resolution of 8 August had pledged the Congress to a federal constitution, 'with the largest autonomy for the federating units and with the residuary powers vested in these units'. Dr Latif, who had talked to

Congress leaders during these critical days before their arrest, was convinced that they were willing to go to the farthest limit to satisfy political aspirations of the Muslim community and to remove its misgivings. Gandhi had in fact gone so far as to propose that the British should quit India by transferring power exclusively to the All India Muslim League.

Dr Latif was not an adherent of the Congress; indeed in his correspondence with Nehru, he had started as a sharp critic. But by the summer of 1942 he had realised that the Congress was prepared to concede to the provinces the widest autonomy with a limited centre – 'the substance of Pakistan'. He begged Jinnah to respond to the Congress gestures; the division of India, he argued, would not solve the communal problem, but only aggravate it. Jinnah dismissed Latif's correspondence with the Congress leaders as 'contradictory, disingenuous and dubious'. Latif replied that:

'Arguments as these only go to confirm the view held by the Congressites that Mr Jinnah was never serious about a settlement with the Congress. For aught I can say, it is clear to my mind, from my talks with its leaders that the Congress on its part appeared sincerely anxious to settle its differences with the League and with its help and willing co-operation to rally the people of India for the defence of the country by forming an interim popular government'.[77]

Latif observed later,

'I have reasons to believe that he [Jinnah] and his Working Committee had neither studied nor attempted to grasp the full implications of Pakistan. He had unfortunately lulled himself into the belief that if he could only carve out two small so-called independent states for the Mussalmans in the north-west and north-east, he would have solved for all times, the problems of Indian Muslims.

'The real Muslim problem does not concern so much the Muslims of those parts where they form a majority, and where they can look after themselves in any constitution, as it concerns the Muslim minority from Delhi, Lucknow, Patna towns to Cape Comorin, who would be rendered eternal orphans under Mr Jinnah's plan. . . . I have found Mr Jinnah incapable of conceiving the hundred million Muslims in India as an indivisible entity and that we can secure all the advantages of his Pakistan without having to labour under its inevitable disadvantages by setting the scheme against an all-India background.'[78]

Dr Latif's plea to Jinnah to grasp the hand of friendship that the Congress leaders were extending before they were removed from the political scene did not evoke a response. The arrest of the Congress leaders immediately after the meeting of the All India Congress Committee, mob violence in some parts of the country and the swift and strong repression by the Government brought Government-Congress relations to the lowest ebb ever, and created a situation which the Muslim League immediately turned to its advantage.

The Muslim League Working Committee hastened to denounce the 'Quit India' movement as an attempt to establish 'Hindu Raj' and 'to deal a death-blow to the Muslim goal of Pakistan. The League's tirade against the Congress was useful to the Government of India which had switched its war-publicity machine with its full force against the Congress, so as to represent it as anti-British, anti-national and pro-Axis.

With the Congress outlawed, its leaders in prison, its publicity media silenced, the political stage was clear for the Muslim League. 'The Government have no love for the League', a Congress leader wrote, 'less for its leader. For them, the League and its leader are the enemy's enemy, the common enemy being the national forces represented by the Congress.'[79] Engaged in the task of an all-out offensive against the Congress, the British Governors and officials were glad to see an ally in the most vociferous opponent of the Congress.

The political gains of the League's new position were not long in coming. In August 1942, Sir Saadullah Khan formed a League ministry in Assam. A month later, Allah Baksh, the Premier of Sind (whose sympathy with the Congress was an open secret) renounced his title of Khan Bahadur and OBE; for these offences he was dismissed from his office even though he commanded a majority in the Legislative Assembly. A League ministry was formed in Sind. In March 1943, Nazimuddin, Jinnah's loyal supporter in Bengal, formed a ministry with the help of the European group. In May 1943, the Muslim League was able to form a ministry in the North-West Frontier Province, as most of the Congress members were in gaol.

'The middle years of the war', a British historian has recently pointed out, 'saw the consolidation of the Muslim League in the

L

Muslim majority provinces.'[80] This consolidation was a direct
result of the breach between the Congress and the Government
and the skill of Jinnah in making political capital out of it. This
was not a new technique: he had practised it since the outbreak
of war.[81] It was only when the estrangement between the Congress
and the Government reached its peak that the dividends to the
League were the highest in the form of League ministries in
provinces which it claimed for Pakistan.

X

As the tide of the war turned against the Axis Powers in 1944
there were indications that the Indian political deadlock might
relax. C. Rajagopalachari, who had been pleading for two years
with his colleagues in the Congress party for the 'recognition of
the right of separation of certain areas from united India',
presented to Jinnah in April 1944 a formula which became the
basis of talks between Jinnah and Gandhi in September 1944.
Gandhi had been released from prison on grounds of health in
May 1944 and was persuaded to take the initiative in seeking an
understanding with Jinnah on the issue of Pakistan. Gandhi did
not accept the two-nation theory, but agreed that after the war
a commission should demarcate contiguous districts in the north-
west and north-east of India wherein the Muslim population
was in absolute majority, and the wishes of the inhabitants of
these areas be ascertained through the votes of the adult population. If the vote went in favour of separation, these areas were to
be formed into a separate state as soon as possible after India
was free from foreign domination. However, there was to be a
Treaty of Separation between the successor states in the sub-
continent, 'for satisfactory administration of foreign affairs,
defence, internal communications, customs, commerce and the
like which must necessarily continue to be matters of common
interest between the contacting parties'.

That Gandhi should have offered these terms to Jinnah in
September 1944, would have been unthinkable four years earlier,
when he had described Pakistan as an 'untruth'. Gandhi had not
merely recognised the principle of partition, but even suggested
a mechanism for it. It is important to note that while Gandhi
suggested links between the two states, he did not insist on a
central government. He was content to have 'a Board of Representatives of both the states' for certain common purposes and

services. He could not, he confessed to Jinnah, envisage the two [successor] states after the partition 'as if there was nothing common between . . . [them] except enmity'. The search for cultural and economic autonomy was legitimate enough, but some safeguards were in Gandhi's view essential to prevent an armament race and an armed conflict between the two states.

Jinnah rejected Gandhi's offer. The demarcation of boundaries by districts was unacceptable to him, though he was to accept it in 1947. He would have nothing less than the 'full' six provinces for Pakistan, even though in two of them (the Punjab and Bengal) the Muslim majority was marginal, and in one province, Assam, it was non-existent. Jinnah did not see why non-Muslim populations in these provinces should have a voice in determining their own fate: if there was to be a plebiscite or referendum, it was to be confined to Muslims. Nor would Jinnah agree to any common links between India and Pakistan for such matters as foreign affairs, defence or customs. Nor would he agree that 'marriage should precede divorce', that partition should come, if at all, after the British departure and after the two parties had an opportunity to co-exist. While these conversations were no more than a kind of re-education for Gandhi, they brought an accession of political strength to Jinnah. That Gandhi had knocked at his door raised Jinnah's prestige in the eyes of Indian Muslims. The fact that the Mahatma had relented so far as to discuss the machinery for the exercise of 'the right of self-determination' by Muslims was a feather in Jinnah's cap.

Two efforts at a short-term solution in 1944–5 met with no more success than Gandhi's attempt at a long-term solution. Early in 1944, the 'Bhulabhai Desai-Liaqat Ali Pact' for Congress-League co-operation in an Interim Government at the centre was published. Liaqat Ali backed out. Desai burnt his fingers in these parleys; the pact was rejected out of hand by Jinnah, but it nevertheless introduced the idea of parity between the Congress and the League in the formation of a national government. At the Simla Conference summoned by Lord Wavell in June 1945, this parity was almost taken for granted: by the time the conference ended, Jinnah had raised his price by demanding a parity between the Muslim League and all other parties. The Simla Conference broke down because Jinnah would not permit the Viceroy to nominate to the Executive Council any Muslim member – not even a non-Congress Muslim 'Unionist' from the Punjab – who did not owe allegiance to the League.

XI

The Simla Conference had failed to break the deadlock. But two important events occurred in the wake of the Conference which made a new initiative possible. With the surrender of Japan on 15 August 1945, the war came to an end, and the Labour Party came into power. Lord Wavell went to London, and on return to India announced on 19 September that the British Government was still working in the spirit of the Cripps offer and intended to convene a constitution-making body. Elections to the central and provincial legislatures, which were in any case overdue, were announced. India politics were again deeply stirred and entered a period of intense excitement, interminable negotiations and bitter controversy.

In the early months of 1945, the Congress leaders could see the beginnings of a change in the British policy, but they were not yet convinced of the British *bona fides*. This was understandable in view of what they had gone through. Nehru himself had spent 3,251 days in British prisons; his latest term from 9 August 1942 to 15 June 1945 had been the longest. A member of the parliamentary delegation has recorded how the members of the Congress Working Committee, 'all ex-prisoners, regarded the British Parliamentarians with a suspicious reserve behind a veil of courtesy'. Nehru had been quoted in the British press as having called the delegation 'a huge hoax'; he had not used these words, but neither he nor his colleagues were impressed by the gesture of a goodwill delegation. Indeed, it was not only the Congress leaders, who had lost faith in British sincerity; the veteran Liberal leader Srinivas Sastri, who was on his death-bed, told Gandhi in January 1946, 'We know nothing can come out of it [the British parliamentary delegation]. Labour or Conservative so far as India is concerned, they are all one and the same.' That this melancholy judgement should have been passed at a time when the transfer of power was about to take place, and by one who had always been a friend of the British connection, showed that the representatives of the British Raj in India, with whom the Indians came into contact, gave no inkling of an early departure.

The Cabinet Mission reached Delhi on 24 March 1946. Nearly fifty persons were summoned for exchange of views with the Mission. 'It is difficult to understand', Vallabhbhai Patel wrote to Nehru on 27 March, 'why this procedure has been adopted and what useful purpose can be served by calling such a group again.

It looks as if they are pursuing the same old process to which this country is accustomed, and it leads one to believe that the local bureaucracy must be behind it.'

As the negotiations with the Cabinet Mission proceeded, the Congress distrust of the British diminished, but it never entirely disappeared. It was not a question of the sincerity of Pethick-Lawrence, Cripps, Alexander and Wavell. They seemed anxious to do the right thing, but they were surrounded by men – senior officials – who could hardly be expected to suddenly unlearn the history of the previous three decades. To the sympathy of some of the senior British officers with the League, testimony has recently been borne by one of its prominent members.[82] There were, it seemed to Congress leaders, 'English Mullahs' around the Viceroy, who were not sorry to give a parting kick to the party who had been primarily responsible for challenging and liquidating the Raj and for wrecking promising British careers in the ICS and the Indian army.

As the negotiations with the Cabinet Mission got under way, it became evident that the main confrontation was between the Congress and the League. For the first time Jinnah had been brought to the negotiating table, made to stay there, and to spell out his terms. Nehru and his colleagues were naturally cautious in dealing with him. For eight years he had defied all attempts at a direct and fruitful discussion. In one important respect, the situation had of course changed. The rift between the Congress and the Government which had given Jinnah his favourable bargaining position was closing. 'It would not be right to allow any minority, however large and important', Sir Stafford Cripps had declared in July 1945, 'to hold up the attainment of self-government in India, any more than it would be right to force the Muslim majority provinces into a new constitutional arrangement. . . .'[83] The Churchill-Amery-Linlithgow team which in the early years of the war had been so sympathetic to the League had been substituted by the Attlee-Pethick-Lawrence-Wavell team, which could be expected to take a more objective view of the Indian political situation.

The Muslim League seems to have realised this; from the beginning of 1946 it increasingly stressed dangers of civil war and issued threats which were calculated to rouse the Muslims, frighten the Hindus and impress the British. In March 1946, Abdur Rab Nishtar, later a League nominee to the Interim Government, declared: 'the real fact is that Mussalmans belong to a martial race and are no believers of the non-violent principles of Mr Gandhi'.[84] Abdul Qaiyum Khan, the League leader of NWFP, threatened that the people in the tribal areas 'who were all armed' were for Pakistan. He was asked by many Muslim students and men in uniform as to when the 'marching orders would be given by the Quaid-e-Azam . . . if they [the British] decide there should be one Constituent Assembly, then the Muslims will have no other alternative but to take out the sword and rebel against it'.[85] Sir Firoz Khan Noon, whose loyalty to the British Raj had never been in doubt, threatened on 9 April: 'I tell you this much. If we find that we have to fight Great Britain for placing us under one Central Government or Hindu Raj, then the havoc which the Muslims will play will put to shame what Chengiz Khan and Halaku did.' Sir Firoz said that if the Hindus and the British did not concede Pakistan, 'the only course left to Muslims was to look to Russia. There was already a great movement in the Punjab, including landlords, in favour of Communism.'[86] This menacing position was a novel one for a political party which had always been careful not to embroil itself with the Government and included among its leaders men who had been instruments, if not pillars of the Raj.

It was to the accompaniment of this tearing propaganda campaign that the Cabinet Mission commenced its work in March 1946. From the record of the negotiations, it is obvious that the Congress Working Committee was subject to three divergent and to some extent, contradictory pulls, which made decisions painfully difficult. In the first place, the Congress was eager to get rid of foreign rule, and to make a constructive response to the gesture of the Labour Government in sending a high-powered mission to India. Secondly, the Congress was prepared to make the widest concessions to the minorities, particularly the Muslims, in the future constitution of India by agreeing to a limited centre, residuary powers in the provinces and the maximum constitutional safeguards for protection of religious and cultural rights. These two considerations had, however, to be balanced against another: the Congress wanted to avoid pitfalls which the ingenuity of the Muslim League or the astuteness of the 'English Mullahs', operating behind the scenes, might devise: it was important not to accept constitutional formulae which would not work, or which would do permanent damage to the future of the country.

The three-month long negotiations in the trying Delhi summer were indeed a great strain on the British ministers. We know that Pethick-Lawrence was exhausted, Cripps became ill and Alexander was exasperated. But the strain on Gandhi, Nehru, Azad and Patel was no less serious. They knew they were engaged in not only a battle of wits but of wills with Jinnah. By sheer tenacity and refusal to make any concession, the League leader had built up his position and made the constitutional problem almost intractable. His price for settlement had progressively risen. It had begun with separate electorates in 1916, gone up to Fourteen Points in 1929, to composite ministries in 1937, and finally to the partition of the country in 1940. The six provinces he claimed for his Pakistan included Assam, where the Muslim population were 33 per cent, and the Punjab and Bengal where the Muslim majority was slight indeed. The League's insistence on holding a position, which seemed untenable, intrigued and exasperated the Congress leaders. They felt that the League was out to achieve its objective by a combination of intransigence and threats of civil war. Why did the League want to include in its homeland predominantly non-Muslim areas? The mental processes of the exponents of partition are illuminated by a letter written on 7 October 1942 by a prominent member of the League Council to Jinnah:

'Further, one of the basic principles lying behind the Pakistan idea is that of keeping hostages in Muslim provinces as against the Muslims in the Hindu provinces. . . . If we allow millions of Hindus to go out of the orbit of our influence, the security of the Mussalmans in the minority provinces will be greatly minimised . . . complete segregation of the Muslim and Hindu population as at present situated is impossible, but there may come a time when it may become feasible. If we allow large territories to go out of our hands in the process of readjustment [of territories] such an exchange of population would be impossible, because the territories which will be left over with us will not be sufficient to receive and maintain large populations migrating from the other land. . . . There is one other factor which should be taken into account. If the whole of Punjab becomes a part of Pakistan zone, Kashmere and other Punjab native states will have no direct communication left with the non-Muslim provinces. They will naturally desire union with them and shall be forced to ask the Pakistan Union for a right of transit. In that event, the Pakistan Government can fairly claim the same right for

Hyderabad and other Muslim estates [*sic*] to establish contact with the Pakistan Union.'[87]

XII

The negotiations with the Cabinet Mission were conducted by Azad on behalf of the Congress, though Nehru, Patel and Abdul Ghaffar Khan were associated with him. The Working Committee was continually in session and Gandhi was available for consultations. Nehru was very much in the picture, but it was Gandhi whose scepticism, particularly about the grouping of provinces, influenced the Congress attitude in the early stages of the negotiations.

Torn between their desire for an early end of British rule and their anxiety about being out-manoeuvred by the Muslim League into a wrong decision, the Congress Working Committee had many an agonising reappraisal before it passed its resolution on 25 June 1946 accepting the long-term Cabinet Plan. In the final decision, Vallabhbhai Patel's influence was probably dominant, but he was able to carry with him his colleagues in the Working Committee, including Nehru. Gandhi's doubts were not entirely resolved, but when the time came for ratification by the All India Congress Committee, Gandhi threw his weight behind the Working Committee. The All India Congress Committee met at Bombay on 7 July 1946. It was at this meeting that Nehru took charge of the Congress Presidency from Abul Kalam Azad and delivered a speech which has been described as a 'serious tactical blunder'[88] and even an act of direct sabotage of the Cabinet Mission Plan. This speech is alleged to have wrecked the Cabinet Mission Plan, and the last hope of preserving the unity of the Indian subcontinent. The charge is based on some remarks made by Nehru, but without reference to the context in which he spoke. Nehru was replying to the attacks made by socialist speakers. One of them, Achyut Patwardhan, had argued that 'the Cabinet Mission Plan foreboded ill both for Congress integrity and the communal problem',[89] and suspected the influence of 'Clive Street European capitalists' in the proposals for grouping of provinces. Another speaker, Aruna Asaf Ali had pointed to the 'traps laid by British imperialists', and called for a mass civil disobedience struggle to throw out the alien rulers.[90] A number of critics had cast doubts on the status and power of the Constituent Assembly, which was to be convened by the Government

JAWAHARLAL NEHRU AND THE PARTITION OF INDIA   169

and could exist only on its sufferance. It was this criticism that
Nehru attempted to answer in his speech of 7 July. The oft-
quoted sentence from this speech: 'We are not bound by a single
thing except that we have decided to go to the Constituent
Assembly', was not the most important part of it. The whole
tenor of his 6,000-word speech was to justify the acceptance of
the Cabinet Mission Plan. 'We cannot forget', he pleaded with
his socialist critics, 'that while we have to be revolutionary, we
also have to think in terms of statesmanship – not in shouting
slogans and escaping responsibility but in terms of facing the big
problems. The world looks to you and the Congress for great
decisions and it is no use to sit cursing, fuming and fretting. . . .'[91]
Nehru refuted the charge that the Constituent Assembly would
be a 'sham', or a nursery game at which Indian politicians would
play while the British Government supervised them. This was
why he declared that no 'dictation' from the British Government
would be tolerated.

Three days later, on 10 July, Nehru covered the same ground
at a press conference in Bombay. Here again, while he emphasised
the sovereign character of the Constituent Assembly, he affirmed
that the Congress was determined to make a success of the constitutional mechanism outlined by the Cabinet Mission. 'Once the
Congress went into the [Constituent] Assembly', Nehru said, 'its
main objective would be to see how to make it a success . . . and
in so doing the Congress would certainly have to take into consideration the situation created by the Cabinet statement of
16 May.'[92]

With some emphasis he added,

'the Constituent Assembly would never accept any dictation or
any other directive from the British Government in regard to its
work. The only two factors which limit the sovereignty of the
Constituent Assembly are those relating to the minorities and
the Indo-British treaty. . . . When the Congress had stated that
the Constituent Assembly was a soverign body, the Cabinet
Mission replied, "Yes, more or less subject to two considerations.
Firstly, proper arrangement for minorities; and the other, treaty
between India and Britain." I wish the Mission had stated both
these matters are not controversial. It is obvious that the minorities
question has to be settled satisfactorily. It is also obvious that if
there is any kind of peaceful change-over in India, it is bound to
result in some kind of a treaty with Great Britain.'[93]

Clearly, Nehru had no intention to repudiate the framework of the Cabinet Mission Plan. All the available evidence points to his anxiety to arrive at a satisfactory solution of the minority problem, and of Indo-British relations after the withdrawal of British power. In so far as Nehru was outspoken, even provocative, in his utterances at Bombay on 7 and 10 July, his words were directed not to the Muslim League, but to the critics of the Congress policy within the Congress organisation or to the British Government.

On the grouping of provinces in the Cabinet Mission Plan, Nehru told the press conference that,

'the probability is, from any approach to the question, that there will be no grouping. . . . Section A would decide against grouping. There was but little chance of the NWFP supporting grouping. . . . Further, there was a good deal of feeling against grouping in the Punjab, in the NWFP and in Sind for economic and other reasons. . . . Both these provinces were afraid of being swamped by the Punjab.'

This statement has often been cited as a destructive piece of work. In fact Nehru was doing no more than stating the political probabilities as they appeared to him in July 1946: the lack of majority support in the Punjab (which had a non-League coalition ministry), the natural reluctance of even Muslims in Sind to be swamped by the Punjabis; the presence of a Congress government in NWFP with its solid base in the Muslim community, and opposition to the League, to grouping and to Pakistan.

It is arguable that Nehru should have avoided a public discussion of political probabilities, which could not but provoke the League. But he was committing neither a breach of faith with the Cabinet Mission, nor an act of sabotage. Neither in his speech at the All India Congress Committee, nor at the press conference did he intend to wreck the Cabinet Mission Plan. His ideas on how the Constituent Assembly would function were given in his broadcast on 7 September 1946 after the formation of the Interim Government. In this he said,

'There has been much heated argument about sections and groupings in the Constituent Assembly. We are perfectly prepared to, and have accepted, the position of formation of groups. . . . We do not look upon the Constituent Assembly as an arena for conflict or the forcible imposition of one view-point on another. That would not be the way to build up a contented and united India. We seek agreed and integrated solutions with the largest measure of goodwill behind them. We shall go to the Constituent Assembly with the fixed determination of finding a common basis for agreement on all controversial issues.

'And so, in spite of all that has happened and the hard words that have been said . . . we invite even those who differ from us to enter the Constituent Assembly as equals and partners with us with no binding commitments. It may well be that when we meet and face common tasks, our present difficulties will fade away.'[94]

The meeting of the All India Muslim League Council, which was to withdraw acceptance of the Cabinet Mission Plan, had been called by Nawabzada Liaqat Ali Khan, its General Secretary, *before* Nehru held the press conference in Bombay. The Nawabzada's statement announcing the meeting referred to 'the grave possibility of All-India Muslim League not participating in the Constituent Assembly for lack of assurance that the fundamental principles of the Cabinet Mission Scheme will be adhered to'. The League had been sore at not being invited to form the Interim Government though it had conveyed its acceptance of the Cabinet Mission Plan, while the Congress had not. The Nawabzada charged the Viceroy and Cabinet ministers with breaking their pledge.[95] 'I ask the Muslims', he said, 'to be prepared and ready. We want peace with honour, but if there is to be war, we should accept the challenge.' Nehru's remarks at Bombay were thus not the initial, or even the primary factor in provoking the League to revoke its earlier resolution. As Pethick-Lawrence told an Indian visitor, 'those remarks gave Jinnah the excuse he was looking for to get out of the Constituent Assembly and the Cabinet Mission Plan'.[96]

In the resolution which the All-India Muslim League passed on 29 July, countermanding its acceptance of the Cabinet Mission Plan, it asserted that 'of the two major parties, the Muslim League alone has accepted the statements of 16 and 25 May acceding to the spirit and letter of the proposals embodied therein'. This assertion is not borne out by the very terms of the resolution passed by the League's Council on 6 June 1946. One of the reasons given in this resolution for the acceptance of the Cabinet Mission Plan was that the League saw in it 'the basis and the foundation of Pakistan . . . [which] are inherent in the Mission plan by virtue of the compulsory grouping of six Muslim provinces in sections B and C'. The resolution went on to affirm that the Muslim League agreed 'to co-operate with the constitution-making machinery proposed in the scheme outlined by the Mission in the hope that it would ultimately result in the establishment of [a] complete[ly] sovereign Pakistan'.[97]

Clearly, the League did not consider the Cabinet Mission Plan, with its three-tier structure, as a final compromise between the Congress ideal of a strong and united India and the League objective of two separate sovereign states. On the contrary, the League made no secret of its hopes and plans that the Cabinet Mission Plan would be a stepping-stone to an independent Pakistan. In his speech to the Muslim League Council on 5 June, Jinnah made no secret of his intentions or tactics:

'Let me tell you that Muslim India will not rest content until we have established full, complete and sovereign Pakistan. . . . The Lahore Resolution [of March 1940] did not mean that, when Muslims put forward their demand, it must be accepted at once. . . . It is a big struggle and continued struggle. The first struggle was to get the representative character of the League accepted. That fight they had started and they had won. Acceptance of the Mission's proposal was not the end of their struggle for Pakistan. They should continue their struggle till Pakistan is achieved.'[98]

As for 'groups of provinces', Jinnah told his Council, they 'should have powers on all subjects except defence, communications and foreign affairs. But so far as defence was concerned, it would remain in the hands of the British till the new constitution was enforced. They would fight in the Constituent Assembly to restrict "communications" to what was absolutly necessary for defence only.'[99] The Cabinet Mission Plan was thus to be made a prelude to Pakistan in two ways. In the first place, the 'grouping' of provinces in the east and the west was to be made compulsory, the widest powers were to be conferred on the 'groups', and provincial autonomy was practically to cease to exist. In the second place, the Central Government was to be made as weak and ineffective as possible, by the narrowest interpretation of its functions and by denying it any right for taxation. A Central Government which lived on doles, had no say in trade, industry, communications (except for defence) and was composed of representatives of antagonistic units in its executive and legislature, could scarcely be expected to prevent the secession of the League's groups of provinces in the north-west and east.[100]

A three-tier constitution, such as the Cabinet Mission had outlined, was a delicate mechanism with numerous checks and balances. Unless the two major parties, the Congress and the League, entered the Constituent Assembly with tremendous good-will and determination to co-operate, it was impossible to draft a workable constitution, much less to enforce it. In retrospect, it is clear that the Muslim League's idea of a central government for a sub-continent like India, in the mid-twentieth century was completely out-of-date. A weak central government might endanger the security of the country and its economic growth, but was likely to create the ideal conditions in which units could break off. The Congress, of course, had no intention of letting the League get away with the Pakistan of its own conception, with 'full' six provinces by disguising them as groups of provinces in the first instance. This was the background of the opposition by Gandhi, Nehru, Patel, and indeed the entire Congress leadership, to compulsory grouping of provinces. This opposition could have been softened, if Jinnah had tried to assure the Hindus of Assam and West Bengal, the Congress Muslims of NWFP, and the Sikhs of the Punjab, that grouping of provinces was a voluntary and constructive association of neighbouring provinces for mutual advantage, and that it would not involve coercion of minorities. By failing to give this assurance, Jinnah sealed the fate of the grouping scheme, and thus of the Cabinet Mission Plan: it is true he thus made sure of Pakistan, but it was to be a Pakistan minus East Punjab, West Bengal, and the major portion of Assam.

XIII

After the rejection of the Cabinet Mission Plan by the Muslim League, events moved fast. The Congress Working Committee passed a resolution, reaffirming its acceptance 'in its entirety' of the Cabinet Mission Plan, The Viceroy, who had invited both the parties to join an Interim Government, decided to go ahead with the proposal even though the Muslim League refused to come in. Nehru went to see Jinnah, but the League leader declined to co-operate in the formation of the Interim Government.

The formation of the Interim Government raised the frustration and bitterness of the League to a high pitch. Its leader spoke of 'the Caste Hindu, Fascist Congress and their few individual henchmen of other communities who wanted to be installed in power and authority in the Government of India to dominate and

rule over Mussalmans . . . with the aid of British bayonets'.[101]
The Congress knew what it was to be in the wilderness; that had
been its portion for a quarter of a century. But for the League it
was the first occasion when it was on the wrong side of the
Government.

The resolution withdrawing the League's acceptance of the
Cabinet Mission proposals had included a threat of 'direct action'.
'This day we bid good-bye to constitutional methods', Jinnah had
told the League Council on 29 July, 'Today we have also forged a
pistol and are in a position to use it.'[102] The League declared 16
August as a 'Direct Action Day', and asked Muslims to observe
it all over India. One wonders whether League leaders had thought
out the implications of 'direct action'. This was a technique the
Congress had employed against the Government on a number of
occasions, but in each case it had been under the leadership of
Gandhi for whom *Satyagraha* had been a life-long discipline. No
other Congress leader had ventured to launch a mass movement.
Evidently, League leaders did not realise that 'a direct action
movement' required more than angry feelings and strong words.

It is not necessary here to go into the details of the communal
riots which began at Calcutta on 16 August with the observance
of the 'Direct Action Day', and spread like a chain-reaction from
Calcutta to East Bengal, from East Bengal to Bihar, and from
Bihar to the Punjab. Unfortunately, the League leaders reacted to
the riots with a political rather than a human bias. Even though
a League ministry was in office in Calcutta, Jinnah blamed the
riots on 'Gandhi, the Viceroy and the British'. Each communal
outbreak was cited as a further endorsement of the two-nation
theory, and of the inevitability of the partition of the country.

Shaken by the Calcutta riots, the Viceroy, Lord Wavell,
decided to bring the Muslim League into the Interim Government
where the League members functioned from the outset as an
opposition bloc. As one of them put it: 'We are going into the
Interim Government to get a foothold to fight for our cherished
goal of Pakistan.'[103] This meant disruption of the Interim Government from within. There was hardly an issue of domestic and
foreign policy on which the representatives of the two parties
saw eye to eye. An unfortunate result of this antagonism was that
the civil service was affected by the communal virus.

By March 1947, when Mountbatten replaced Wavell, the
Congress leadership had been sobered by its experience in the
Interim Government as well as by the growing lawlessness in the

country. A *modus vivendi* with the League seemed not remote, but impossible. Partition of India as demanded by the League was bad enough, but even worse possibilities had begun to loom ahead. In the twilight of the British Empire in India, some of the Indian princes were nursing new ambitions. The Political Department of the Government of India was proceeding on the assumption that British paramountcy over the Indian States would lapse with the withdrawal of British power, and each of the rulers of 562 states would be free to decide his future. The princes of western and central India, under the inspiration of some of the larger states, especially Bhopal, were thinking in terms of leagues of princes. It was the intrigue by the ruler of Bastar, a small state in central India with the Nizam of Hyderabad, and the attitude of the Political Department to it, which finally convinced Patel that it was imperative to secure immediate British withdrawal even if it meant acceptance of the partition of India. A similar conclusion was reached by Nehru after the frustrating experience of the working of the Interim Government, where he noticed a 'mental alliance' between British officials and the League members.

It has been suggested that Nehru and Patel agreed to the partition of India because they were avid for power. It is important to recall that the decision in favour of partition was not that of Patel and Nehru alone; it was endorsed by the Working Committee; and in the All India Congress Committee 157 voted for it and only 15 against it. It was a painful decision taken with a heavy heart, but there seemed no alternative to it at that time. The immediate problem, as Nehru saw, it, was 'to arrest the swift drift to anarchy and chaos'.

In retrospect it appears that Congress acceptance of the partition was not such a sudden development as it may have seemed at the time. It was the culmination of a process which had begun immediately after the passage of the Pakistan resolution by the Lahore session of the All India Muslim League. Gandhi had opposed the two-nation theory and the 'vivisection' of India, but he had nevertheless written as early as April 1940:

'I know no non-violent method of compelling the obedience of eight crores of Muslims to the will of the rest of India, however powerful a majority the rest may represent. The Muslims must have the same right of self-determination that the rest of India has. We are at present a joint family. Any member may claim a division.'[104]

This was perhaps an inevitable position for a leader, who was committed to non-violence, but another leader such as Abraham Lincoln could have insisted that there could be no compromise on the unity of country. Two years later, the Congress Working Committee in its resolution on the Cripps proposals affirmed that 'it cannot think in terms of compelling the people of any territorial unit to remain in the Indian Union against their declared and established will'.[105] Under the impact of the League propaganda and the political deadlock with the Government, the Congress position on the question of partition was gradually softening. In 1944, Gandhi in his talks with Jinnah not only accepted the principle of partition, but even discussed the mechanism for the demarcation of boundaries. In 1946 the Congress, after much heart-searching, accepted the Cabinet Mission Plan with its loose three-tier structure, and a central government which was unlikely to have the powers or the resources to maintain the unity of the sub-continent.

The Cabinet Mission Plan proved still-born. The Interim Government revealed the incompatibility of the two major parties. Henceforth, there were only two options: partition of the country as demanded by the League, or a moratorium on political controversy and conflict for a couple of years to allow tempers to cool and to produce the climate in which a compromise solution could be secured. Unfortunately communal rioting unleashed on the land in August 1946 made respite impossible. In April 1947 when the situation looked grim, one man still hoped to build bridges of understanding between the communities. Gandhi toured the villages and towns of Bengal and Bihar, condemning violence irrespective of who perpetrated it, rehabilitating refugees, restoring confidence, and preaching the brotherhood of man. His greatest triumphs in this self-imposed mission lay ahead: in Calcutta in August 1947 and in Delhi in January 1948. But he was convinced that the tension, however serious it might look, was a temporary phase, and that the British had no right to impose partition 'on an India temporarily gone mad'.[106] He suggested to Mountbatten that Jinnah should be invited to form a Muslim League Government; by this supreme gesture the Mahatma hoped to win over the League leader. One wonders whether this proposal was seriously considered by the Viceroy, and whether Nehru, Patel and their colleagues, who had the frustrating experience of the Interim Government, would have liked to hand over all power to the League. Jinnah's reaction to

Gandhi's proposal has not been recorded, but it is doubtful whether it could have been different from what he had said about a similar proposal made by Gandhi in August, 1942.

'If they [the Congress] are sincere I should welcome it. If the British Government accepts the solemn declaration of Mr Gandhi and by an arrangement hands over the government of the country to the Muslim League, I am sure that under Muslim rule non-Muslims would be treated fairly, justly, nay, generously; and further the British will be making full amends to the Muslims by restoring the government of India to them from whom they have taken it.'[107]

The crux of the problem was whether the delay, such as Gandhi envisaged, could have staved off the partition. The political temperature had risen; it did not suit the Muslim League to have it lowered; for the League it was a case of 'now or never'. Gandhi's plea that there should be 'peace before Pakistan' did not impress the League. In fact the League's argument was that there could be no peace until Pakistan was established; that it was either to be a 'divided or destroyed India'. Having declared their resolve to leave India by June 1948, the British Government did not want to and perhaps could not antagonise the Muslim League, or compel it to a particular course of action. Three or four years earlier the British could have exercised a moderating influence on the League; in 1947 the scope for this influence was limited. The sins of Linlithgow were visited on Wavell and Mountbatten.

It is arguable that communal tension or disorder could not have lasted indefinitely. But it is difficult to judge such situations with any degree of confidence when events are moving fast. The mounting tension in 1947 could have touched off a civil war; alternatively it could have been brought to an abrupt end by some unforeseen, and spectacular incident, such as a fast by Gandhi. In the event, Mountbatten's judgement in the summer of 1947 that division of the country was the only practical solution was accepted by the three main parties to the decision: the British Government, the Indian National Congress and the All India Muslim League.

XIV

The final result, the partition of India, was a personal triumph for Jinnah. By arousing deep emotions, by avoiding the details of

M

his demand for Pakistan, and by concentrating on a tirade against Hindu Raj and Congress tyranny, Jinnah was able to sustain a large consensus in his own community. By keeping his cards close to his chest, he was able to keep his following in good order. Such was the magical effect of his insistence on the full six provinces – Pakistan – that large numbers of his adherents in Bengal and the Punjab failed to see the consequences of the division of the country. Even a seasoned politician like Suhrawardy confessed later that he had never expected the partition of Bengal.[108] As for Muslims in the Hindu majority provinces, they had in any case nothing to gain from the secession of provinces in the east and west; the two-nation theory and the theory of hostages were to do them no good at all. Jinnah had played his cards skilfully. From near political eclipse in 1937 he had brought his party to a position where it could decisively influence events. His success was, however, due not only to his skill and tenacity, but to the tension between the Congress and the Government, which prevailed throughout this period, except perhaps for the two years in which the Congress held office in the provinces.

The Government of India Act of 1935 was not the radical measure of constitutional reform it is being made out to be by some historians. It retained the levers of ultimate authority in British hands; the federal structure, with its communal and princely checks and balances, if it had come into being, could have been capable of sustaining British rule for many years. In 1939 the British hierarchy in India may not have had the optimism of earlier generations of the ICS, but the Raj seemed a solid enough structure. Sir S. P. Sinha, an able and patriotic man, the first Indian to be appointed to the Viceroy's Executive Council, had estimated before the First World War that British rule would last 400 years. Twenty-five years later, on the eve of the Second World War, most Britons in India would have confidently predicted a lease of fifty years if not longer for the Raj. It was the aim of the Indian National Congress to wear down the British reluctance to part with power. The antagonism between Indian nationalism and British rule was inherent in the unnatural relation between the two countries. This antagonism helped the Muslim League in two ways: in securing it at crucial moments the support of certain British politicians and civil servants who were embittered with the Congress, and in ensuring to the League almost the exclusive possession of the political stage when the Congress was not only out of office, but outlawed. The brunt of the struggle for liberation of India was borne by the Congress. The Muslim League had no lot or part in this struggle, of which the establishment of Pakistan was a by-product. Others forced open the doors through which Jinnah walked to his goal.

Nehru has been criticised by latter-day writers for estranging the Muslim League and for driving it to extremist policies. Much of this criticism is due to an inadequate appreciation of Nehru's ideas and attitudes and of the political framework within which he and the Congress Party had to function.

Nehru's secularism was not a tactic against the Muslim League, but a deep conviction which he held in his years of office with the same tenacity as in the years of opposition. The 'mass contact movement' was not a conspiracy against the Muslim League, but an integral part of the Congress programme since 1920 for educating the people of all communities in all parts of India on political and economic issues. There were good reasons for stressing mass contact in the late thirties – the electorate had expanded from 2 to 10 per cent of the population, and was bound to increase further if the Congress aim of adult franchise was to be realised. The idea that only the Muslim League had the right to approach Muslim masses was a totalitarian doctrine which made nonsense of democracy and political life, as they were commonly understood.

It has already been indicated that the failure of the coalition talks in the UP in 1937 was in the circumstances of the time almost inevitable: in the face of Jinnah's minatory posture, the Congress could hardly have hamstrung itself in its very first attempt at ministry-making. It was not failure of these talks, but the electoral disaster of 1937, which seems to have driven Jinnah – who had his roots in the Victorian age and was trained as a rationalist and constitutionalist in the school of Dadabhai Naoroji and Gokhale – to use the dynamite of religious emotion for blasting his way to political influence and power. The new strategy brought quick results. The cry of religion in danger, the reiteration of 'Congress tyranny', and the spectre of 'Hindu Raj' roused the Muslims, widened the communal gulf and created the climate in which the proposal for the partition of the country could be mooted.

It is difficult even today to contest the validity of the argument of Nehru and his colleagues, that religion is not a satisfactory basis for nationality in the modern world, that multi-religious, multi-lingual and even multi-racial societies should seek a political solution within the framework of a federal structure. This is what has been done under widely different conditions by the USSR, USA, Canada and South Africa.

No serious attempt at a compromise solution could, however, be made. From 1937 to 1940, Jinnah refused to begin a dialogue with the Congress until it conceded the League's right to be the exclusive representative of the Muslim community. From 1940 onwards, he refused to begin a dialogue until the Congress conceded the principle of the partition of India. He did not elaborate the constitutional, economic and even geographic content of his proposal. While the Congress attitude towards the constitutional future of India underwent important changes between 1939 and 1946, Jinnah did not meet the Congress half-way, not even quarterway. He did not budge an inch from the position he had adopted. Every overture was rejected; every concession treated as a bargaining counter for a better deal. Only once, in June 1946, he seemed to agree to a compromise by accepting the Cabinet Mission Plan; but this acceptance (as already explained in this essay) was more apparent than real; in any case it was withdrawn within seven weeks.

If Jinnah's position had little flexibility, his political style was hardly calculated to assist in a compromise. He heaped ridicule and scorn on all Congress leaders from Gandhi and Nehru downwards. Some critics have suggested that Nehru was on occasions too theoretical, too proud and impatient to deal with Jinnah successfully. It is well to remember that the patience and humility of Gandhi, the cool calculation of Rajagopalachari, the militant radicalism of Subhas Chandra Bose, the sedate realism of Abul Kalam Azad and the gentleness of Rajendra Prasad equally failed to work on the League leader.

Biographical Notes

AGARKAR, GOPAL GANESH, b. 1856; writer and social reformer; first editor of *Kesari;* life-member of Deccan Education Society; principal of Fergusson College 1892–5; editor of *Sudharak;* d. 1895.

ANDREWS, CHARLES FREER, b. 1871; educated at Birmingham and Cambridge; fellow and lecturer at Pembroke College 1899; professor in St Stephen's College, Delhi; taught at Visva-Bharati, Santiniketan 1913; went to South Africa to help Gandhi-Smuts Agreement 1913–14; d. 1940.

ANSARI, MUKHTAR AHMAD, b. 1880; medical practitioner at Delhi; President of the All-India Muslim League 1920, of the Indian National Congress 1927, and of the All-Parties Conference 1928; d. 1936.

APTE, HARI NARAYAN, b. 1864 in Maharashtra; educated in Bombay and Poona; edited the *Karmanuk* from 1890 to 1917; President of Poona Municipality 1915–18; participated in the Congress session in Poona 1895; Marathi novelist of repute; d. 1919.

BANERJEA, SURENDRANATH, b. 1848; entered Indian Civil Service 1871; dismissed from Indian Civil Service 1874; teacher and journalist at Calcutta; President of the Indian National Congress 1895 and 1902; Minister in Bengal Government 1921–3; d. 1925.

BASU, BHUPENDRANATH, b. 1859; attorney of the Calcutta High Court; President of the Indian National Congress 1914; member of the Secretary of State's Council 1917–23; d. 1924.

BHOWNAGGREE, MANCHERJEE MERWANJEE, b. 1851; educated at Elphinstone College, Bombay; elected member of British Parliament from Bethnal Green NE 1895–1906; took part in the agitation against treatment of Indians in South Africa; d. 1933.

BIRDWOOD, GEORGE, b. 1832; educated at University of Edinburgh; established Victoria and Albert Museum and Victoria Gardens, Bombay; Sheriff of Bombay 1864; Royal Commissioner for Indian and Colonial Exhibitions 1886; served India Office, 1971–1902; d. 1917.

BONNERJEE, WOMESH CHUNDER, b. 1844; educated at Calcutta and London; called to bar in 1867; President of the first session of the Indian National Congress in 1885 and also of the session in 1892; member, Bengal Legislative Council, 1894–5; d. 1906.

BOSE, SUBHAS CHANDRA, b. 1897; President of the Indian National

Congress 1938 and 1939; escaped to Germany 1942; formed the Indian National Army 1943; d. 1945.

CHANDAVARKAR, NARAYAN GANESH, b. 1855; educated Elphinstone College; judge of the Bombay High Court 1901; leader of social reform movement; President of the Indian National Congress, 1900; d. 1923.

CHINTAMANI, C. Y., b. 1880; in Visakhapatnam; educated at Madras; plunged into politics; one of the leaders of the Liberal Party; edited the *Leader* 1909–23, 1926–41; Minister of Education and Industries in UP 1921–3; d. 1941.

DAS, CHITTA RANJAN, b. 1870; barrister of the Calcutta High Court; President of the Indian National Congress 1921; formed with Motilal Nehru the Swaraj Party 1922; d. 1925.

DESAI, MAHADEV, b. 1892; educated at Bombay (Elphinstone College and Law College); Secretary to Mahatma Gandhi 1917–42; edited *Harijan* 1935–42; d. 1942.

DEVADHAR, GOPAL KRISHNA, b. 1871; social worker and reformer; President, All-India Social Conference, Lucknow 1929 and Madras 1933; editor *Dnyanprakash;* d. 1935.

DUTT, ROMESH CHUNDER, b. 1848; educated Presidency College, Calcutta, and University College, London; ICS, 1871; divisional Commissioner, 1894; President of Indian National Congress, 1899; d. 1909.

HAMILTON, LORD GEORGE FRANCIS, b. 1845; Under-Secretary for India 1874–80; First Lord of the Admiralty 1885–6 and 1886–92; Secretary of State for India 1895–1903; d. 1927.

HUNTER, WILLIAM WILSON, b. 1840; entered Bengal Civil Service 1861; President, Indian Education Commission 1882; member of Viceroy's Legislative Council 1881–7; d. 1900.

HUQ, A. K. FAZLUL, b. 1873; educated at Calcutta; elected member Bengal Legislative Council 1913–35; Chief Minister, Bengal, 1937–43; founder-leader and President of Krishak Praja Party; migrated to Pakistan 1947; d. 1962.

IRWIN, LORD (Edward Frederick Lindley Wood, 1st Earl of Halifax), b. 1881; educated at Eton, Oxford; entered British Parliament 1910; appointed Viceroy of India 1926 and held this post up to 1931; d. 1959.

IYER, G. SUBRAMANIA, b. 1855; educated at Tanjore; headmaster Anglo-Vernacular School, Triplicane 1879; editor, *Hindu*, 1878–98; helped to start a Tamil newspaper, *Swadesamitran*, 1882; associated with Indian National Congress; d. 1916.

JAYAKAR, MUKUND RAMRAO, b. 1873; barrister of the Bombay High Court; member of the Bombay Legislative Council 1923–5; member of the Indian Legislative Assembly 1926–30; Judge of the Federal Court of India 1937–9; d. 1959.

JINNAH, MUHAMMAD ALI, b. 1876; enrolled in Bombay High Court 1906; opposed Gandhi's non-co-operation movement; President of the Muslim League 1916, 1920 and from 1934 onwards; Governor-General of Pakistan 1947–8; d. 1948.

JOSHI, G. V., b. 1851; educated at Elphinstone College, Bombay; served in Educational Department of Bombay Presidency; vice-principal, Training College, Poona; well informed critic of the economic and fiscal policies of the Government; d. 1911.

JOSHI, N. M., b. 1879; father of the Indian trade union movement; member, Servants of India Society; founder, All India Trade Union Congress; member, Central Pay Commission, 1947; d. 1955.

KHALIQUZZAMAN, CHOUDHRY, b. 1889; educated at Aligarh; a leading Congressman of UP till 1937; then joined All-India Muslim League; migrated to Pakistan; d. 1973.

KUNZRU, HRIDAY NATH, b. 1887; President, Servants of India Society since 1936; member, Indian Constituent Assembly; President, Indian Council of World Affairs.

LOHIA, RAMMANOHAR, b. 1910; educated at Bombay, Banaras and Calcutta; edited *Congress Socialist;* General Secretary, Praja Socialist Party 1954; d. 1967.

MALAVIYA, MADAN MOHAN, b. 1861; UP lawyer and politician; President of the Indian National Congress 1909 and 1918; member of the Imperial Legislative Council 1910–20; Vice-Chancellor of Benaras Hindu University 1919–40; d. 1946.

MEHTA, ASOKA, b. 1911; founder-member of Congress Socialist Party; elected to Lok Sabha 1954 and 1957; Deputy Chairman Planning Commission 1963–6.

MEHTA, PHEROZESHAH, b. 1845; Parsi lawyer and politician; barrister of the Bombay High Court; President of the Indian National Congress 1890; d. 1915.

MINTO, LORD (4th Earl of, Gilbert J. M. K. Elliot), b. 1847; educated at Eton, Trinity College, Cambridge; Governor-General of Canada 1898–1904; Viceroy of India 1905–10; d. 1914.

MONTAGU, EDWIN SAMUEL, b. 1879; Liberal MP, 1906–22; Parliamentary Under-Secretary of State for India, 1910–14; Secretary of State for India, June 1917–March 1922; d. 1924.

184 GOKHALE, GANDHI AND THE NEHRUS

MOONJE, BALKRISHNA SHEORAM, b. 1872; eye-surgeon and medical practitioner, Nagpur; one of the secretaries to the first political conference, Nagpur 1904; member, Central Legislative Assembly; President, Hindu Mahasabha 1927; d. 1948.

MORLEY, JOHN, b. 1838; statesman and man of letters; Chief Secretary for Ireland 1886 and 1892–5; Secretary of State for India 1905–10; d. 1923.

NAIDU, SAROJINI, b. 1879; poetess and politician; President of the Indian National Congress 1925; Governor of the United Provinces 1947–9; d. 1949.

NAMBOODIRIPAD, E. M. S., b. 1909; educated at St Thomas College, Trichur; gave up his studies while studying for the BA and joined the Congress Socialist Party and later the Communist Party of India; Chief Minister of Kerala 1957–9.

NAOROJI, DADABHAI, b. 1825; one of the eminent leaders of Indian opinion in the nineteenth century; first Indian Member of British Parliament 1892–5; President of the Indian National Congress 1886, 1893 and 1906; d. 1917.

NARYAN, JAYAPRAKASH, b. 1902; Sarvodaya leader; educated in Bihar and USA; founder-secretary, Congress Socialist Party.

NARENDRA DEVA, b. 1889; educated at Allahabad and Benaras; a staunch nationalist from his student days, he attended every session of Indian National Congress during 1918–48; participated in Gandhi's movements; sentenced to imprisonment several times; founder of Congress Socialist Party 1934; d. 1956

PAL, BIPIN CHANDRA, b. 1858; Bengali journalist and politician; imprisoned for sedition, 1911; d. 1932.

PARANJPYE, RAGHUNATH PURUSHOTTAM, b. 1876; life-member of Deccan Education Society; first Indian to become Senior Wrangler in Cambridge; Principal, Fergusson College, Poona; Minister of Education; Bombay Presidency 1921–4; d. 1966.

PATEL, VALLABHBHAI, b. 1875 at Nadiad, Kaira, of Patidar family; brother of Vithalbhai Patel; Gujarati lawyer, municipal councillor and politician; joined Gandhi in Kaira *satyagraha* and rose to be leading Congress organiser, politician and Deputy Prime Minister of India; d. 1950.

PATWARDHAN, ACHYUT, b. 1905; educated at Banaras Hindu University; founder-member of the Congress Socialist Party; participated actively in the underground movement during the Second World War.

PRASAD, RAJENDRA, b. 1884; lawyer and politician; President of Indian

National Congress 1934, 1939; President of Indian Republic; d. 1963.

RANADE, MAHADEV GOVIND, b. 1842; Judge of the Bombay High Court 1893–1901; economist, social reformer and writer; founder of the Indian National Social Conference; d. 1901.

RANGA, N. G., b. 1900; one of the leaders of the peasant movement in India during the 1930s; became leader of Swatantra Party in the Indian Parliament.

ROY, M. N., b. 1893; founder-member of Communist Party of India in 1920 at Tashkent; doyen of Indian Communism; founder of Radical Democratic Party 1940; d. 1954.

ROY, RAMMOHUN, b. 1772; eminent Bengali reformer and educationalist; one of the founders of Hindu College and founder of Brahmo Samaj 1828; d. 1833.

SAMPURNANAND, b. 1891; educated at Allahabad; thrice secretary to United Provinces Congress Committee; Chief Minister, Uttar Pradesh 1955–60; Governor of Rajasthan 1962–7; d. 1969.

SANDHURST, WILLIAM MANSFIELD, b. 1855; educated at Rugby; Governor of Bombay 1895–9; d. 1921.

SAPRU, TEJ BAHADUR, b. 1875; advocate of the Allahabad High Court; Law Member of Viceroy's Council 1920–3; President of the National Liberal Federation of India 1923 and 1927; d. 1949.

SASTRI, V. S. SRINIVASA, b. 1869; President of the Servants of India Society 1915–27; President of the National Liberal Federation of India 1922; Agent of the Government of India in South Africa 1927–9; d. 1946.

SEN, KESHUB CHUNDER, b. 1838; leader of religious reform movement in Bengal; exponent of Brahmo Samaj; d. 1884.

SRI PRAKASA, b. 1890; educated at Allahabad; Cambridge; Bar-at-Law 1914; General Secretary, UP Congress Committee 1922–34; Minister in the Nehru Cabinet 1950–2; d. 1971.

TAGORE, RABINDRANATH, b. 1861; poet and philosopher; awarded Nobel prize for literature 1913; sought synthesis of Eastern and Western cultures by founding at Santiniketan an international university called Visva-Bharati 1921; d. 1914.

THAKKAR, A. V., b. 1869; graduated from Engineering College at Poona; served in various departments of Government and public bodies as an engineer; joined the Servants of India Society in 1914; Secretary of

All India Harijan Sewak Sangh, 1932–50; started All India Adimjati Sevak Sangh; Member of Constituent Assembly; d. 1951.

TILAK, BAL GANGADHAR, b. 1856; teacher, journalist and politician of Poona; helped to found *Kesari* and *Mahratta;* eminent nationalist leader; gaoled for sedition 1897–8 and 1908–14; rejoined the Congress, having been excluded by the Moderates, 1916; d. 1920.

VIVEKANANDA (NARENDRANATH DATTA), b. 1863; disciple of Ramakrishna and founder of Ramakrishna order; represented Hinduism at the World's Parliament of Religions in 1893 at Chicago; d. 1902.

WACHA, DINSHAW EDULJI, b. 1844; Bombay politician, journalist; President of the Congress 1901; d. 1936.

WEDDERBURN, WILLIAM, b. 1838; entered Indian Civil Service 1860; Judge of the Bombay High Court 1885; officiating Chief Secretary to the Government of Bombay 1886–7; retired 1887; Member of Parliament 1893–1900; Chairman of the Indian Parliamentary Committee; President of the Indian National Congress 1889 and 1910; d. 1918.

WILLINGDON (1st Marquess of), b. 1866; Liberal MP, 1900–10; Governor of Bombay, 1913–18; Viceroy of India, 1931–6; d. 1941.

References

CHAPTER 1

1. *Speeches and Writings of Sarojini Naidu* (Madras, First Edition, 1918), p. 33.
2. Curzon to George Hamilton, 25 March 1903, Curzon Papers.
3. Curzon to Gokhale, 31 December 1903, Curzon Papers.
4. Minto to Morley, 22 August 1906, Morley Papers.
5. M. K. Gandhi, *An Autobiography or My Experiments with Truth* (Ahmedabad, 1945), p. 286.
6. D. G. Karve and D. V. Ambekar, *Speeches and Writings of Gopal Krishna Gokhale* (Bombay, 1966), vol. 2, p. 217.
7. Quoted in John S. Hoyland, *Gopal Krishna Gokhale* (Calcutta, 1947), p. 131.
8. *Speeches and Writings of Sarojini Naidu*, p. 39.

CHAPTER 2

1. W. K. Caine (1842–1903) temperance reformer and Liberal MP. Attended Indian National Congress as a delegate in 1890. Visited Poona in 1897.
2. R. P. Masani, *Dadabhai Naoroji* (London, 1939), pp. 379–80.
3. Viceroy to Secretary of State, 30 June 1896, Hamilton Papers.
4. K. Subba Rao, *Revived Memories* (Madras, 1933), p. 253.
5. B. M. Bhatia, *Famines in India* (Bombay, 1963), p. 239.
6. D. D. Karve (ed.), *The New Brahmans* (Berkeley, 1963), p. 141.
7. Hamilton to Elgin, 21 January 1897, Hamilton Papers.
8. Elgin wrote to Hamilton on 7 April 1897: 'I am sorry to hear that Dr Lowson was not satisfied with the measures taken at Bombay to stamp out the plague . . . I venture to say that he was rash in assuming that the advisers of the Governor were "unduly afraid of exciting caste or religious prejudice". It is true that our Home Department were inclined to think that the risk must be run, and we urged the Bombay Government to take a stronger line . . .' Elgin to Hamilton, 7 April 1897, Hamilton Papers.
9. *Kesari*, 30 March 1897.
10. *Dnyan Prakash*, 19 April 1897 (Native Newspapers, Bombay, 1897).
11. *ibid.*, 22 April 1897.
12. H. N. Apte to Gokhale, 27 May 1897, Gokhale Papers.
13. Letter dated 18 May 1897 to the editor, *Guardian* reproduced in *India*, August 1897.
14. *India*, August 1897.
15. Secretary of State to Governor of Bombay, 23 June 1897, Hamilton Papers.
16. Secretary of State to Viceroy, 3 July 1897, Hamilton Papers
17. Elgin to Hamilton, 17 August 1897, Hamilton Papers
18. Station Staff Officer Datta Khel to Military Simla, 10 June 1897, Elgin Papers.
19. Elgin to A Mackenzie, Lt Governor of Bengal, 17 June 1897, Elgin Papers.

188 GOKHALE, GANDHI AND THE NEHRUS

20. Elgin to Hamilton, 6 July 1897, Hamilton Papers.
21. Sandhurst to Elgin, 25 June 1897, Elgin Papers.
22. Governor of Bombay to Secretary of State, 4 July 1897, Hamilton Papers.
23. *The Times*, 17 July 1897.
24. This opinion was later expressed by G. Subramania Iyer, editor of *The Hindu*, who had also appeared before the Welby Commission 'I cannot but think that on the whole we have received a heavy blow.' Subramania Iyer to Gokhale, 21 September 1897, Gokhale Papers.
25. D. E. Wacha: *Reminiscences of the late Hon. Mr G. K. Gokhale* (Bombay, 1915), p. 45.
26. On 28 July 1897.
27. Gokhale's letter to the *Times of India*, 8 January 1898.
28. Indian Parliamentary Debates, 1897.
29. To Motilal Ghose in P. Dutt, *Memories of Motilal Ghose* (Calcutta, 1935), p. 98.
30. W. S. Caine to Gokhale, 29 October 1897, Gokhale Papers.
31. Dadabhai Naoroji to Gokhale, 27 August 1897, Gokhale Papers.
32. A. O. Hume to Gokhale, 24 August 1897, Gokhale Papers.
33. A. O. Hume to Gokhale, 24 August 1897, Gokhale Papers.
34. Wedderburn to Gokhale, 24 August 1897, Gokhale Papers.
35. Secretaries of the Bombay Presidency Association to Gokhale, 2 August 1897, Gokhale Papers.
36. Gokhale to G. V. Joshi, 9 December 1897, Gokhale Papers.
37. *Times of India*, 8 January 1898; also *Indian Social Reformer*, 16 January 1898.
38. 'By the way, is it true', wrote V. V. Khatidarkar to Gokhale on 24 August 1897, 'that students of your own college treat you with hisses?' Gokhale Papers.
39. Gokhale to G. V. Joshi, 8 February 1898, Gokhale Papers.
40. W. S. Caine to Gokhale, 29 October 1897, Gokhale Papers.
41. Gokhale to A. K. Ghosh, 15 January 1898, Gokhale Papers.
42. Gokhale Papers; also reproduced in V. S. Srinivasa Sastri: *Gopal Krishna Gokhale* (Bangalore, 1937), pp. 32–3.
43. Gokhale to Pherozeshah Mehta, 15 January 1901, Gokhale Papers.
44. To serve for twenty years as a life member of the Deccan Education Society.

CHAPTER 3

1. G. S. Sardesai, 'The Pilgrimage of My Life' in D. D. Karve and Ellen E. McDonald (eds), *The New Brahmins, Five Maharashtrian Families* (Berkeley, 1963), p. 118.
2. Bipin Chandra Pal, *Memories of My Life and Times* (Calcutta, 1932), p. 331.
3. A. Waley Cohen (ed.) *H. M. Kisch, A Young Victorian in India* (London, 1959), pp. 118–9.
4. 6 June 1897.
5. April 1895, p. 5.
6. Minute 'On the Age of Consent' by Lord Lansdowne, 5 September 1890, circulated to Members of the Executive Council, Lansdowne Papers.

7. Mrs Ramabai Ranade (ed.), *The Miscellaneous Writings of the late Honble Mr Justice M. G. Ranade* (Bombay, 1915), pp. 231–2.
8. *ibid.*, p. 234.
9. *ibid.*, p. 236.
10. *Speeches of Gopal Krishna Gokhale* (Madras, 1920), pp. 880–1.
11. *ibid.*, p. 882.
12. *ibid.*, p. 883.
13. *ibid.*, pp. 471–2.
14. *ibid.*, p. 898.
15. R P. Paranjpye, *Gopal Krishna Gokhale* (Poona, 1916), p. 28.
16. D. E. Wacha, *Reminiscences of the Late Hon. Mr G. K. Gokhale* (Bombay, 1915), p. 21.
17. Ranade to Gokhale, 3 January 1901, Gokhale Papers.

CHAPTER 4

1. B. R. Nanda, *The Nehrus* (London, 1962), p. 39.
2. *ibid.*, p. 122.
3. *ibid.*, p. 60.
4. *ibid.*, p. 61.
5. *Congress Presidential Address*, Second Series (Madras 1935), p. 865.
6. *Tribune*, 30 December 1928.

CHAPTER 5

1. Chandrashanker Shukla (ed.), *Incidents of Gandhiji's Life* (Bombay, 1949), p. 118.
2. Edwin S. Montagu, *An Indian Diary* (London, 1930), p. 58.
3. S. C. Bose, *Indian Struggle* (Bombay, 1964), p. 74.
4. G. I. Patel, *Vithalbhai Patel* (Bombay, 1950), p. 1219.
5. *Harijan*, 11 January 1936.
6. *ibid.*, 14 October 1939.
7. R. Coupland, *Indian Politics 1936–1942* (London, 1944), p. 295.
8. The notification prohibiting the import of the book was issued by the Government of India (Department of Commerce and Industry) on 30 July 1910. In the Home Department, a senior official noted: 'It is in my opinion a most pernicious publication'. Home Department Political A, 1910 Proceedings 96–103.
9. *Young India*, 26 January 1921.
10. See 'Gandhi the Man', by Rabindranath Tagore reproduced in *Visva-Bharati Quarterly* (Gandhi Number), vol. 35, p. 32.
11. *The Diary of Mahadev Desari*, vol. 1 (Ahmedabad, 1953), p. 321.
12. *Harijan*, 24 February 1946.
13. *ibid.*, 24 December 1938.
14. *ibid.*, 15 October 1938.
15. *ibid.*, 29 September 1946.
16. Quoted by E. Stanley Jones, *Mahatma Gandhi* (London, 1948), p. 164.

CHAPTER 6

1. Subhas Bose to Nehru, 4 March 1936, Nehru Papers in Nehru Memorial Museum and Library, New Delhi.

2. J. P. Narayan to Nehru, 20 July 1940, Nehru Papers.
3. Percival Spear, 'Nehru' in *Modern Asian Studies* I (January 1967), p. 18.
4. M. N. Roy, 'Jawaharlal Nehru: An Enigma or a Tragedy' in A. B. Shah (ed.) *Jawaharlal Nehru, A Critical Tribute*, (Bombay, 1965), p. 39.
5. Hiren Mukerjee, *The Gentle Colossus: A Study of Jawaharlal Nehru* Calcutta, 1964), pp. 71–5.
6. B. R. Nanda, *The Nehrus*, p. 23.
7. Tibor Mende, *Conversations with Mr Nehru* (London, 1956), p. 23.
8. *ibid.*, pp. 24–31.
9. J. Nehru to G. A. Lambert, Chief Secretary, Government of UP, 4 July 1921, Nehru Papers.
10. J. Nehru, *An Autobiography* (London, 1942), p. 77.
11. *ibid.*, p. 81.
12. *ibid.*, p. 86.
13. Gandhi to J. Nehru, 4 January 1928, Nehru Papers.
14. Gandhi to Motilal, 3 March 1928, Nehru Papers.
15. Pyarelal, 'Gandhi-Nehru, A Unique Relationship' in *Link*, New Delhi, 30 May 1965.
16. Nehru, *An Autobiography*, p. 194.
17. Quoted by D. G. Tendulkar, *The Mahatma* (Bombay, 1952), vol. 3, p. 31.
18. Gandhi told Lord Irwin (Halifax) that Jawaharlal had wept on his shoulder, 'over this tragedy of the betrayal of India'. See *Talking of Gandhi*, Francis Watson (ed.) (Bombay, 1957), p. 63.
19. Nehru, *An Autobiography*, pp. 257–9.
20. *ibid.*, pp. 129–30.
21. *ibid.*, pp. 370–1.
22. *ibid.*, p. 490.
23. J. Nehru to Gandhi, 13 August 1934, Nehru Papers.
24. Nehru, *An Autobiography*, p. 403.
25. J. Nehru to Colonel J. C. Wedgewood, 23 April 1941, Nehru Papers.
26. Nehru, *An Autobiography*, p. 547.
27. *ibid.*, p. 544.
28. *ibid.*, p. 525.
29. Quoted in *Indian Annual Register*, 1933, vol. 2, p. 358.
30. According to J. B. Kripalani, but for the powerful backing of Gandhi, the resolution had little chance of being accepted by the Congress leadership at that time. J. B. Kripalani, *Indian National Congress* (Bombay, 1946), p. 12.
31. Narendra Deva to J. Nehru, 9 February 1929, Nehru Papers.
32. J. P. Narayan, *Why Socialism?* (Benares, 1936), p. 84.
33. Hari Kishore Singh, *A History of Praja Socialist Party* (Lucknow, 1959), p. 42.
34. Narendra Deva, *Socialism and the National Revolution* (Bombay, 1946), p. 28.
35. Sampurnananda, *Memories and Reflections* (Bombay, 1962), p. 77.
36. Telegram, Government of India to the Secretary of State for India, 24 October 1933. Home Political Confidential F. 31 of 1933. National Archives of India.
37. Quoted by Shanti S. Gupta in *The Economic Philosophy of Mahatma Gandhi* (Delhi, n.d.), p. 136.

38. *Indian Annual Register*, 1936, vol. 2, p. 238.
39. Nehru, *An Autobiography*, p. 515.
40. J. Nehru to Sri Prakasa, 3 May 1936, Nehru Papers.
41. J. Nehru to Syed Mahmud, 5 May 1936, Nehru Papers.
42. *Indian Annual Register*, 1936, vol. 2, p. 285.
43. Gandhi to Jawaharlal, 15 July 1936, Nehru Papers.
44. *ibid.*, 8 July 1936.
45. *News Chronicle*, 12 November 1936.
46. J. Nehru to Subhas Bose, 4 February 1939, Nehru Papers.
47. *ibid.*, 3 April 1939.
48. Gandhi to Jawaharlal, 15 July 1936, Nehru Papers.
49. Mukerjee, *The Gentle Colossus*, p. 71.
50. E. M. S. Namboodiripad, *The Mahatma and the Ism* (New Delhi, 1958), p. 74.
51. Gandhi to Jawaharlal, 5 April 1937, Nehru Papers.
52. *ibid.*, 25 April 1938, Nehru Papers.
53. *ibid.*, 30 April 1938, Nehru Papers.
54. On 30 July 1937 Gandhi sent Jawaharlal extracts from a speech of Yusuf Meherally with the remark, '[it] is an eye-opener for me. I wonder how far it represents the general socialist view. . . . I call it a bad speech of which you should take note. This is going contrary to Congress policy.' Nehru Papers.
55. Rafi Ahmed Kidwai to J. Nehru (undated), Nehru Papers.
56. Narendra Deva to J. Nehru, 10 December 1937, Nehru Papers.
57. J. P. Narayan to J. Nehru 23 November 1938, Nehru Papers.
58. Gandhi to Jawaharlal, 11 August 1939, Nehru Papers.
59. J. Nehru to Gandhi, 28 April 1938, Nehru Papers.
60. Gandhi to Jawaharlal, 26 October 1939, Nehru Papers.
61. J. Nehru to Subhas Bose, 4 February 1939, Nehru Papers.
62. J. Nehru, *Discovery of India* (Calcutta, 1946), p. 536.
63. Abul Kalam Azad, *India Wins Freedom* (Bombay, 1959), p. 65.
64. Quoted by Michael Brecher in *Nehru: A Political Biography* (London, 1959), p. 286.
65. Nehru, *Discovery of India*, pp. 576–7.
66. *ibid.*, p. 576.
67. *Dawn*, 28 June 1942.
68. Brecher, *Nehru: A Political Biography*, p. 379.
69. Congress Bulletin No. 4, 10 July 1947, p. 9.
70. Ram Manohar Lonia gives an account of the Working Committee meeting in his *Guilty Men of the Partition* (Allahabad, 1960), p. 9.
71. Pyarelal, *The Last Phase* (Ahmedabad, 1958), vol. 2, p. 251.
72. Quoted in Pyarelal, 'Gandhi-Nehru', p. 32.
73. Mukerjee, *The Gentle Colossus*, p. 31.
74. *Young India*, 3 October 1929.
75. Gandhi to Agatha Harrison, 30 April 1936, Nehru Papers.
76. Gandhi to Jawaharlal Nehru, 17 January 1928, Nehru Papers.
77. *ibid.*, 4 November 1929, Nehru Papers.
78. Quoted in Pyarelal, *Towards New Horizons* (Ahmedabad, 1959), p. 5.
79. Nehru, *An Autobiography*, p. 511.
80. N. K. Bose and P. H Patwardhan in *Gandhi in Indian Politics* (Bombay, 1967), p. 85.

192 GOKHALE, GANDHI AND THE NEHRUS

81. M. Chalapathi Rau *Gandhi and Nehru* (Bombay, 1967), p. 102.
82. Bose and Patwardhan, *Gandhi in Indian Politics*, p. 85.
83. *Statesman*, 1 December 1958.
84. Quoted in Shriman Narayan, *Letters from Gandhi, Nehru, Vinoba* (Bombay, 1968), p. 10.
85. Foreword by Nehru to Narayan, *Letters*.

CHAPTER 7

1. Irene Collins, 'Liberalism in Nineteenth-Century Europe', in W. N. Medlicott (ed.), *From Metternich to Hitler: Aspects of British and Foreign History*, 1814–1939 (London, 1963), p. 25.
2. *Times of India*, 9 September 1918.
3. *Young India*, 24 November 1921.
4. Muzaffar Ahmed, *Communist Party of India: Years of Formation*, 1921–1933 (Calcutta, 1959), p. 5.
5. X. J. Eudin and R. C. North, *Soviet Russia and the East, 1920–7* (Stanford, 1957) pp. 181–3.
6. Ahmed, *Communist Party of India*, p. 8.
7. L. Shapiro (ed.) *Soviet Treaty Series*, vol. 1, 1927–8 (Washington, 1950), p. 102.
8. Trotsky had suggested that the revolutionary road might lead to Paris and London through Kabul, Calcutta and Bombay. See I. Deutscher, *The Prophet Armed-Trotsky: 1879–1921* (London, 1954), pp. 456–7.
9. Gene D. Overstreet and Marshall Windmiller, *Communism in India* (Berkeley, 1959), pp. 44–5.
10. *Congress Presidential Address: From the Silver to the Golden Jubilee* (Madras, G. A. Natesan, 1934), p. 572.
11. Jane Degras (ed.), *The Communist International*, vol. 2, 1923–8 (London, 1965), p. 544.
12. Muzaffar Ahmed (introduction), *Communists Challenge Imperialism from the Dock*, pp. 176–7, 236 and 268–9.
13. *M. N. Roy's Memoirs* (Bombay, 1964) p. 543.
14. This was how it was described by the accused in the Meerut Conspiracy Case. See Ahmed, *Communists Challenge*, p. 86.
15. B. R. Nanda, *The Nehrus*, p. 202.
16. *ibid.*, p. 96.
17. *Congress Presidential Addresses*, p. 894.
18. J. Nehru, *An Autobiography* (Bombay, 1962), p. 659.
19. Acharya Narendra Deva, *Socialism and the National Revolution* (Bombay, 1946), p. 28.
20. Hari Kishore Singh, *A History of the Praja Socialist Party: 1934–59* (Lucknow, 1959), p. 42.
21. Sampurnanand, *Memories and Reflections* (Bombay, 1962), p. 81.
22. D. G. Tendulkar, *Mahatma: Life of Mohandas Karamchand Gandhi* (Delhi, 1952), vol. 3, p. 363.
23. Subhas Chandra Bose to J. Nehru, 4 March 1936, Nehru Papers.
24. M. K. Gandhi to J. Nehru, 26 October 1939, Nehru Papers.
25. Jayaprakash Narayan, *Socialism to Sarvodaya* (Calcutta, 1958), p. 11.
26. M. R. Masani, *The Communist Party of India* (London, 1954), p. 71.

CHAPTER 8

1. Jawaharlal to Motilal, 18 August 1911, Nehru Papers.
2. J. Nehru, *An Autobiography* (London, 1936), p. 77.
3. Motilal to Jawaharlal, 26 February 1920, Nehru Papers.
4. Jawaharlal to Motilal, 1 September 1922, Nehru Papers.
5. J. Nehru, *Soviet Russia* (Allahabad, 1928), p. vii.
6. J. Nehru, Foreword to *Letters from a Father to His Daughter* (Allahabad, 1931), first published in 1929 (Allahabad).
7. J. Nehru, *Glimpses of World History* (Allahabad, 1935), vol. 2, p. 1499.
8. J. H. Horrabin to J. Nehru, 29 December 1955, Nehru Papers.
9. *Saturday Review*, 20 June 1964.
10. *Leader*, 10 June 1936.
11. *Mahratta*, 28 June 1936.
12. *The Sunday Times*, 10 May 1936.
13. *The Listener*, 27 May 1936.
14. *Spectator*, 15 May 1936.
15. *The Economist*, 11 July 1936.
16. C. F. Andrews to J. Nehru, 6 November 1935, Nehru Papers.
17. J. Nehru, *India and the World* (London, 1936).
18. J. Nehru, *Recent Essays and Writings* (Allahabad, 1934); *Eighteen Months in India* (Allahabad, 1938); *China, Spain and War* (Allahabad, 1940); *The Unity of India* (London, 1941).
19. P. E. Dustoor's article in P. D. Tandon (ed.), *Nehru Your Neighbour* (Calcutta, 1946), p. 62.
20. A. J. P. Taylor *et al.* (eds.), *Churchill: Four Faces and the Man* (London, 1969), p. 137.
21. Thomas Jones, *A Diary with Letters*, 1930–1950 (Oxford, 1954), p. 177.

CHAPTER 9

1. J. Nehru, *An Autobiography* (London, 1936), p. 544.
2. *ibid.*, p. 544.
3. J. Nehru, *India and the World* (London 1936), p. 86.
4. *ibid.*, p. 86.
5. *ibid.*, pp. 91–2.
6. For details, see B. R. Nanda, *Mahatma Gandhi* (London 1958), pp. 332–44.
7. J. Nehru to Lord Lothian, 9 December 1935, Nehru Papers.
8. *Congress Presidential Addresses*, 1911–34 (Madras, 1934), second series p. 893.
9. J. Nehru to Lord Lothian, 17 January 1936, Nehru Papers.
10. Rafiq Zakaria (ed.), *A Study of Nehru* (Bombay, 1959), article by N. B. Khare, p. 215.
11. Nehru, *An Autobiography*, p. 470.
12. J. Nehru to Lord Lothian, 17 January 1936, Nehru Papers.
13. Nehru, *An Autobiography*, p. 137.
14. C. Khaliquzzaman, *Pathway to Pakistan* (Lahore, 1961), p. 153.
15. UP Government Fortnightly Report on the Political Situation for the first half of December 1936, Government of India Home Department File 18 December 1936 Poll.

N

16. Circular No. K-70/C.W. 886/34 dated 9 July 1936 from Secretary, Court of Wards, UP Allahabad to all district officers in the UP, except Kumaun, Nehru Papers.
17. The Hindu Mahasabha did not win a single seat in the UP Legislative Assembly.
18. UP Government Fortnightly Report on the Political Situation for the first half of September 1936, Government of India Home Department File 18 September 1936 Poll.
19. Khaliquzzaman, *Pathway to Pakistan*, p. 141.
20. As suggested in Abul Kalam Azad's *India Wins Freedom* (Calcutta, 1959), p. 161.
21. Ramnarayan Chaudhary, *Nehru in His Own Words* (Ahmedabad, 1964), p. 87.
22. Sajjad Zaheer, a young left-wing Congress Muslim in 1937, has recorded that he pleaded with Abul Kalam Azad 'against any kind of compromise with the Muslim League, which in our view was a reactionary organisation . . . ridden as it was at the time with jaded Muslim landlords and Nawabs . . .' Quoted from 'Notes on Hindu-Muslim Unity', *Mainstream*, 17 June 1967.
23. *Leader*, 28 April 1937.
24. *ibid.*, 6 May 1937.
25. *ibid.*, 6 May 1937.
26. *ibid.*, 9–10 May 1937.
27. Interview with the writer, 18 October 1966, Oral History, Nehru Memorial Museum and Library.
28. Total strength of the UP Legislative Assembly was 228, as shown below:

General (including 20 seats reserved for Scheduled Castes and 4 for women)	144
Muhammadans	66
Anglo-Indians	1
Europeans	2
Indian Christians	2
Commerce	3
Landholders	6
University	1
Labour	3
	228

The state of parties in the UP Legislative Assembly in 1937 was as follows:

Congress	134
National Agriculturist Party	29
Hindu Sabha	0
Muslim League	26
Liberal	1
Independent Hindus	8
Independent Muslims	24
Independent Christians	2
Europeans and Anglo-Indians	4
	228

29. Notes in the Home Department, Government of India File 4 October 1937 Poll, National Archives of India.
30. *Star of India*, 31 December 1938.
31. Press statement, Allahabad, 30 June 1937, *Tribune*, 2 July, 1937.
32. Khaliquzzaman, *Pathway to Pakistan*, p. 175.
33. Jamil-ud-din Ahmad, *Some Recent Speeches and Writings of Mr Jinnah* (Lahore, 1946), p. 30.
34. *ibid.*, p. 40.
35. Dr Mahmudullah Jung in the *Pioneer*, 7 November 1937.
36. Jamil-ud-Din Ahmad, *Some Recent Speeches*, p. 25.
37. *ibid.*, p. 122.
38. *ibid.*, p. 225.
39. *ibid.*, p. 154.
40. *ibid.*, p. 426.
41. *ibid.*, p. 567.
42. *Hindustan Times*, 4 October 1947.
43. *Star of India*, 15 October 1938.
44. S. Wazir Hasan to J. Nehru, 11 February 1938, Nehru Papers.
45. J. Nehru to Nawab Mohammad Ismail Khan, 4 and 5 February 1938, Nehru Papers.
46. R. Coupland, *Indian Politics*, 1936–1942 (Madras, 1944), p. 187.
47. 'In 1938, of the members of the ICS serving in the Provinces, 490 were British and 529 were Indians', R. Coupland, *Indian Politics*, 1936–1942, pp. 118–9.
48. Of the eight Inspectors-General of Police who attended the Home Ministers' Conference in May 1939, only one was Indian.
49. The Viceroy, in a White Paper, stated in October 1939 that the Congress ministers had conducted their affairs 'with great success'. For details see Cmd Paper 6121.
    Compliments to the Congress ministers' administrative ability and general impartiality were paid by Sir Harry Haig, Governor of the United Provinces 1934–9, in an article entitled 'The United Provinces and the New Constitution', in the *Asiatic Review* (July 1940); and by Lord Erskine, Governor of Madras, in an article entitled 'Madras and the New Constitution' in *Asiatic Review* (January 1941).
50 J. Nehru to Sir Sikandar Hyat Khan, 4 January 1939, Nehru Papers.
51.. Rajendra Prasad, *India Divided* (Bombay, 1946), p. 155.
52. V. P. Menon, *Transfer of Power* (Calcutta, 1957), p. 60.
53. Lord Linlithgow to Lord Zetland, 28 December 1939, quoted in Zetland, *Essayez* (London, 1956), p. 277.
54. See R. J. Moore's paper 'British Policy and the Indian Problem 1936–40', in C. H. Phillips and M. D. Wainwright (eds), *The Partition of India* (London, 1970), pp. 79–94.
55. Gwyer and Appadorai, *Speeches and Documents on the Indian Constitution* (London, 1957), vol. 2, p. 492.
56. Report from the UP Government to the Government of India, 5 January 1940, Government of India, Home Department File 18 December 1939 Poll, National Archives of India.
57. Jamil-ud-Din Ahmad, *Some Recent Speeches*, p. 126.
58. *ibid.*, p. 36.
59. *The Hindu*, 27 March 1940.

N*

60. *The Hindu*, 8 April 1940.
61. *The Tribune*, 11 September 1940.
62. *The Hindu*, 17 April 1940.
63. *The Tribune*, 29 March 1940.
64. *The Hindu*, 4 April 1940.
65. *Manchester Guardian*, 2 April 1940.
66. A Yusuf Ali, Sir Muhammad Zafrullah Khan and Dr Shuja-ud-Din cited in Rajendra Prasad, *India Divided*, p. 207.
67. Khaliquzzaman, *Pathway to Pakistan*, p. 211.
68. *ibid.*, p. 234.
69. *Dawn*, 23 March 1946, and Jamil-ud-Din Ajmad, *Some Recent Speeches*, p. 443.
70. B. R. Nanda, *Mahatma Gandhi* (London, 1958), p. 440.
71. Hugh Tinker, *Experiment with Freedom* (London, 1967), p. 24.
72. Khaliquzzaman, *Pathway to Pakistan*, p. 257.
73. Gwyer and Appadorai, *Speeches and Documents*, vol. 2, p. 522.
74. Jamil-ud-Din Ahmad, *Some Recent Speeches*, pp. 418–20.
75. *ibid.*, p. 423.
76. C. Khaliquzzaman, *Pathway to Pakistan*, p. 288.
77. Nazir Yar Jung (ed.), *The Pakistan Issue* (Lahore, 1943), p. 125.
78. *ibid.*, pp. 137–8.
79. J. B. Kripalani, 'League and War Effort' in *National Herald*, 5 October 1941.
80. Tinker, *Experiment*, p. 30.
81. V. P. Menon records that in February 1940, Jinnah in the course of an interview with Lord Linlithgow sought the support of the Governor Sir George Cunningham in teaching 'a salutary lesson to the Congress' by forming a League ministry in the NWFP, the Congress ministry having resigned a few months earlier. See V. P. Menon, *Transfer of Power*, p. 78.
82. Khaliquzzaman, *Pathway to Pakistan*, p. 333.
83. Gwyer and Appadorai, *Speeches and Documents*, vol. 2, p. 566.
84. *Dawn*, 26 March 1946.
85. *The Indian Annual Register*, Jan.–June 1946, p. 197. See also *Dawn*, 26 March and 8 April 1946.
86. *ibid.*, p. 196, see also *Dawn* 11 April 1946.
87. Khaliquzzaman, *Pathway to Pakistan*, pp. 425–7.
88. Michael Brecher, *Nehru: A Political Biography* (London, 1959), p. 317.
89. *Bombay Chronicle*, 8 July 1946.
90. *ibid.*
91. *ibid.*
92. *Bombay Chronicle*, 11 July 1946.
93. *ibid.*
94. Dorothy Norman, *Nehru: The First Sixty Years*, vol. 2 (Bombay, 1965), p. 251.
95. *Statesman*, 1 July 1946.
96. Sudhir Ghosh, *Gandhi's Emissary* (London, 1967), p. 180.
97. Gwyer and Appadorai, *Speeches and Documents*, vol. 2, p. 601.
98. *The Indian Annual Register*, Jan.–June 1946, vol. 1, p. 181.
99. *ibid.*, p. 182.

100. For Muslim League's conception of the functions and resources of the Central Government, see the 'Terms of the offer made by the Muslim League as a basis of agreement 12 May 1946', reproduced in Gwyer and Appadorai, *Speeches and Documents*, vol. 2, pp. 573–4.
101. *Indian Annual Register*, July–Dec. 1946, p. 226.
102. *ibid.*, p. 178.
103. *ibid.*, p. 79.
104. D. G. Tendulkar, *Mahatma: Life of Mohandas Karamchand Gandhi* (Bombay, 1952), vol. 5, pp. 333–4.
105. Gwyer and Appadorai, *Speeches and Documents*, p. 525.
106. Pyarelal, *Mahatma Gandhi: The Last Phase* (Ahmedabad, 1958), vol. 2, p. 208.
107. Jamil-ud-Din Ahmad, *Some Recent Speeches*, p. 447.
108. Khaliquzzaman, *Pathway to Pakistan*, p. 397.

Index